D0873963

George B. Yeater
24 May 1995

CONFEDERATE EDGED WEAPONS

Other books by William A. Albaugh III

Confederate Swords
The Original Confederate Colt
The Confederate Brass-Framed Colt & Whitney
Confederate Arms
Tyler, Texas, C.S.A.

CONFEDERATE

EDGED

WEAPONS

by WILLIAM A. ALBAUGH III

Illustrated by CARL J. PUGLIESE

R&R BOOKS
Livonia, New York

This 1993 Edition Printed by
R & R BOOKS
3020 East Lake Road
Livonia, New York 14487

DEDICATION

To my very good friend—
the late Richard D. Steuart

CONTENTS

LIST OF ILLUSTRATIONS, AND RELATIVE VALUE

The weapons depicted were drawn roughly to the following scales: full size for swords, short swords and bayonets, three-quarter size for knives and bowies, and one-half size for pikes and lances. In printing this was reduced one third.
(Figures 119 and 120 were drawn half size.)

PART II. ARMS WHOSE MAKERS HAVE NOT BEEN IDENTIFIED

ACKNOWLEDGMENTS

No book is ever the sole product of one person's mind. Much from many goes into every book I have ever written and such it is with the present work. I am sure that each sincere author must regret that full acknowledgment is rarely possible. I do the best I can, and my apologies to any whom I have overlooked.

In depicting the weapons shown, the illustrator has relied heavily upon his own collection and that of the author. In addition, the following persons and institutions have graciously permitted access to specimens which otherwise might have been unavailable.

Robert Abels, New York City; Robert Berryman, East Point, Ga.; Battle Abbey, Richmond, Va.; William A. Bond, Vernon, Texas; Philip Colavita, Jr., Richmond, Va.; The Confederate Museum, Richmond, Va.; Major J. V. Cremonin, New York City; Norman Flayderman, Greenwich, Conn.; Col. Leon C. Jackson, Dallas, Texas; George Knight, Alexandria, Va.; Ben Palmer, Baltimore, Md.; M. Hume Parks, Nashville, Tenn.; Nick Penachio, Scarsdale, N.Y.; Jack Rawls, Vienna, Va.; J. O. Shelton, Lynnville, Tenn.; William Shemerluk, Hartford, Conn.; Smithsonian Institution, Washington, D.C.; Hermann N. Williams, Washington, D.C.; and Adrian P. Wilson, Memphis, Tenn.

In addition to the above, the author wishes to extend thanks to those whose ideas and enthusiastic contributions have been of incalculable value. They are: W. Herbert Bahlke, Chesterton, Ind.; Donald Baird, Princeton, N.J.; John L. Beck, Fort Worth, Texas; Hugh Benet, Baltimore, Md.; Harry Berry, Baltimore, Md.; Robert Berryman, East Point, Ga.; William A. Bond, Vernon, Texas; William J. Boylhart, Whittier, Calif.; Richard Brady, Baltimore, Md.; Mrs. Judson Briefer, Stow, Mass.; Miss Eleanor Brockenbrough, Richmond, Va.; Edmond Budde, Amityville, N.Y.; Mrs. George W. Craven, Chesterton, Ind.; Major J. V. Cremonin, New York City; Col. Alston Deas, Mount Pleasant, S.C.; Michael DeLuca, New York City; Oscar DePrato, Silver Spring, Md.; Tom Donahue, Memphis, Tenn.; W. W. Eubanks, Concord, N.C.; Col. Charles W. Fritz, Norwood, Ohio; John B. Gilmer, Richmond, Va.; Herb Glass, Bullsville, N.Y.; Robert Glover, Tyler, Texas; Cecil Godman, Memphis, Tenn.; Craddock Goins, Washington, D.C.; Walter Goldstein, New Orleans, La.; Col. William Harden, Augusta, Ga.; T. Sherman Harding, Arcadia, Fla.; Ralph W. Heavner, Lincolnton, N.C.; Robert Held, New York City; Peter Hlinka, Greenwich, Conn.; Robert I. Howard, Richmond, Va.; Edgar M. Howell, Washington, D.C.; Mrs. Elsie Jackson, Dallas, Texas; Col. Leon C. Jackson, Dallas, Texas; Henry Jacoby, Sandusky, Ohio; Bruce Kusrow, Falls Church, Va.; Walter Lawrence, Akron, Ohio; Robert Leavy, Jr., South Corning, N.Y.; Sam McClaren, Richmond, Va.;

Robert McDonald, Dearborn, Mich.; Alexander McDonnell, New York City; Robert Miller, Arlington, Va.; Bernard J. Mitchell, Falls Church, Va.; Robert Moore, Houston, Texas; Ashby Morton, Lexington, Ky.; James Moser, Falls Church, Va.; R. H. Myers, Brodhead, Wisc.; Ben Palmer, Baltimore, Md.; Tom Parvin, Lombard, Ill.; C. Meade Patterson, Hyattsville, Md.; Harold Peterson, Arlington, Va.; Bud Purvis, Alexandria, Va.; Jack Rawls, Vienna, Va.; Ray Riling, Philadelphia, Pa.; Herman Schindler, Charleston, S.C.; James Serven, Santa Ana, Calif.; J. O. Shelton, Lynnville, Tenn.; Edward N. Simmons, Chatsworth, Calif.; Fred Slaton, Jr., Madisonville, Ky.; Wyman Spaulding, San Francisco, Calif.; W. Thomas Smith, Richmond, Va.; William C. Steuart, Baltimore, Md.; Miles Standish, Kansas City, Mo.; Walter W. Stephen, Oxford, Ala.; Mrs. Clayton Torrence, Richmond, Va.; Miss India Thomas, Richmond, Va.; Lee Wallace, Arlington, Va.; Major Charles West, Wilton, Conn.; Robert Wheeler, Baltimore, Md.; Adrian P. Wilson, Memphis, Tenn.; Ken Wyatt, Granite City, Ill.; and The Hon. Ralph W. Yarborough, Tyler, Texas.

In particular, the author would like to acknowledge the assistance of two persons well known to arms enthusiasts: Bob Abels and M. Hume Parks.

Bob Abels, an author as well as a dealer in antique arms, has guided countless neophites into full-fledged collectors. In this instance he has given much of his excellent advice and encouragement and made available with the utmost grace his own personal collection of bowie knives.

Hume Parks, of the Tennessee Gun Collector's Association, has long felt that organizations such as the one of which he is president should lend their weight to the betterment of not only their own members but gun collectors at large. Consequently the bulletin of this worthy club has consistently exposed fakes, given information valuable to those interested in arms collecting, and special encouragement and assistance to persons such as myself engaged in new publications. I am very proud to be a member of the organization which Hume heads.

FOREWORD—A

The Identification of Confederate Edged Weapons

THE MOST COMMON question asked by the collector new to the field of Southern edged weapons is: "How can a Confederate sword be distinguished from a Yankee?" The only true answer to this question is, of course, "Experience." Lacking this, there are certain guides the initiate may follow.

I have a good friend who swears that he has an infallible answer to the above question which can be applied not only to swords but to any other item as well. According to my friend, he simply holds the object in question to his ear, shuts his eyes and listens. If he hears "Dixie" in sweet and dulcet tones, then to him there is no question as to its authenticity.

Unfortunately few of us are so gifted as my friend says he is. It is suggested that in addition to listening for "Dixie" the following pages also be considered in determining the identity of a Southern-made sword.

Figure 1.

Figure 1 was taken from the U.S. Ordnance Manual of 1861 and shows the various types of edged weapons in use in the United States Army at that time. If it seems strange that any book dealing with the Confederacy would be prefaced with such an illustration let us remember that just as the Confederate Constitution was taken from that of the United States, so were the army and ordnance manuals. The arms used by the South were the same ones used in the North—but with variations, and it is with these variations that we are concerned. But first, let us examine the Northern counterparts from which almost all Southern cavalry weapons were imitated—the U.S. Heavy Cavalry Sabre, Model 1840, and the U.S. Light Cavalry Sabre, Model 1860.

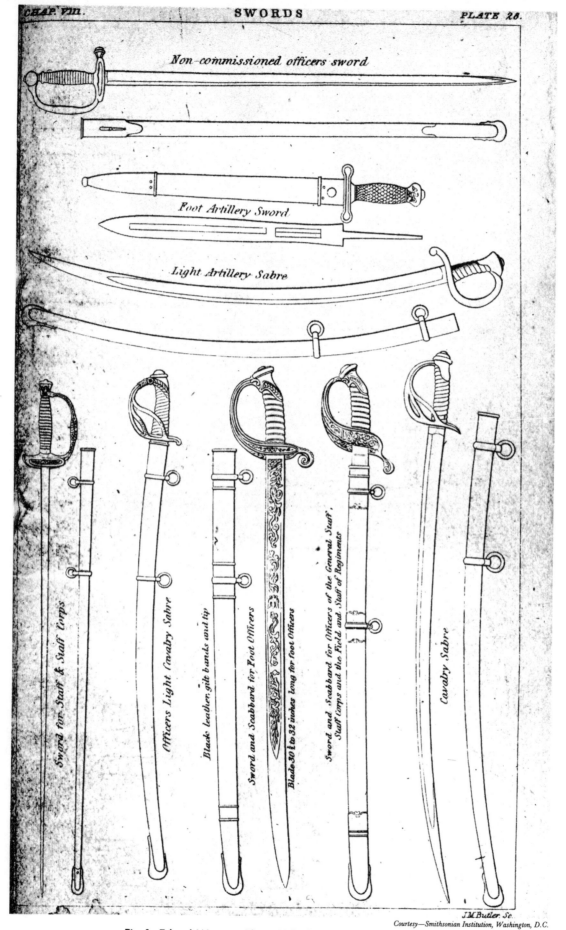

Fig 1. Edged Weapon Plate, U.S. Ordnance Manual 1861

Figure 2.

IN THE 1830S AND 1840s the U.S. Cavalry was not known as such. Our mounted service sprang from the U.S. Regiment of Dragoons, created in 1833, and at the time our only mounted troops. The weapon they carried does not concern us but was termed a "dragoon" sabre, being closely related to the British light cavalry sabre of 1822. By 1840 the Dragoons had increased to three regiments and in that year the War Department adopted for their use a new model sabre. With this model we are concerned. It is now known as the Heavy Cavalry (Dragoon) Sabre, Model 1840.

This weapon conformed closely to the French light cavalry model of 1822. The 35¾-inch blade is distinctly curved, 1 inch wide at the guard and flat on the back. Each side of the blade contains two fullers, one wide one running from the ricasso to within 10 inches of the point. The ricasso end of the fuller comes to a full right-angled stop, the other end tapers, or "runs out." The other fuller is deep and narrow, tapering on both ends and is located near the back edge of the blade. The guard is of brass, half-basket type, with a knuckle bow joined by two branches. The grip is somewhat cone-shaped with a slight curve forward. The wide end of the cone rests on the guard. The grip has been wound with heavy cord and then covered with leather after which it is wound with twisted brass wire, the wire following the lays made by the cord. The pommel is of the Phrygian helmet pattern with an encircling ring at the top, and of the style now termed "standard cavalry." The ricassos of these weapons are stamped on the obverse (front side) with "U.S." and the initials of the inspecting officer. The reverse (back) ricasso contains the manufacturer's name and year of manufacture. The scabbards are of iron, with no brasswork and the drag is usually stamped with the inspecting officer's initials.

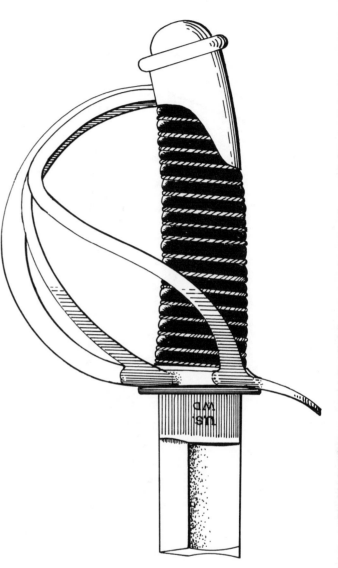

Fig. 2. U.S. Cavalry Sabre, Model 1840

Figure 3. U.S. Cavalry Sabre, Model 1860

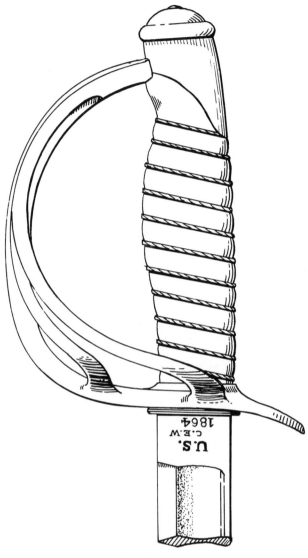

Fig. 3. U.S. Cavalry Sabre, Model 1860

ACCORDING TO HAROLD PETERSON in *American Swords*, "About 1860 a light sabre was introduced for [the U.S.] cavalry. In this new model which did not immediately supplant the heavy saber, the blade was reduced in width, and the entire weapon was lightened. . . .

"The light saber can quickly be distinguished from the model of 1840 by the lighter blade with its rounded back and by the shape of the grips which have a swell in the center. In all other characteristics, however, the light cavalry saber is essentially like its predecessor."

Another difference lies in the grips being ridged prior to being covered with leather, the twisted wire following the ridges. No cord is used.

The blade is 34 inches long with rounded back, and two fullers identical to those of the Model 1840. The guard is of brass with two branches. The pommel cap is of the standard cavalry design. The ricasso on the specimen shown is stamped "U.S., C.E.W., 1864," in three lines. The "U.S." is, of course, for "United States," the initials "C.E.W." for the inspector and the "1864" the year the sword was made. The reverse ricasso of this particular sabre is stamped with the name of the manufacturer, "Ames Mfg. Co., Chicopee, Mass."

Most Confederate swords or sabres conform generally to their Northern counterparts, but the departures from the standards as set up by the U.S. ordnance officers place the Southern weapons apart. Below are listed the major of these "departures," which were not made willfully so that in years to come collectors would be able to identify one from the other, but simply because Southern manufacture was not equivalent to that of the North.

Most Southern swords or sabres contain one or more of the following variations:

1. The blade may be only single-fullered on either side, the fullers running out on either end, or possibly even made flat without any fullers.

2. The blades of many were literally beaten out by hand not rolled, and by holding at arm's length and looking down the blade one can see the unevenness and irregularities of both blade and fullers.

3. The grips may be wrapped with oilcloth rather than leather. Where leather is used, it is usually brown. Rarely is sharkskin to be found on the grip of a Confederate sword.

4. The grips may be wound with untwisted wire—of brass, copper or even iron.

5. The ridges in the grip usually slant up from the front of the grip to the back—opposite from U.S. weapons.

6. The branches on the guard may be flat with squared edges as though stamped from sheet brass, or may be heavy, awkward and completely round in cross section rather than symmetrical and oval, as is consistently found in the Union weapons.

7. The pommel cap may be crude and heavy and may contain no encircling ring at the top. The pommels on officers' swords are frequently without decoration.

8. The casting of the brass parts may be poor, containing faults and flaws.

9. Roman or Arabic numbers may be found on blade, guard or pommel, sometimes on all three. However, just because a sword is so marked does not definitely mean that it is Confederate.

10. Contrary to belief, very few Confederate swords are stamped "C.S.A." Most weapons so found were stamped in the 1950s.

11. Many are completely without marks or stamps.

12. Any suggestion of high-speed tool marks indicates twentieth-century handiwork—not the 1860s.

13. Leather scabbards are sometimes sewed at top or bottom side, French fashion, rather than on the reverse middle as found on the Yankee models.

14. Metal scabbards are usually brass-mounted, sometimes to include throat, drag and the carrying rings as well as the ring mounts. Some scabbards are of the wrap-around type with brazed or leaded seams.

None of the above are infallible guides, but they at least are indications, and a bit more scientific than listening for the strains of "Dixie." It might also be well to remember that because of unstopped fullers and apparent absence of makings, many English, French or other foreign blades are mistaken for Southern. Although it sometimes takes a bit of looking to find, many foreign edged weapons contain a proof mark of some sort either on the blade or guard, which feature is not known to extend to those of Southern manufacture.

FOREWORD — B

Comparable Value

THE FIELD of Confederate edged weapons is a new one for most collectors. To date little has been written on the subject, the only known publication being a small booklet entitled *Confederate Swords* which appeared in 1951. Good as far as it went, present-day knowledge has caused it to become obsolete.

Arms collecting seems to pass through various phases. In the 1920s the most desirable of all weapons were the Kentucky rifles, followed by military shoulder arms. Handguns ran a poor third and edged weapons could scarcely be given away. The depression years saw an increasing interest in handguns, due, I believe, to the fact that homes were then made smaller and such items could be displayed in less space than shoulder arms. Then too, there was considerable difference in the expense of crating and shipping a pistol compared with that of a long gun, and in those days every penny counted.

Now, we are living in an inflationary period. Almost every new home has a "rec" room and, in addition, most collectors have what they term a "gun room." Space is no longer to be considered in the acquisition of a new item. Hence, shoulder arms are once again coming into their own, particularly since revolvers and pistols seem to have reached a plateau in the price scale. The "hottest" two items in today's arms collecting are carbines and edged weapons. As yet, these have not approached their final ultimate sales price, when they too will reach a plateau. As more and more is written on the subject of carbines and edged weapons, higher and higher will become their prices, mainly because each collector likes to turn to a book and proudly say, "There is a picture of a sword (or gun or pistol) exactly like the one you now see hanging on my wall." Prior to the publication of the particular book which pictures this item, the sword in question was just a sword, but with publication, this item becomes documented, and thus increases in price.

Not so many years ago swords were just swords. Dealers listed them as such with slight qualification. Prices at that time seemed consistently to fall into the $5 bracket. Gradually swords evolved in interest and in price until in dealer's catalogues they were given rather lengthy descriptions which included type, style, period, etc. The publication of Harold Peterson's excellent book *American Swords* aroused considerable interest in the edged weapon field and has now enabled the dealer to list his sword simply as "American sword of such and such period (Peterson's Sword Book plate so-and-so)." The lengthy description is no longer necessary. The prices, incidentally, have increased according to the knowledge available on the weapon. To a lesser degree this same technique has been followed on Confederate swords by reference to *Confederate Swords,* Mr. Peterson having omitted any reference to Southern swords in his book.

As yet, however, the point has not been reached in many edged weapons where their sales price actually bears too close a relationship to the four aspects which usually govern price on more established items: eye appeal, rarity (availability), historical background and condition. The time is still with us when unmarked Confederate swords sell for $35 to $50. "Marked" Confederate swords sell from $125 to $200, regardless of how they are marked, or their comparative rareness. While this is quite a step from the days when all swords, regardless of what they might be, sold for $5, it still does not indicate any approach to the end of the price ladder.

Many books contain a portion devoted to "value." Such books often consider value and price as being one and the same, forgetting that value usually remains constant, while prices constantly change, being dependent upon national economy, the fad at the moment, etc. Far be it from me to try to give a fixed price to anything. On the other hand, it is possible roughly to assign a relative value. With this in mind the author has arbitrarily set "values" to the weapons illustrated in this book. We have assigned the value of "A" to the sword of General Robert E. Lee. Obviously, nothing could be more Confederate, or more desirable from a collector's standpoint than the sword carried by Lee at the time of his surrender to Grant. While I cannot attempt to put a "price" on this weapon described under "Devisme" of this book, its value relative to other Confederate swords should remain constant throughout eternity, regardless of economic conditions, wars, floods or plagues.

Under the "B" classification fall those swords which are associated with some well-known historical figure. These include those with sufficient documentation to establish such to be the case, or whose blades by etching or engraving prove the fact beyond question. These can fall into a plus or minus category depending upon: (a) who carried the weapon and (b) the sword itself (eye appeal, etc.).

In the "C" classification are those swords that can be identified as to maker and which are marked "C.S." The "C.S." carries a terrific amount of eye appeal and adds a great deal to the value and price. These fall into a "plus" or "minus" category depending upon comparative rarity and also upon whether the "C.S." is contained as a portion of the guard decoration, or just appears on the blade. If the former is the case, it means the collector can exhibit his sheathed item as Confederate. If the latter, he is required to unscabbard his weapon before some doubter will actually believe it to be what it is.

Weapons classified "D" are those which show only by the maker's name that they are Southern. Naturally some are more desirable than others through rarity or manner of marking.

Into the "E" classification fall those many weapons which can be determined as Confederate only by style—in other words, they are unmarked. Like the others, these too fall under the subdivisions of plus and minus.

Carrying this same line of reasoning farther, there could be an "F" classification consisting of arms which either might be Confederate, or which, through documentation, can be established as carried by a Southern soldier.

From the values assigned illustrated pieces the reader should be able to relate these to a current "sales" price. It should be remembered, however, that swords, bowies, bayonets and pikes each have their own scale of value. A sword assigned the value of "C" does not necessarily have the same "sales" price as a bayonet or pike assigned the same classification.

The above is written with full realization that I will be damned by many, who will contend that I should be man enough to say such and such a sword is worth either $2 or $200. However, I have seen too many others fall into this quicksand wherein value and price are treated as one and the same, and the "sales" value they ascribed to various weapons in 1950 must, in 1960, keep them awake at nights.

In the 1860s the only ones interested in collecting swords were the Ordnance Departments of the United and Confederate States respectively. The department heads had no difficulty in assigning both a price and a value to various weapons, this figure representing what they had to pay to get them. A comparison between the U.S. and C.S. prices might be interesting. This information has been taken from the U.S. and C.S. Army Regulations of 1863.

Type	United States Army	Confederate Army
Cavalry sabres	$7.50	$14.00
Cavalry sabres (foreign)	5.50	no price given
Horse artillery sabres	5.50	10.00
Noncommissioned swords	5.50	11.00
Musician's swords	4.00	8.00
Foot artillery	4.00	8.00
Musketoon sabre bayonet	no price given	10.00

In addition to the above, the C.S. Army Regulations listed the following swords: artillery swords, new pattern; cavalry sabres, English; sergeant's swords, Prussian; foot officer's swords, $30\frac{1}{2}$ inches; foot officer's swords, new pattern, 32 inches; and field officer's swords. No prices are given for any of these.

PART I

MAKERS WHOSE ARMS ARE

IDENTIFIABLE

Introduction

At this late date it is impossible to give any accurate figures on the number of firms and persons who supplied the Confederacy with various types of edged weapons. It is supposed, however, that such a list would embrace at least a thousand individuals and/or firms. The part of this book that follows gives what information is available on those whose weapons can be identified as to their manufacturer.

The list of those whose arms can be traced back to their source is pitifully small—clearly we have yet a long way to go.

CONTENTS

1. L. Bissonnet, Mobile, Ala.

(SWORDS)

Figure 4

THE OPERATIONS of L. Bissonnet of Mobile, Ala., must have been very small. Very few of his weapons have survived the years, and available Confederate records make no mention of his name. Apparently he made only one type of sword, of which several specimens exist.

This cavalry weapon has a straight, double-edged 36½-inch blade, 1⅜ inches wide, which gradually tapers to a width of ¾ of an inch, one inch from the tip, then to a point. It has a modified diamond cross section. The blade is well etched with vines and "L. Bissonnet, Maker, Mobile, Ala." on the reverse, and "Patria Honneur" (Honor to the Fatherland) on the obverse. The grip of wood is leather-covered, wound with 12 turns of twisted brass wire. The brass guard conforms closely to the U.S. Cavalry Officer's Sabre, Model 1840, which in turn was adopted from a French style, popular in that country for 20 years. The pommel is undecorated. Scabbard is of brass, leather-covered with brass mounts. The weapon has an overall length of 43½ inches.

A sword of this description is to be found in the Jefferson Memorial, St. Louis, Mo., and is known to have been carried by a Captain A. G. Moore, 38th Regiment of Infantry, Alabama Volunteers.

Some authorities have expressed the opinion that L. Bissonnet predated the Confederacy by about 10 years.

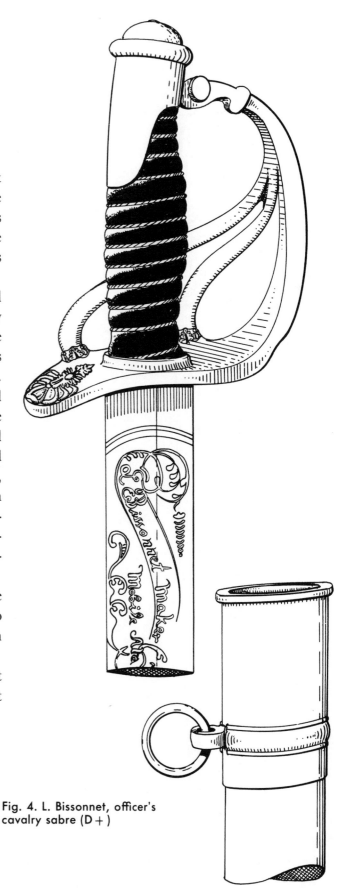

Fig. 4. L. Bissonnet, officer's cavalry sabre (D +)

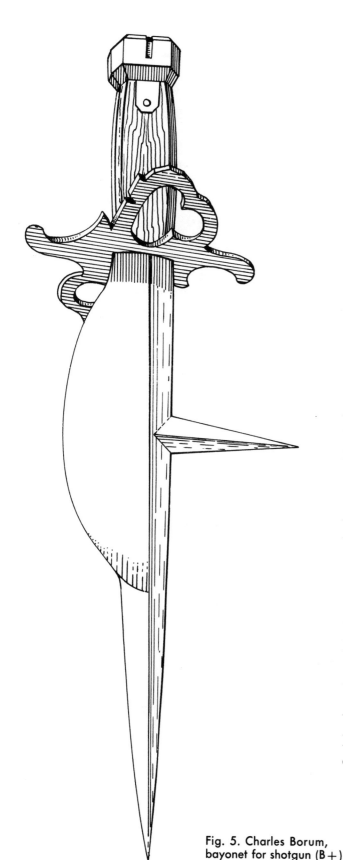

Fig. 5. Charles Borum,
bayonet for shotgun (B+)

2. Captain Charles Borum, C.S.A., Norfolk, Va.

(BAYONETS)

Figure 5

AMONG THE RAREST of Confederate items, but not necessarily the most desirable, are the bayonets made to fit double-barreled shotguns or fowling pieces. Such were weapons of desperation, and in 1861, the South was desperate for any type of arm to put into the hands of the volunteers swarming to points of enlistment.

The daily Richmond *Examiner* of May 29, 1861, contains the following advertisement of General (then, Colonel Commanding) Jubal A. Early:

Lynchburg, Va., May 27, 1861. Notice is hereby given that all companies coming here to be mustered into service, whether organized as infantry, riflemen or artillery, must come with the understanding that they are to be armed with such arms as the authorities think proper to give them. Muskets are the only weapons on hand here and the companies must take them whether they be percussion or flint lock. Companies not willing to take muskets will not be received or furnished transportation. It is a great mistake to suppose that the musket can not be relied on. It is the weapon that must be relied on and it does the most execution in close conflict.

A "Proclamation" of October 19, 1861, states: "No volunteer will be mustered in unless he has in serviceable order a good country rifle, double-barreled gun or other Military arm." (*Confederate Records of Georgia,* page 45.) So desperate were some enrolling officers that it was stipulated that volunteers, to be received as such, must come armed with at least an ax.

Those of us old enough to remember World War I, World War II and the Korean disturbance (not labeled a war by our *leaders*) either joined the army or received a draft card whose "Greetings" made no note that the recipient, in order to be drafted, must carry with him grandpa's old fowling piece; but in 1861 things were different. A whole lot farther from socialism then than we are now, a war was properly considered every man's business, and it was not only hoped, but expected, that each would share his responsibility to his community, not only by enlisting, but also by bringing with him something that would inflict damage upon the enemy.

In this year of 1960 we seem to be more than one hundred years away from the ideas and ideals of the 1860s, when the Southern recruits came in to enlist trailing fowling pieces and double-barreled shotguns. These men came from an agricultural country whose populace was thoroughly acquainted with this type of arm, and it is not at all unusual that they were gathered up and distributed not only to cavalry, but to infantry soldiers as well. The men who received them were no strangers to their use and accepted them gladly, but grew long in the face upon seeing other troops armed with muskets or rifles which carried a triangular or sabre bayonet at their ends.

Many attempts were made to fit fowling pieces or double-barreled shotguns with bayonets. Both L. Haiman & Brother and Leech & Rigdon advertised bayonets for this type of arm. Such attempts, however, were never wholly successful, perhaps because these guns were simply not of a basic design suited to the addition of a bayonet. Their original manufacturers had clearly envisioned the shooting of game, but the idea of bayoneting a rabbit or bobwhite had never occurred to them.

Without doubt there were any number of this type bayonet made, but judging from the very few still in existence, most must have been discarded as soon as issued. This is not because the shotgun disappeared from the Confederate Army. Moore's *Rebellion Record,* page 175, states: "Of ten to fifteen thousand small arms surrendered at Fort Donelson, most of them were shotguns, hunting rifles and flintlock muskets." This was true in 1861–1862, and a number of men in the Southern Army fought through the entire war with grandpa's old hunting rifle.

Pictured is an awkward-appearing contraption from the mind of Captain Charles Borum, of Norfolk, Va., to be used under the end of a double-barreled shotgun as a bayonet. Only the model is known to exist, this bearing the name "Capt. Charles Borum, Norfolk, Va., 1861" engraved on the brass butt. It is to be found in the Washington & Lee Museum, Lexington, Va.

3. Boyle & Gamble; Boyle, Gamble & MacFee (Mitchell & Tyler), Richmond, Va.

(SWORDS AND BAYONETS)

THOSE INTERESTED IN any phase of Confederate ordnance should not be surprised at "mysteries." One which hangs heavy is the difference (if any) between the firms of Boyle & Gamble and Boyle, Gamble & MacFee. As both operated in Richmond, Va., and the names are rather unusual, there must be some close connection between the two, but judging from the weapons alone, the two firms operated independently, there being little resemblance in style of manufacture. To date it is not established whether they operated as separate entities or if there was some corporate connection which is not now apparent.

Figure 6

Taken either jointly or separately, the operation of Boyle & Gamble and/or Boyle, Gamble & MacFee was not a small one. One of the commonest of Confederate swords—if any Confederate sword can be

called common—is the staff officer's, the counterguard of which contains the letters "C.S." on a ribbon
encircled by a wreath which in turn is surmounted
by a star. Floral designs and an ear of corn also appear
in the guard. These swords are found with and without
etched blades but always with a number stamped on
the underside of the guard, on the pommel where it
engages the knuckle bow, and on the tang of the blade
as well (if anyone is so foolish to separate blade from
guard). As this number is consistently found to be no
higher than two digits, the idea of its being a serial
number, reflecting the number of swords made, is
discounted. More than likely it either applied to a
worker, or was used to facilitate the matching of
component parts which were all hand-fitted.

On the blades that are etched, the design is usually
standard, consisting of a Confederate battle flag, a
shield bearing the letters "C.S.A.," floral designs and
stands of flags and trophies. Some vary from this in
that they contain a likeness of President Jefferson
Davis, or some patriotic inscription such as "Liberty
or Death."

The star which is part of the counterguard design
has been thought by some to relate to the State of
Texas, but the writer is of the firm opinion that it
does not, any more than the ear of corn which also
appears in the counterguard relates to the State of
Iowa. It is just a part of the design, with no particular
significance one way or the other. Many with the
etched blade include the following inscription on the
ricasso: "Boyle & Gamble, made for Mitchell &
Tyler, Richmond, Va." It is possible that all swords
of this design were marketed through the firm of
Mitchell & Tyler.

Mitchell & Tyler were a firm of military outfitters
and jewelers, located at 108 Main Street, Richmond,
Va. They did no manufacturing, but as witness the

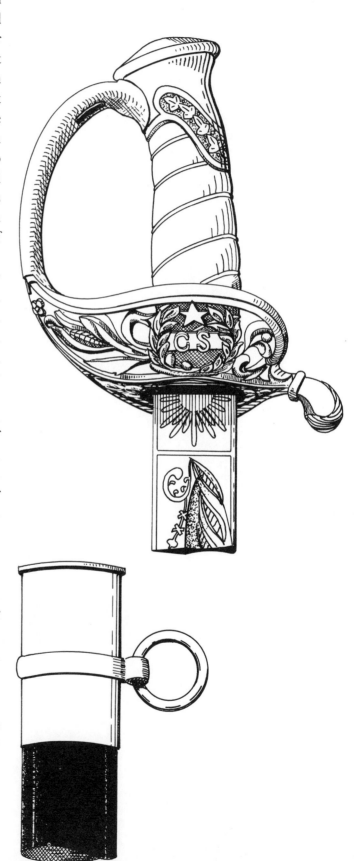

Fig. 6. Boyle & Gamble, staff
or field officer's sword (C+)

following advertisement from the Richmond *Dispatch* of March 25, 1861, they supplied the South with much military equipment:

Military Notice—Arms for Volunteers. Volunteer companies desiring arms are hereby informed that we have made arrangements for a supply of the best English and American guns, including the Minnie musket, Enfield rifle, rifled musket, with either angular or sword bayonets, fine navy pistols, also French cavalry sabres, a superior article at a low price. Samples may be seen at our store. Also on hand our usual large variety of officer's swords, belts, sashes, epaulettes, passants, gloves, spurs, together with buttons, laces, biding, binding and all necessary trimming for uniforms.

The name of "Mitchell & Tyler, Richmond, Va." is frequently found on the backs of Virginia State seal buttons of the Civil War period.

The grip of the sword just described is of leather, wound with 7 turns of single-strand brass wire, and most conform to this style. However, one which has a blade inscribed "Presented to Lieut. Col. C. G. Coleman of the 23rd Reg. Va. Vols. by his friends in Co. G., April 22, 1862" has a grip wrapped in sharkskin and wound with twisted gilt wire.

The scabbards of all these swords are of leather with brass mounts, said to have been made by the R. H. Bosher Carriage Factory of Richmond, Va. They are consistently found with the seam sewed at the top.

The writer has observed what appears to be copies of the sword just described. The casting is crude, the knuckleguard has no slot for sabreknot, and no numbers are to be found stamped on the underside of the guard. These "copies" are usually found in a wooden scabbard, painted black, with brass mounts. Their background is not known, but they are not believed to be the work of Boyle & Gamble. Inasmuch as a number of them have been around for over 50 years or more, certainly they are not to be considered fakes.

Figure 7

Although the staff officer's sword made by Boyle & Gamble appears its most common product, the firm also produced edged weapons of other varieties. They made a foot officer's sword that conforms to the standard of this period. These too were made with or without etched blades. Those that are etched usually bear a furled Stars and Bars Confederate flag, a floral design and a large "C.S.A." as a part of the blade decorations. Some are also etched with "Boyle & Gamble" on one side of the ricasso and "Richmond, Va." on the other. The guards are consistently of rose design. The grips of leather, usually brown with a trace of white, are wound with single-strand or twisted brass wire. The pommel caps are very similar to those of the staff pattern, with either ivy or laurel leaf decoration on their forward edge. Scabbards are leather, seam at the top, with brass mounts.

Whether etched or not, all are stamped on the underside of guard, tang of blade and pommel cap with a number (not higher than two digits), as are the staff officer's swords.

A foot officer's sword such as described is in a private collection. The etched blade indicates that it was presented to "Capt. J. S. Mitchell, by Company E, August, 1863."

The firm also turned out fine presentation swords, some of which differ from the two types already described. One known is of the field officer's variety, but surprisingly with the guard literally taken off of a Yankee U.S. Model 1850 field officer's sword of the kind with the large "U.S." between the branches. On this particular sword the "U" in the guard has been altered to form a "C," so that at first glance the letters appear to be "C.S." The grip is of sharkskin, wound with twisted gilt wire. The blade is of Confederate manufacture, having a single unstopped

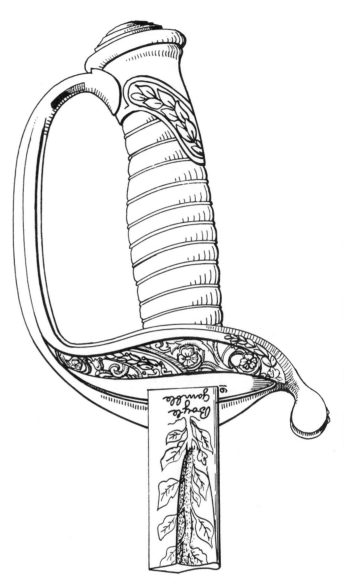

Fig. 7. Boyle & Gamble, foot officer's sword (C)

fuller, as do all swords by this manufacturer. It is finely etched with "Boyle & Gamble" on the ricasso, and the blade with stands of Confederate flags, crossed cannon, floral designs, etc. and "Presented to Gen'l J. H. Winder from some of his friends in Richmond as a token of their esteem, July 15, 1864." Those students of Southern history who know of Winder will be amazed that he possessed even one friend in 1864, but here is living proof that he apparently did. The scabbard is of metal with ornamented brass mounts.

A peculiarity of the etching observed on swords made by Boyle & Gamble is that it is very lightly applied, almost a frosting, which wears badly and will disappear under almost any type of abrasive.

Figure 8

In a private collection is the sword that was carried by Julian Allusi. This interesting soul was born at Lucca, Italy, in 1830, the son of an engineer. First educated as a priest, he later studied sculpting at the Royal Academy. He came to America in 1851, but not before having been employed by Princess Mondanti of Poland as an interpreter. In America he went first to Washington, D.C., then to Charleston, S.C., and finally ended in Richmond, Va.

At the outbreak of war he enlisted for one year as a private in the Virginia Rifles on April 21, 1861, only a few days after Virginia seceded from the Union. At the expiration of this enlistment he became a lieutenant in Company K, 19th Regiment, Virginia Militia, and so served throughout the war.

The hilt of the sword carried by Lieutenant Allusi consists of a flat knuckle guard with two branches, somewhat similar to a cavalry sabre. The pommel, however, is typically Boyle & Gamble, with ornamented laurel leaf fore edge, and its casting matches exactly another sword which contains the firm's name

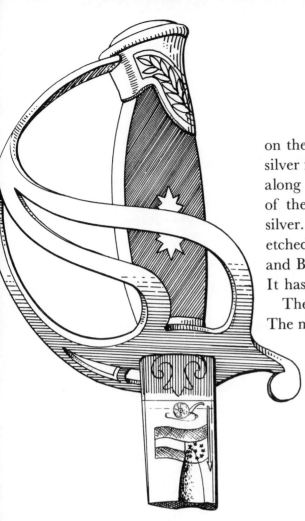

Fig. 8. Boyle & Gamble,
foot officer's sword (D+)

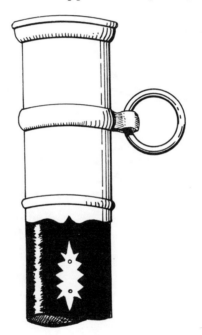

on the blade. The grip is of rosewood with a German silver ferrule at the base, and a strip of the same metal along the front and back. In the middle of each side of the grip is an 18-pointed oval, also of German silver. The 33-inch blade is slightly curved, finely etched with the same design on either side: two Stars and Bars flags, cannon, drums and floral decorations. It has a single unstopped fuller on either side.

The scabbard is of leather, seam at the bottom. The mounts are of copper with superimposed German

silver ring mounts and borders of the same metal. Between the mounts on the obverse are two 12-pointed ovals. The entire is finely made, and is the only sword of this type ever seen.

From Boyle & Gamble, we now pass to the weapons which are the product of Boyle, Gamble & MacFee, all of which are distinctive in their hiltings, the oval counterguard turning down cup-fashion on all sides. On many the name "Boyle Gamble & MacFee,

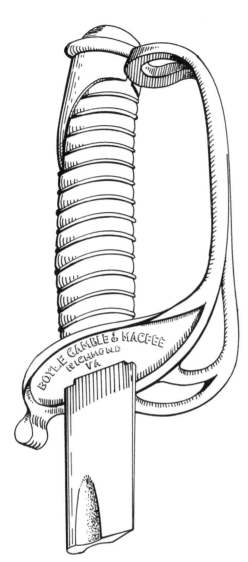

Fig. 9. Boyle, Gamble &
MacFee, foot officer's sword
(D+)

Richmond, Va." appears on the underside of the counterguard, being cast thereon in raised letters, but some are devoid of markings other than the same type numbering (no higher than two digits) already described as being found on swords made by Boyle & Gamble.

Figure 9

The foot officer's swords by the maker in question invariably have a wide heavy blade. Those that do not, indicate a replaced blade. Some are flat without fullers but usually they have a single unstopped fuller on either side. The brass guard has open spaces between the branches rather than the usual floral design. The pommel cap, of standard cavalry design, is undecorated. The black leather grip is wound with a single heavy strand of brass wire. A two-digit number is usually found on blade, guard and pommel. The illustrated piece carries a "34," stamped on the top of the pommel. Scabbards for these weapons are identical to those sheathing the swords of Boyle & Gamble. Over-all length is 35 inches.

Most contain the firm's name and address in raised letters cast in the underside of the guard (reverse), but some are devoid of markings.

Figure 10

Cavalry sabres made by the subject firm copy the two-branched U.S. Model 1860, but with the peculiarly turned-down counterguard bearing the firm's name and address on the obverse underside. Scabbards are of metal with brass ring mounts. A sabre such as this was carried by Captain William Storke of the Engineer Corps, C.S.A., and may now be seen at the Robert E. Lee House in Richmond, Va.

Figure 11

Almost identical with the above but without any identifying marks is the pictured cavalry sabre. The

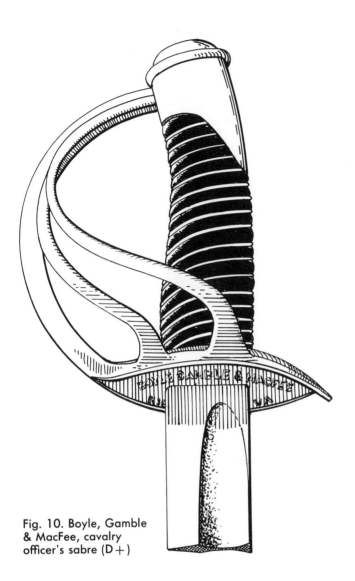

Fig. 10. Boyle, Gamble
& MacFee, cavalry
officer's sabre (D+)

turned-down guard, so distinctive of Boyle, Gamble &
MacFee, would lead the writer to suppose it to be a
product of this firm even though devoid of markings.

Figure 12

The author at one time had in his collection a
noncommissioned officer's sword that must have been
made by this manufactory. The brass knuckle guard
joined an oval counterguard, peculiarly turned down
around the entire circumference. It had no branches.

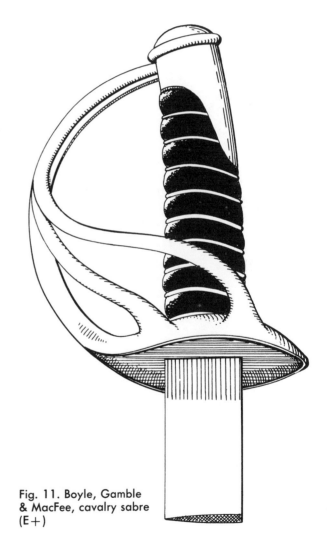

Fig. 11. Boyle, Gamble
& MacFee, cavalry sabre
(E+)

BBBBBBBBBBB

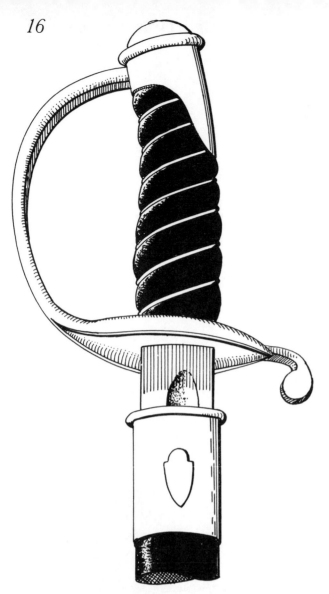

Fig. 12. Boyle, Gamble & MacFee, noncommissioned officer's sword (E+)

An attempt at decoration appeared on the top of the guard but the pommel cap was undecorated. The leather-covered grip was wound with single-strand brass wire. This weapon bore the number "2" stamped on the same places as other products of Boyle, Gamble and MacFee. The scabbard was of leather with brass drag and top mount, the latter having a stud for a frog.

Figure 13

Another arm made by Boyle, Gamble & MacFee was a bowie bayonet which has found much favor with today's collector. The blade is flat, without fullers, 15 inches long, 1½ inches wide, straight with semi-clipped point. The grip is of brass, and cast in raised letters on the cross guard appears the firm's name and "Richmond, Va." A number is stamped on the brass parts. The scabbard is of tooled leather, finely made. Over-all length is 19¾ inches.

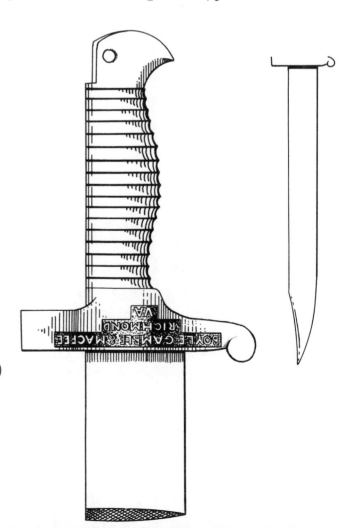

Fig. 13. Boyle, Gamble & MacFee, bowie bayonet (B+)

Figure 14

A bayonet very similar to the one above, but un-marked with the firm's name, is the most commonly encountered of all Confederate bayonets. It is found in several variations: straight blade, yataghan blade or with blade slightly curved. These were made with unstopped fullers, or flat with no fuller at all. All viewed are stamped with a one- or two-digit number on the bottom of the cross guard. These bayonets are very distinctive in appearance and although not rare are eagerly sought after. Their blade lengths vary, but are usually about 20 inches, over-all 25 inches.

In addition to bayonets the firm also patented and made what was known as a "bayonet adapter." This was a brass ring made to fit over the barrel of a rifle and/or a musket. A screw tightened the ring to the barrel. On the ring was a lug designed to fit the female portion at the base of the sabre bayonet. Thus, any gun could be made to carry a sabre bayonet. The

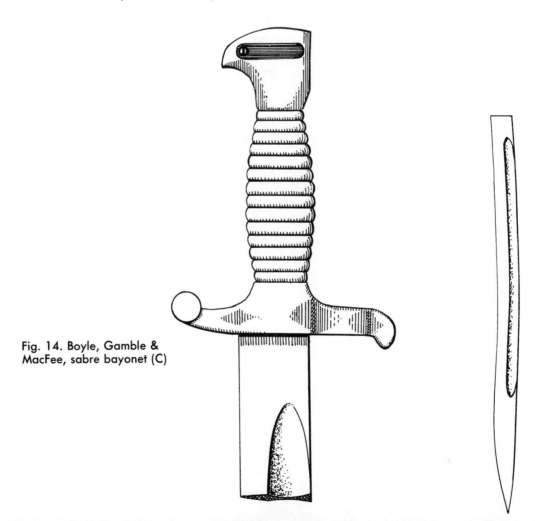

Fig. 14. Boyle, Gamble & MacFee, sabre bayonet (C)

adapters were stamped "B.G. & M., Richmond, Va., Pat. Sept. 2, 1861," and the serial. Today, they are not plentiful.

The described bayonets and "adapter" can all be found in the Battle Abbey collection in Richmond, Va.

Although the weapons of the firms in question are relatively plentiful, information concerning the manufactory is meager. Directories for Richmond, Va., for 1859 reflect a "Boyle & Burger" engaged in the saw-manufacturing business at the corner of 8th and Arch streets. The principal in this firm was Edwin Boyle, whose home was on St. Stephen's Street between Baker and Duval. The directory makes no mention of either a "Gamble" or a "MacFee."

A news item from the weekly Missouri *Republican* of May 30, 1861, states:

The following paragraph from the Richmond *Dispatch* of Wednesday indicates that there are still opponents of secession in that city. "Messres Boyle & Gamble, who have established a saw factory in this city, have for some time engaged in the manufacture of swords for the Southern troops. We learn that their factory was set fire yesterday morning, about half past three o'clock by a party of daring, but dastardly scoundrels, who to the number of seven or eight, came and attacked the watchman stationed there beating him badly. . . ."

Again on September 1, 1861, the "Boyle & Gamble's stock of saw steel was damaged to the extent of $10,000," declared the Richmond *Examiner* of September 2, 1861. This damage was the result of a fire, cause of which was not stated.

The *Dispatch*, September 24, 1862, contains an advertisement of "Boyle Gamble & Co., sword manufacturers, 13th Street" for "5,000 pounds of old brass and 5,000 pounds of zink."

Although the above advertisement and news accounts refer only to "Boyle & Gamble," we know that Boyle, Gamble & MacFee were also in operation during this same period of time—witness their bay-onet "adapter" which bears the patent date of September 2, 1861. Thus, both firms must have been operating at one and the same time. Possibly, they were one and the same, Boyle & Gamble selling only to individuals and outfitters such as Mitchell & Tyler, while Boyle, Gamble & MacFee attended only to government contracts.

On December 9, 1863, General William Harvey Richardson assessed the profits of Boyle & Gamble at $18,000.

4. College Hill Arsenal (L. T. Cunningham), Nashville, Tenn.

(ALL TYPES OF SWORDS)

L. T. CUNNINGHAM of Nashville, Tenn., began his activities to aid Confederate Ordnance early in the war. Contract Book, Chapter VIII of the *Captured Rebel Records*, reflects a letter dated June 29, 1861, addressed to the Confederate Secretary of War from Cunningham and a Robert E. Dury, advising that they were in a position to buy "muskets, pistols and sabres for gold, to be delivered in Nashville."

We hear no more of Robert Dury but Cunningham secured an advance from the State of Tennessee upon his promise to manufacture swords. With this advance he organized an arsenal on College Hill, which became known as the College Hill Arsenal. Here, swords and sabres were turned out in large quantity.

Figure 15

Cunningham made swords and sabres of various kinds. Most common of these is a cavalry sabre which closely resembles those made by the Nashville Plow Works, the guards being the same but without the name "Nashville Plow Works" in the design. It does have, however, the large block letters "C.S.A." It also differs from the Plow Works in consistently having an iron backstrap instead of brass. The grip is leather-covered, wound with twisted wire and with an iron ferrule at its base. The blades are slightly curved, flat back with a single tapering fuller on either side. Their lengths vary from 30 to 36 inches. The scabbards are iron with brass mounts.

Another cavalry sabre made by Cunningham conforms closely to the regulation U.S. two-branched model of 1840. It is 44 inches over-all with a 37-inch curved blade (unstopped fullers) etched on the reverse side only with a Confederate Stars and Bars flag, "C.S.A." and in old English letters: "A. A. Dysant." This sabre is Item #180 in the Battle Abbey collec-

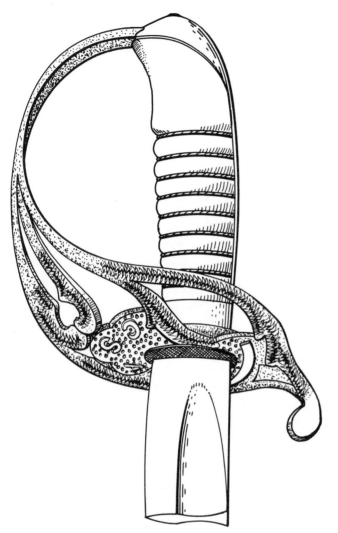

Fig. 15. College Hill Arsenal, cavalry officer's sabre (C)

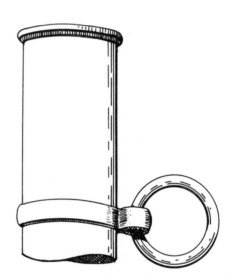

tion, Richmond, Va. Captain Alfred A. Dysant, Company D, 4th Tennessee Cavalry, was killed at Thompson's Station, March 8, 1863. He is a man who had a strong premonition of his death, an account of which is to be found in the *Confederate Veteran*, October, 1913, Vol. 21, page 487.

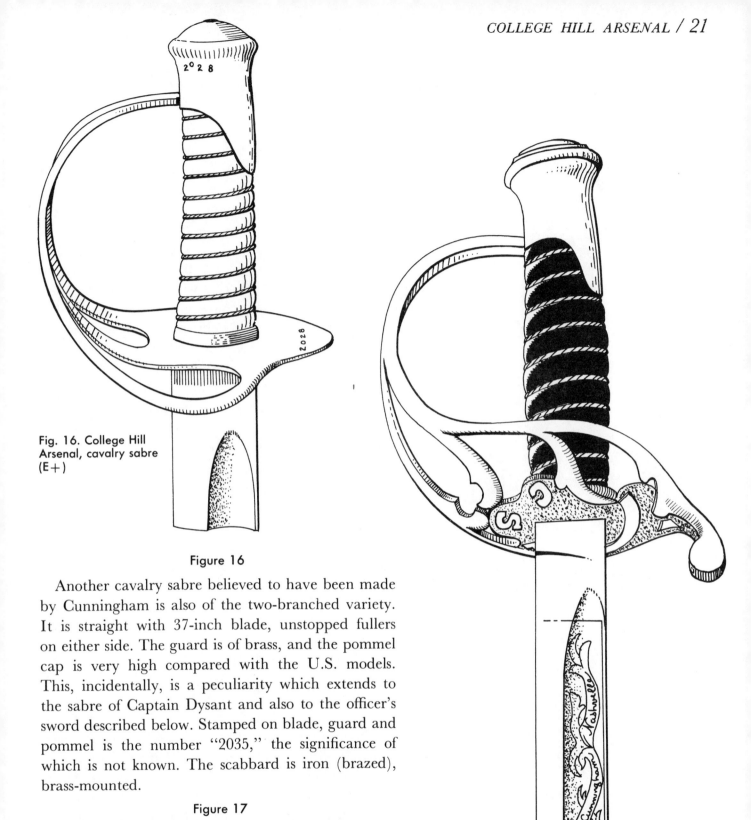

Fig. 16. College Hill Arsenal, cavalry sabre (E+)

Fig. 17. College Hill Arsenal, officer's sword (C+)

Figure 16

Another cavalry sabre believed to have been made by Cunningham is also of the two-branched variety. It is straight with 37-inch blade, unstopped fullers on either side. The guard is of brass, and the pommel cap is very high compared with the U.S. models. This, incidentally, is a peculiarity which extends to the sabre of Captain Dysant and also to the officer's sword described below. Stamped on blade, guard and pommel is the number "2035," the significance of which is not known. The scabbard is iron (brazed), brass-mounted.

Figure 17

A very handsome and fine sword made by Cunningham is an officer's sabre which, although reasonably common, is most desirable. It is very light, its

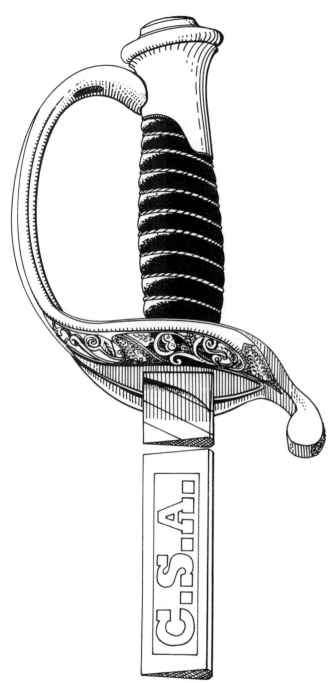

Fig. 18. College Hill Arsenal,
foot officer's sword (C)

curved slender blade being only 29 inches in length, and etched with "C.S.A.," a Confederate Stars and Bars flag and floral designs. A portion of the floral design includes the name "L. T. Cunningham, Nashville." This, however, is so small that it can be perceived only with the aid of a magnifying glass. The guard is identical with those manufactured by the Nashville Plow Works, with large block letters "C.S.A." It does not contain any firm name. The undecorated pommel is high, as already mentioned, and has no backstrap. The scabbard is of leather, seam at the bottom, with all brass mounts.

According to *Forrest's Artillery*, by John W. Morton, page 23: "Swords with CSA in the guard and CSA and a Confederate flag on the blade were made at the Arsenal on College Hill, Nashville, where flintlock guns were converted into percussion." Morton must have had the above sword in mind.

A sword similar to this is in the Battle Abbey collection (Item #144), although the blade etching is somewhat different in that it consists of a field cannon and an 11-starred Confederate flag on one side and at the ricasso "L. T. Cunningham," and on the other, an 11-starred shield bearing "C.S." in small letters and a large "C.S.A." along with the name "J. W. Head." Head was colonel of the 30th Tennessee Infantry Regiment and was Attorney General for the State under Governor Harris.

Figure 18

A foot officer's sword by Cunningham is here pictured. It will be noted that the 31-inch blade is flat, without fullers but is etched in the distinctive design of the College Hill Armory. The blade is unusual in that it has an 18-inch false edge. The weapon was carried by First Lieutenant S. C. Bowers of the 18th Tennessee Infantry, who was captured by the Yankees

February 16, 1862, and imprisoned at Johnson's Island, Sandusky, Ohio, September, 1862, later transferred to Fort Delaware on July 20, 1863, exchanged March 10, 1864, and killed in action near Marietta, Ga., June 22, 1864. Lieutenant Bowers enlisted in the Confederate Army at Nashville, Tenn., on May 22, 1861.

Cunningham also made field officer's swords very similar to those of James Conning, the counterguards of which bear the large letters "C.S." (slanted backward) surrounded by floral designs. The weapon is only 35 inches over-all, with a 30-inch blade, single-fullered on either side. It is etched with the identical design found on the officer's sword above described. The scabbards are also identical. A specimen of such a sword is exhibited at Battle Abbey, Item #168.

As Nashville fell to the Federals in the spring of 1862, Cunningham could have been in operation for only about a year. Judging from the number of his weapons still extant, he must have had a sizable armory.

5. Confederate States Armory (L. Froelich & B. Eastvan), Wilmington and Kenansville, N.C.

(SWORDS, BAYONETS, CUTLASSES AND LANCES)

IN APRIL, 1861, Louis Froelich and a "Colonel" B. Eastvan (sometimes spelled "Estvan"), a Hungarian, secured a contract to supply the State of North Carolina with edged weapons. Operations were begun at Wilmington, N.C.

June 6, 1861, Governor Henry T. Clark of North Carolina wrote to General Anderson, C.S.A., as follows:

Colonel Eastvan at Wilmington proposes to instruct a company in the use of the lance which he recommends as a very effective weapon and says a company or regiment armed with it becomes a most formidable corps. In the great scarcity of arms of every description I am willing to arm a company with the lance which Colonel Eastvan proposes to instruct and drill. If this meets with your approval and you can find or raise such a company you may order the lances forthwith and add the company to your defenses. (Ellis-Clark letters.)

The following year, March 11, Governor Clark wrote to the Confederate Secretary of War, Judah P. Benjamin:

We tried in vain to get swords or carbines for Colonel Spruill's regiment of cavalry. They are yet without sabres although we spared neither effort nor money. We did engage from the Eastvan & Froelich sword factory at Wilmington, and paid high prices, but three-fourths of the swords proved worthless. (*Official Records of the War of the Rebellion*, Vol. 1, Part 4, page 987.)

Eastvan, who posed as a "colonel" and sometimes as a "count," deserted to the Yankees and once safe from the perils of war wrote a book *War Pictures from the South*, supposedly an account of his adventures as a Confederate colonel. These adventures put those of Baron Munchausen to shame.

The affair came to the attention of the Richmond *Examiner*, which on August 10, 1863, declared Eastvan to be neither "count" nor "colonel," as he posed, but a "sleek rascal, smooth-spoken and slimey as the serpent in the garden. He cheated his partner out of all funds and ran away from North Carolina where the factory was located. Eastvan's real name was said to have been 'Raussey' and his occupation prior to his venture into sword-making, a 'discarded valet.' "

Evidently Froelich had already found out something about his partner's background, for on March 12, 1862, he advertised locally that the partnership had been dissolved and that henceforth the sword-making business would be operated by himself alone. Thereafter he moved to Kenansville, N.C., and continued operations under the name of Confederate States Armory, although his business had no official connection with the government, other than on a contract basis.

The Confederate States Armory operated until destroyed by Federal raiders in the fall of 1864. Fortunately we have a pretty good account of its production during this period through the Wilmington (N.C.) *Journal* of April 28, 1864. This source states that from April 1, 1861, to March 1, 1864, "Messrs. L. Froelich & Co., Kenansville, produced: 3,700 lance spears, 800 gross military buttons, 6,500 sabre bayonets, 11,700 cavalry sabres, 2,700 officer's sabres, 600 navy cutlasses, 800 artillery cutlasses (short swords), 1,700 sets of infantry accoutrements, 300 sabre belts and 300 knapsacks."

Such a production indicates a large operation and it is foolish to suppose that it was carried on by fifteen or twenty hands such as a previous account of the author's may have indicated.

The last official account of the enterprise consists of a letter signed "Louis Froelich" on the letterhead of the "Confederate States Armory, L. Froelich & Co.," dated June 7, 1864, addressed to Captain James Dinwiddie, Ordnance Department, Richmond, Va.: "Yours of June 1st received. In reply I would respectfully inform you that I received about the beginning of February last, an order from Colonel Brown through Mayor Taylor to discontinue the manufacture of knapsacks. What I had then on hand have been delivered." This letter is to be found in our National Archives, *Captured Rebel Records*, Vol. 94, Chapter 4. The answer from Captain Dinwiddie can be found in Vol. 91.

Figure 19

Of all the arms made by Froelich only one has been positively identified. This is an officer's sword, and one of the most common and most attractive of all Confederate arms. The blades are almost straight, 32 inches in length, slim, barely 1 inch wide, each side of which has an unstopped fuller. The guard, although actually cast, appears to have been stamped from a sheet of brass and forms the letters "C.S.A." The knuckle guard has no slot for sabre knot. The grip is leather-covered, with a swell in the middle, and wound with single-strand untwisted brass wire. A brass collar encircles the base of the grip at the guard. The reverse of the quillon is always cut with a Roman numeral, the highest of which noted is "XXXVII" and the lowest "VII." The significance of this numeral is not known, although it also appears on the brass throat of the red-lacquered metal scabbard, which has brass ring mounts but iron rings and drag.

A sword as described bears Roman numeral "XXII" and is noted to have an etched blade, the only one ever seen so decorated. The etching is so faint that the complete pattern cannot be made out beyond the general floral designs. The scabbard of this sword, apparently original, is stamped with the Roman numeral "XI."

Swords such as these are found only in the wake of the Army of Northern Virginia. Specimens may be seen at the Smithsonian Institution, Washington, D.C., or at Battle Abbey, Richmond, Va.

Figure 20

Noted in the report of the Wilmington *Journal* was the statement that Froelich had turned out 11,700 cavalry sabres. Now this is a large number and it is odd that to date none have been identified.

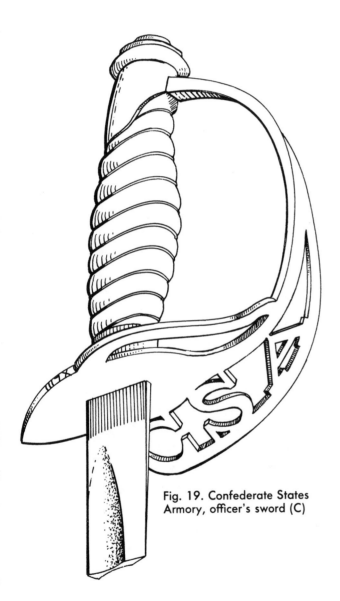

Fig. 19. Confederate States Armory, officer's sword (C)

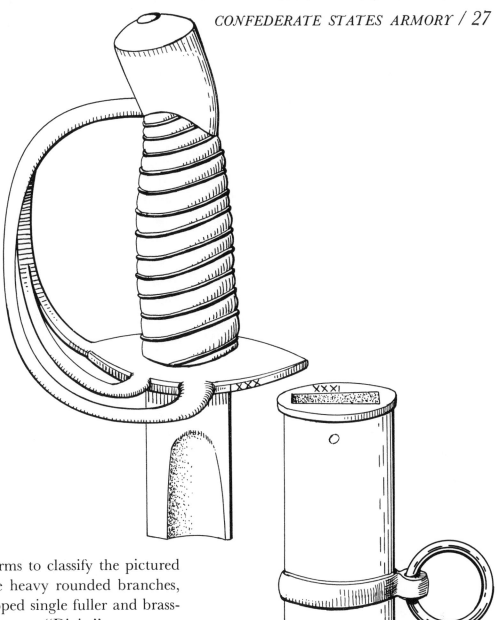

It takes no student of arms to classify the pictured sabre as Confederate. The heavy rounded branches, crude pommel cap, unstopped single fuller and brass-mounted scabbard fairly cry out "Dixie."

All of them appear to be marked with only a Roman numeral cut into the obverse edge of the back portion of the counterguard. The same numeral consistently appears on the brass throat of the scabbard. The significance of such marking is not known, although it is improbable that it applies in any way to the total number made. More likely it has to do with the total of weapons made during a certain period—say, a week or a month.

An exact description of the sketched sword is as follows and all examined adhere closely to these measurements: Slightly curved blade, 35 inches long,

Fig. 20. Confederate States Armory, cavalry sabre (E+)

with modified round back and single fuller tapering out on either end. Over-all length, 41½ inches. Guard is of brass with two heavy and rounded branches joining a rounded knuckle guard and eliptical counterguard. The leather-wrapped grip is wound with heavy untwisted copper wire (some with iron wire). The pommel cap is heavy and knob-like. Scabbard is of iron, brazed, with brass throat and ring mounts. The carrying rings and drag are of iron. Only marks: "XXXI" on side of guard and reverse top (throat) of scabbard. Originally, the scabbards were red-lacquered.

In the writer's collection is such a sabre, marked "IIII" on the edge of the guard, which belonged to Charles B. Foster of Kempsville, Princess Anne County, Va. Purchased with the sword was a photograph of the owner—a young bearded Confederate officer in double-breasted gray frock coat with wide-brimmed black hat, pictured in the act of withdrawing a sword from its scabbard.

After almost a hundred years the photograph has faded, but not so badly that the heavy pommel cap and rounded branches do not clearly show this sword to be the one under discussion. The stamped photographer's name indicates his studio to have been in Norfolk, Va., and as this city fell to the Federals on May 8, 1862, the manufacture of this particular weapon must have started business pretty early in the war.

The U.S. Archives list only one Confederate officer named "Charles B. Foster," as having been senior second lieutenant of Company C, 3rd Confederate Engineers, formerly known as Presstman's Battalion.

Another sabre of this type is in the Battle Abbey collection in Richmond, Va., Item #148, and was carried by Charles H. Powell, Company F, 4th Virginia Cavalry, company bugler. The 4th Virginia

Regiment of Cavalry bears the distinction of having been selected by General J. E. B. Stuart to first try out the imitation of the Sharps breech-loading carbine as made by S. G. Robinson Co., of Richmond, Va.

The similarity between the cavalry sabres and the officer's swords previously described is marked, both in method of manufacture of the sword itself as well as the scabbards, and in the manner of markings. Although not by any means definitely established, it is the writer's firm belief that these cavalry sabres are the product of L. Froelich at Kenansville, N.C. Like the officer's swords, they are to be found only in the wake of that superb Army of Northern Virginia.

Figure 21

Other weapons of L. Froelich have never been identified, although in the Battle Abbey collection, Richmond, Va., are two edged weapons which the late Richard D. Steuart always felt came from Kenansville. For those too young, or too new in the collection field, Richard Steuart was the peer of all Confederate collectors and writers on the subject of Civil War ordnance. In 1949, Mr. Steuart presented his outstanding collection of Confederate relics to the Virginia Historical Society in Richmond, Va., and it is permanently housed in the home of the Society at Battle Abbey. Included in this collection are the following: Item #191: "Confederate navy cutlass (Kenansville, N.C.?) 21 inches overall, 16 inch straight double-edged blade, 1¾ inches wide, iron guard, wooden grip. Cut in grip 'Roanoke, Feb. 8, 1862.' Probably made by Froelich & Co., Kenansville, N.C." Item #200: "Confederate knife, 20 inches overall, 15 inch heavy clip blade, wooden grip, iron guard. Apparently factory made and may have been manufactured by Froelich & Co. of Kenansville, N.C. as a navy cutlass."

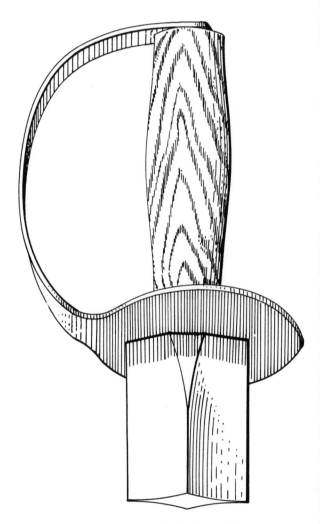

Fig. 21. Confederate States Armory, naval cutlass (E+)

Somewhat similar to the cutlass pictured, although a great deal better constructed, is one in a private collection, mentioned here only because of its similarity and eye appeal. Its double-edged blade is 18½ inches long, diamond cross section, wasp waist, 2¼ inches wide. The metal guard is similar to the Froelich cutlass. The grip is round, of fine flame maple, at the base of which is a zinc collar. There is no pommel, but a copper washer is set at the top of the grip over which the blade tang is peened. The scabbard is most unusual, being of tin, covered with leather and entirely outlined by a frame of wrought iron. Two iron carrying rings are attached to this frame. This is a very handsome and very heavy weapon.

6. James Conning, Mobile, Ala.
(ALL TYPES OF SWORDS)

STEPHEN ENSKO in his *American Silversmiths* lists James Conning as a New York silversmith *circa* 1840. Conning was first brought to the writer's attention in connection with a typical sword of the period 1835, which had an ivory grip, eagle's-head pommel and 30-inch straight blade. The leather scabbard had brass mounts, the throat of which was engraved: "Made by James Conning, Mobile, Ala., 1776." The reverse bore the engraved name "J. H. Carr." The blade was stamped with the number "20." The meaning of the engraving is not known but obviously the sword was not made in 1776.

Since this weapon appeared, some 30 or 40 years ago, a number of other swords by Conning have become known. A peculiarity seems to be that many bear the maker's name on the scabbard throat and another name on the obverse side.

Figure 22

Perhaps the best known of Conning's swords are

those of the field officer type, basket guard with large "C.S." in the counterguard, which also contains a rose pattern. The blade is almost straight, single un-stopped fuller on either side, modified rounded back, 29½ inches long. The guard is of brass, as is the pom-mel, the forward edge of which is decorated with a laurel leaf design. The leather-covered grip is wound with twisted brass wire. Scabbards for these swords were usually of leather, brass-mounted, although the specimen in the writer's collection has a metal scab-bard with fancy brass mounts, the throat of which is engraved "Made for James Conning, Mobile," in three lines. One formerly owned bore the maker's name with "H. A. Lowe" engraved on the obverse. Most are stamped with a serial number on the ricasso and under the guard at the front of the blade.

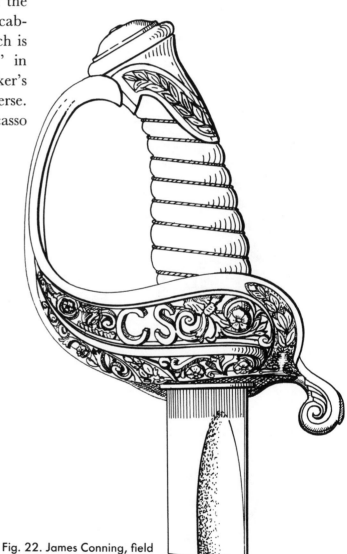

Fig. 22. James Conning, field officer's sword (C)

Conning also made foot officer's swords which conform pretty closely to standard. One in a private collection has a straight blade, 30 inches long, with single unstopped fuller on either side. The guard and pommel are of brass, once gold-plated. The pommel is decorated with a laurel leaf design on the forward edge, and the guard contains the customary rose pattern. The scabbard is of leather, seam in the middle of the back, with brass ring mounts, throat and drag, each of which is stamped with the number "204." The same number is to be found on the underside of the guard at the front of the blade and also on the ricasso of the blade itself. The top mount is engraved on the obverse: "Lieut. R. M. Rogers, from L. S." (in four lines). The reserve is engraved: "Made by James Conning, Mobile" (three lines). This weapon was once owned by Major James Walter Spradty, Quartermaster Corps, C.S.A., on the staff of General Gardner, C.S.A., and used at the siege of Port Hudson after the original owner, Rogers, had been killed.

It would appear that Conning was under no contract on officer's swords, but made and sold them privately. However, he was under contract with the State of Alabama for both artillery and cavalry sabres.

Figure 23

A contract cavalry sabre by Conning has a 36-inch curved blade, flat back, unstopped fullers, $1\frac{3}{8}$ inches wide. The $5\frac{1}{2}$-inch brass guard (knuckle bow with two branches joining an eliptical counterguard) is stamped with the number "180" on the back top, along with "152" and "40." The number "180" also appears on the back of the blade, and "James Conning, Mobile" on the reverse ricasso. The obverse of

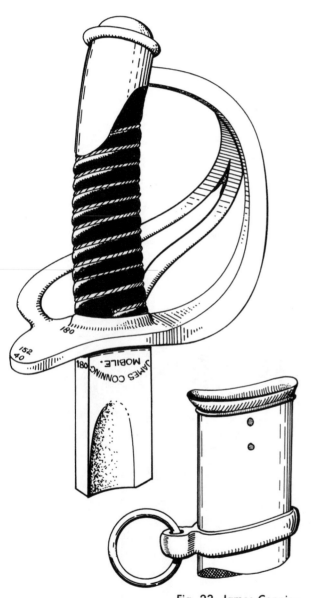

Fig. 23. James Conning, cavalry sabre (D+)

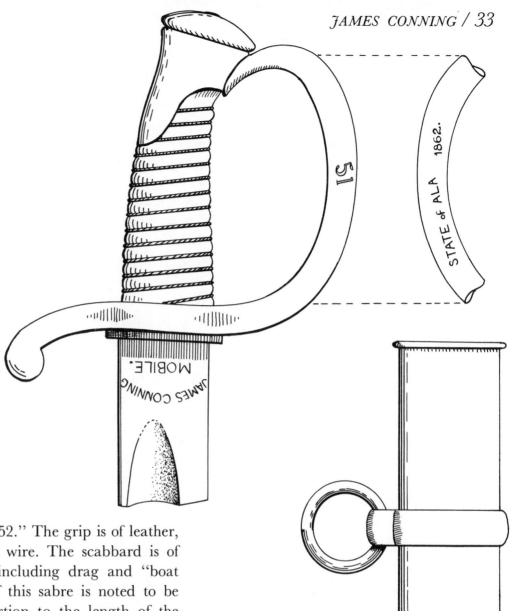

Fig. 24. James Conning,
artillery sabre (D+)

the pommel is stamped "152." The grip is of leather,
wound with twisted brass wire. The scabbard is of
iron with brass mounts, including drag and "boat
type" throat. The grip of this sabre is noted to be
unusually small in proportion to the length of the
blade.

Figure 24

An artillery sabre made under contract for the
State of Alabama is pictured. It has a 28¼-inch blade
which is only slightly curved, single tapering fullers
on either side. It is stamped with the maker's name on
the reverse ricasso in a semicircle above "Mobile."
The "D" guard and standard artillery pommel are of
brass, the former being stamped with the number
"51," as shown. The obverse is stamped "State of
Ala." and the date "1862." The all-iron scabbard is
braze-welded. In the Battle Abbey collection, Rich-

mond, Va. Item #178 is an artillery sabre similar to the one pictured, bearing the serial number "127." It too has a grip of wood, grooved, but not covered with leather, although wound with twisted brass wire.

The contract swords of Conning are very rare.

Of Conning, personally, nothing is known. The City Directory for Mobile, 1873, lists as follows: "Virginia Conning, widow of James, residence South-side Davis Ave., 2 W. Ann St."

During the war Conning is known to have operated from Dauphin and Water streets, according to an advertisement which appeared in a local Mobile paper on October 21, 1862: "Military buttons, just received a few gross of very fine gilt gold staff buttons. Sold by the gross or set. James Conning, Dauphin and Water Sts."

After the war John G. Conning, evidently a son of James, continued the business, as he and a John H. Pippen are listed in the 1873 Directory at Dauphin and Water streets as "Watchmaker and jeweler, N.E. corner, residence 2 W. Ann St., Southside Davis Ave."

7. Cook & Brother, New Orleans, La., and Athens, Ga.

(CUTLASSES, SWORDS AND BAYONETS)

IN JUNE, 1861, Ferdinand W. C. Cook, engineer and architect, with his brother Francis opened the Cook & Brother rifle manufactory at #1 Canal Street, New Orleans, La. Their initial contract was with the State of Alabama. Operations were begun with 27 men and 8 or 10 rifles per day were turned out. By August, 1861, in addition to the contract with the State of Alabama, the operation had increased to such a degree that they accepted $5,000 to arm a full company of Mississippi volunteers.

On April 1, 1862, another contract was secured with the Confederate Government for 30,000 rifles upon receipt of an advance of $150,000. By this time Cook & Brother, according to the daily *True Delta*, was "the largest gun and rifle factory in the Confederacy; and although in its infancy, it turns out twenty rifles and a vast number of artillery swords and sword bayonets each day. They employ nearly four hundred men. . . ."

New Orleans fell to the Federals shortly thereafter but the firm escaped with a small portion of their original machinery, eventually relocating in Athens, Ga., where a mill and 63 acres of land were purchased from the Messrs. Hodgson and Colonel William A. Carr. Here they operated until the end of the war, although during the last days of the Confederacy the plant was closed because of lack of funds. About 500 men were employed and the plant was capable of producing 600 rifles and/or carbines per month, although this production was never realized.

Major Ferdinand Cook formed an "Armory Guard," which was called out at the battle of nearby Griswoldville, Ga., in November, 1864. In December, 1864, the Major was killed at the head of his troops at Goose Pond, S.C.

A number of the rifles, carbines and musketoons made by Cook & Brother have survived the years. Only a very few of their edged weapons are known still to exist. Their triangular bayonets have never been identified.

James W. Camak writing in the magazine *Antique Firearms* in January, 1911, states: "The armory also made a fine triangular bayonet, bayonet scabbards, belts, cartridge boxes. An attempt was also made to manufacture sabres, but they were crude affairs with an iron hilt of Revolutionary type. Their manufacture was not a success and the attempt was soon abandoned.

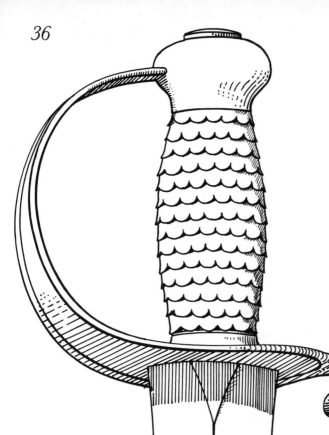

Fig. 25. Cook & Brother,
naval cutlass (D+)

No attempt was made to manufacture pistols or revolvers.''

None of Cook's "crude Revolutionary type" sabres are known to have survived but a few of the naval cutlasses are still extant.

Figure 25

The Cook naval cutlass is patterned after the U.S. Model 1841, the blade being double-edged, with a diamond cross section 1¾ inches wide at the hilt, 21

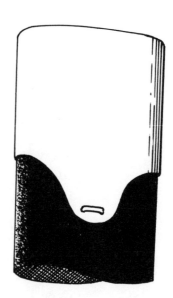

inches long, gradually tapering to the point, with a triangular ricasso. The brass guard consists of a broad strip, beaded on either outer edge, gradually expanding from pommel to form a wide flat counterguard which ends in a quillon terminating in a flat disk. Grip and pommel are cast in one piece, the former of simulated fish scales. Unlike the U.S. model, but like most Confederate ones, the grip is not held to the tang of the blade by rivets through the grip, being peened at the top of the pommel. The name "Cook & Brother" in small stamping is on the top of the guard. The scabbard is of black leather with brass mounts.

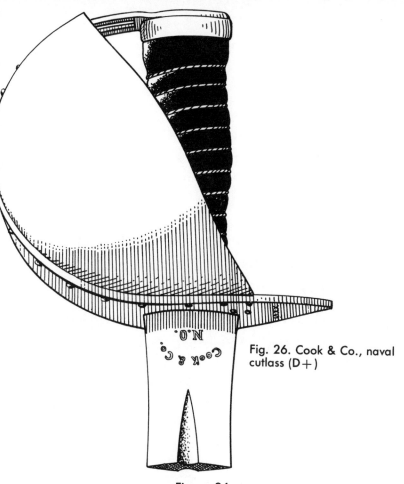

Fig. 26. Cook & Co., naval cutlass (D+)

Figure 26

The writer has never seen an artillery sword or sabre which could be attributed to Cook. However, the pictured navy cutlass presumably is his. The blade is 21¾ inches long, double-edged with a 7¼-inch fuller, and 1⅜ inches wide. The grip is brown leather, wound with 10 turns of twisted brass wire. There is a brass ferrule at top and bottom of grip. The guard is of brass, stamped, the number "XXVI" appearing on the underside. As shown, the blade is stamped "Cook & Co." in a semicircle over "N.O." (New Orleans).

Figure 27

A sabre bayonet which might have been made by Cook & Brother is here pictured, it being the only bayonet ever encountered which would fit a rifle made by this firm, barrel dimensions of which were constant. The fact that these bayonets are found with varying sizes of guard ring suggests that if they were

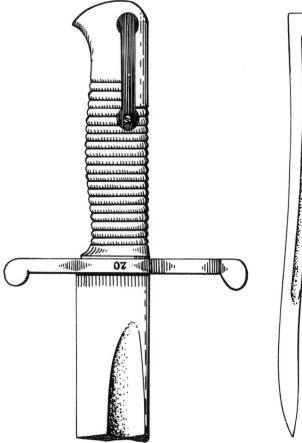

Fig. 27. Cook & Brother, sabre bayonet (E+)

made by Cook & Brother the firm was also supplying them to fit other makes of rifles or muskets. They are marked only with a serial number on the cross guard, and some are devoid of such markings.

8. Courtney & Tennant, Charleston, S.C. (Robert Mole, Birmingham, England) (See also Firmin & Sons.)

(SWORDS AND CUTLASSES)

COURTNEY & TENNANT contributed considerably to the Confederate war effort. The "Courtney" of the firm is unknown, but early in the war George B. Tennant, of Charleston, a partner in the business, was sent abroad by the Confederate Naval Department to act as agent for Edward Tiball, who held the responsible position of Chief Clerk of that department. Tennant was instrumental in the purchase of practically everything used by the C.S. Navy, from the large-calibre cannon to ship's china bearing the C.S. naval coat-of-arms (fouled anchor superimposed over crossed cannon). It was he, incidentally, who helped design this coat-of-arms, which adorns the face of most Confederate naval buttons.

While abroad, Tennant secured a contract for swords and cutlasses from the old and established sword-making firm of Robert Mole of Birmingham, England. The cavalry sabres received from Mole were patterned after the English Model 1853, having a large, almost straight blade, $34\frac{1}{2}$ inches long, single unstopped fuller on either side. As furnished the English Government, the guards were of iron (knuckle bow joined by two branches), but those supplied Courtney & Tennant had guards of brass, and all such sabres with brass guards whose blades are stamped "Mole" can be considered Confederate. Like all of this model they have a leather two-piece grip riveted to the tang of the blade. They are stamped "Mole" under the guard and on the back of the blade. The scabbards are of iron.

Robert Mole had been in business for a number of years and had supplied the English Government with a variety of edged weapons. As far as is known, the only Mole swords which can definitely be called Confederate are those above described, except those which also contain additional markings or decorations showing clearly that they were made for the South.

Figure 28

Identical with the cavalry sabres in grip and guard are the naval cutlasses, these having the brass cavalry type guard, leather grip, etc. The blades, however, are 20 inches in length, double-edged, 1¾ inches wide at grip with wasp waist. A single tapering fuller is on

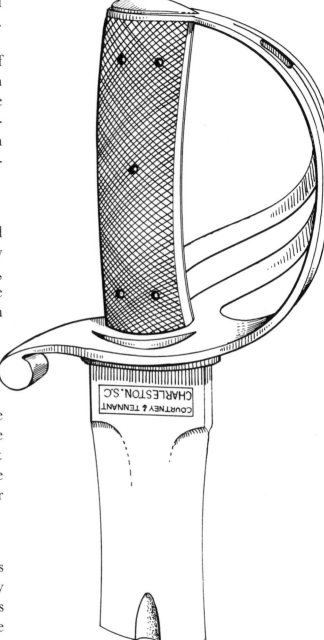

either side. Like the cavalry sabres, they too are stamped "Mole" on the back of blade and on the underside of guard, but also are stamped "Courtney & Tennant, Charleston, S.C." (two lines) in a rectangle on the obverse ricasso. The scabbards are of leather with brass throat and toe, and stud for frog.

Figure 29

Some few of the regulation English cavalry sabres with iron guards must have been purchased by Courtney & Tennant. One in a private collection is known to be of this type, with the firm name on the ricasso (three lines), and "C.S.A." on the other side. The name of the manufacturer does not appear. The scabbard is of iron.

The most desirable of the Courtney & Tennant swords are those made by Mole and which conform

Fig. 28. Courtney & Tennant, naval cutlass (D+)

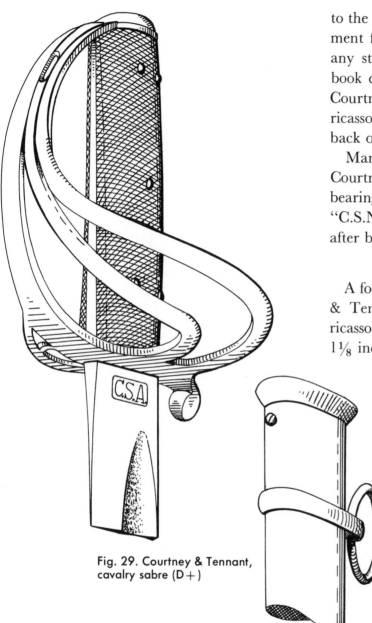

Fig. 29. Courtney & Tennant, cavalry sabre (D+)

to the standard as set forth by the C.S. Naval Department for C.S. naval officers. This is a fine sword by any standard. It is described in the portion of this book devoted to Firmin & Sons. Those imported by Courtney & Tennant bear the firm's name on the ricasso and the manufacturer's name (Mole) on the back of the blade and underside of the guard.

Many Confederate naval buttons bear the name of Courtney & Tennant on their reverse sides, the faces bearing the coat-of-arms with either "C.S." or "C.S.N." beneath. Such buttons are highly sought after by today's collector.

Figure 30

A foot officer's sword bearing the name of Courtney & Tennant, Charleston, S.C., in three lines on the ricasso is here pictured. The blade is 32 inches long, 1⅛ inches wide, with modified flat back. The grip is

of sharkskin, wound with 15 turns of double twisted brass wire. The reverse ricasso of this weapon is stamped "Solingen." The circumstances of its reaching Courtney & Tennant are not known, but it is assumed that Tennant's activities must have extended beyond England to Germany. Also it would appear that all the Mole swords purchased by the subject firm were stamped with the two-line die. On other purchases the three-line die was used.

9. Devisme, Paris, France
(SWORDS)
Figure 31

ONE OF the rarest, if not the rarest treasure housed in the Confederate Museum in Richmond, Va., is the sword of General Robert E. Lee, worn at the time of his surrender to General U.S. Grant at Appomattox, Va. The historical value of this weapon is beyond all calculation, but leaving this aside, its intrinsic worth, even if its owner were not known, is not small.

This sword is almost straight, with a quill-back, 34 inches in length, 1⅛ inches in width. Both sides are exquisitely etched with floral designs, stands of arms and trophies, but in addition, the obverse bears the inscription: "Gen'l Robert E. Lee, C.S.A. from a marylander, 1863." (Note that "Marylander" is spelled with a small "m.") The reverse contains the French motto: "*Aide toi et Dieu L'aidera.*" Translated, this means: "God helps him who helps himself." The motto was a popular one in the South and may also be found on the china ship service made by E. F. Bodley & Co., Burslem, England, for the Confederate States Navy, which in addition to the motto also bears the Confederate naval coat-of-arms, a fouled anchor superimposed over two crossed cannons.

The guard and counterguard of the sword in question are finely cast brass, heavily gold-plated, bearing in high relief, floral designs, draped figures, a snake intertwined throughout the branches, and a shield bearing a cross. The significance of these designs is not known. The pommel and backstrap are shaped to form a lion's head. The ivory grip is wound with 10

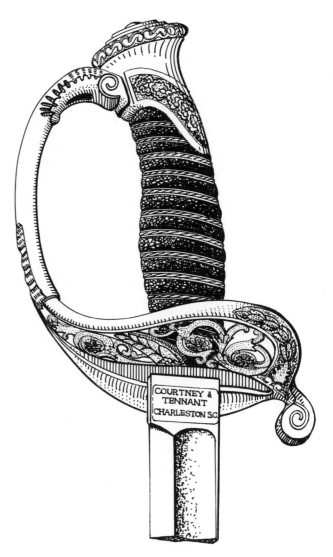

Fig. 30. Courtney & Tennant, foot officer's sword (D+)

turns of 3 twisted gilt wires. Over-all length is 40 inches, excluding the polished gun-metal scabbard with ornamented brass mounts.

The whole is as exquisite a weapon as can be imagined. The back of the blade is inscribed with the maker's name: "Devisme, à Paris."

Richard D. Steuart, whose collection of Confederate arms in the Battle Abbey, Richmond, Va., is the finest in existence, expressed to the author the belief that this particular sword was given General Lee by a Samuel H. Tagart, of Baltimore, Md., at whose home the General stopped both before and after the war. Available records do not disclose the donor, and Maryland having remained in the Union, General Lee would not name him for fear of Federal reprisal upon his benefactor.

Devisme of Paris, France, supplied the South with a number of revolvers and sabres, but as far as is known, the sword described is their only edged weapon made exclusively for the South and which bears Confederate inscriptions.

General John B. Hood, C.S.A. (Texas), carried a Devisme cavalry sabre of French design from which the U.S. Cavalry Officer's Model 1840 was taken. This has a decorated pommel, knuckle bow, branches and counterguard. It was a popular type of sabre in the South and copies of it were made by Thomas, Griswold & Co., William J. McElroy & Co., Leech & Rigdon and Bissonnet.

Fig. 31. Devisme, the sword of General Robert E. Lee (A) Courtesy Confederate Museum, Richmond, Va.

10. Dufilho, New Orleans, La.

(SWORDS)
Figure 32

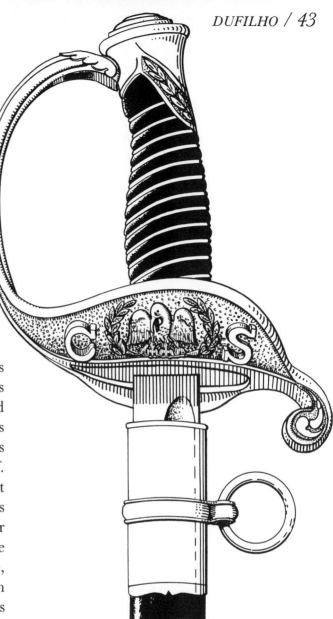

Fig. 32. Dufilho, field officer's sword (C)

EXCEPT for the few swords he left behind, little is known concerning Dufilho. The sword for which he is best known is a beautiful weapon. The counterguard is unpierced and contains in high relief the letters "C.S.," separated by the Louisiana coat-of-arms (pelican on nest feeding her young), also in high relief. The grip is leather-wrapped, wound with twisted gilt wire. The pommel cap is ornamented. The blade is 30 inches long, straight, with single unstopped fuller on either side (a stopped fuller on a sword of this type indicates a replaced blade). Stamped on the ricasso, or in the fuller itself, is "Dufilho, N.O." The "h" in the name is rarely clear and more closely resembles an "n." For this reason this maker is more usually referred to as "Dufilno" than by his correct name.

Although presentation swords of the type described are sometimes encountered with finely etched blades, most are bare of such decoration. The scabbards are leather with all-brass mounts.

Another sword by Dufilho is one which closely follows the U. S. Foot Officer's Sword, Model 1850. The blade is identical with the one described above. The brass guard has the standard rose design. The pommel cap is decorated along its forward edge with laurel leaves. Grip is of leather, wound with twisted gilt wire. Scabbard is of leather, all-brass mounts.

11. Fayetteville Armory, Fayetteville, N.C.

(BAYONETS)

IN MARCH, 1898, Matthew P. Taylor, Major, 6th Batt. Armory Guard, wrote in the Wilmington (N.C.) *Messenger*:

The Fayetteville Armory was located on what is known as "Hay Mount" and no trace remains, having been totally destroyed by Sherman. It overlooked the old city, and was constructed by the U.S. government prior to the war, under the immediate supervision of a Mr. William Bell, as architect; but in charge of various army officers of high distinction as commandants of the post. It was one of the loveliest spots anywhere in the South, and was very often visited by strangers from various States and greatly admired.

Conspicuous octagonal high brick and stone towers were located at the four corners of the enclosure, while symmetrical walls and massive iron railing and heavy iron gates surrounded the premises. Handsome two-story brick and stone buildings for officers' quarters and the accommodation of the troops adorned the front and sides, while in the centre, rear and both sides were large commodious buildings used for the storing of small-arms, fixed ammunition, commissary and quartermaster supplies. In the centre of the enclosure were the gun-carriage and machine shops, the former with Mr. T. S. Barratt as superintendent, who had served the U.S. Government formerly at Old Point Comfort for a number of years before the war, while in the rear part of this enclosure was a large rifle-factory, containing all the rifle works brought from Harpers Ferry, Va., and handsome frame dwellings for various officers' quarters. With the exception of these last, all the other buildings were constructed of brick, trimmed with stone. Mr. Bell continued during the entire war as architect of all buildings, and was a Scotchman of national reputation. Some 100 yards from the rifle-factory were two large brick magazines for the storage of powder and fixed ammunition.

Captain John C. Booth, an old army man was placed in command of the arsenal following its surrender to the C.S. authorities by Lieutenant DeLagnel, who returned North, gave up his commission and then joined the C.S. Army. Booth enlarged the buildings, and added an armory for the rifle machinery. He became ill from over-work and died, but previous to his death and while ill, was promoted to rank of major. At his death, Captain Charles P. Bolles assumed command until Lieutenant Colonel J. A. DeLagnel was placed in command three weeks later. DeLagnel remained at the post for about six months when he returned to the field, being relieved in command by Lieutenant Colonel F. L. Childs who continued in command until the close of the war

The rifles made at Fayetteville were as fine as any made for the U.S. Army—they should have been, as their manufacture was accomplished on machinery originally set up at the U.S. Arsenal and Armory at Harpers Ferry, Va. On the same day that Virginia seceded from the Union her State troops seized the Armory and the property was claimed by the State. The machinery was carried off to Richmond, the portion which had to do with the manufacture of muskets being retained there. The rifle machinery was sent on to Fayetteville. It was said at the time that the works had sufficient machinery on hand to manufacture 10,000 arms per year if provided with 250 hands.

Confederate operations at Fayetteville began early. The Richmond *Dispatch* on June 18, 1861, commented that "all the rifle works recently at Harpers Ferry have been boxed and removed to the armory at Fayetteville, N.C., where the fabrication and alteration of guns will be immediately commenced."

On August 9, the following year, the same source states:

The Confederate Arsenal and Armory at Fayetteville, N.C., may be said to be in full blast; at least, there is nothing pertaining to the Minnie rifle and sabre bayonet that can not be manufactured on the spot and equal to any in the world. A few days since, a large lot of rifles manufactured at the Armory were sent to the Chief of Ordnance, Richmond, Va. Besides making new rifles and altering old ones, the force at the Armory has been engaged lately in restoring and putting in order several thousand Enfield and Belgium rifles, swords, sabres and bayonets, and also several boxes of pistols received from the *Modern Greece* (blockade runner) considerably damaged. They will soon be restored to their original appearance and condition by the industry and skill of the mechanics engaged.

The works continued operations until March, 1865, when upon the approach of General Sherman, U.S.A., the machinery was taken to Egypt, Chatham County, N.C., and there secreted in an old mine. At the time of its seizure by the Federals in 1865, the following arms were captured: 2,028 muskets, 3,000 unfinished rifles and 500 sabres.

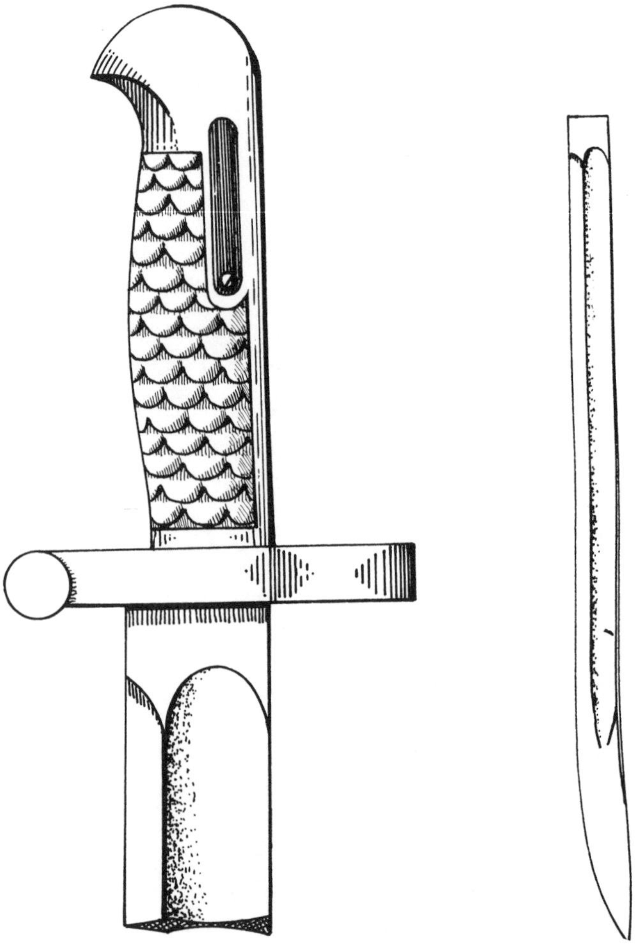

Figure 33

Although the Armory did considerable repair work on various edged weapons, the only such actually made there were the sabre bayonets designed for the Model 1841 rifle. These bayonets all conformed to the same pattern, having a 22-inch blade, straight for 16 inches, after which there is a decided curve to the rear. There is a single deep fuller on each side of the blade, tapered at the point end, the other end terminating in a symmetrical half-curve. The hilt and guard are made in one piece of cast brass, with a single iron rivet through grip and blade tang just above the guard. Grip is cast to represent eagle's feathers. Most are unmarked but some few are stamped "C.S.A." on the blade with the same die that stamped these initials on the brass butt plates of the Fayetteville rifles. The scabbards are of black leather with thin brass mouth and tip.

Manufacture of sabre bayonets was discontinued in the Confederacy as of January 14, 1864, by order of Adjutant General Samuel Cooper, so it is safe to assume that all in existence were made between June, 1861, and January, 1864.

Fig. 33. Fayetteville Armory, sabre bayonet (D+)

12. Firmin & Sons, London, England
(SWORDS)

ONE OF the most fascinating books on the Civil War is *Recollections of a Rebel Reefer*, written by James Morris Morgan and published in 1917. Delightfully told, the story recounts the many adventures which befell Morgan during that time he was a midshipman in the Confederate States Navy, and later a colonel in the Egyptian Army.

Long after the war Colonel Morgan had occasion to go to Richmond, Va., and while there, visited the old home of Confederate President Jefferson Davis, which is now known as "The White House of the Confederacy" or "The Confederate Museum." Says the Colonel of his visit:

The ladies connected with the museum were very kind to me, and I felt very much complimented when they requested me to present to the Museum the Confederate regulation naval sword which I wore when I accompanied Mrs. Davis (wife of the President) South (at the evacuation of Richmond). The sword was made in England, and had the cotton plant chased on one side of the blade, and the tobacco plant on the other; also the first Confederate flag (the Stars and Bars) and the naval coat-of-arms—two crossed cannon and a fouled anchor. This sword now hangs in the Louisiana Room of the Confederate "White House."

Figure 34

All Confederate swords are rare, but the type described by Colonel Morgan is one of the rarest and most beautiful of all the blades that were drawn in defense of the South. Besides the cotton, tobacco, Stars and Bars flag and Confederate naval coat-of-arms chased on the blade itself and mentioned by Colonel Morgan, these same motifs (without the flag) are repeated in high relief on the counterguard. The pommel and backstrap form a sea monster. The reverse of the counterguard is hinged so that the weapon

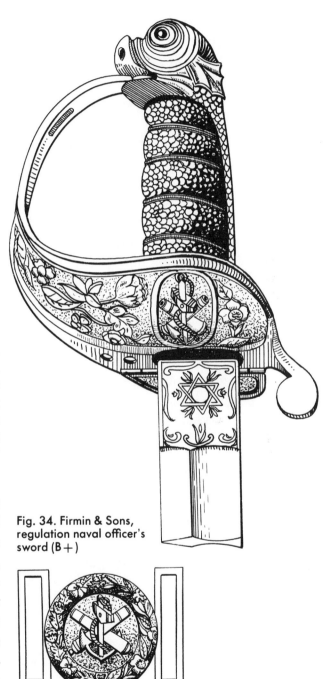

Fig. 34. Firmin & Sons, regulation naval officer's sword (B+)

can hang flat against the officer's side, and on most, there is a small hole on this portion made to engage a stud on the scabbard which "locks" the blade in the scabbard. The grip is of sharkskin, wound with three separate strands of twisted gilt wire. The black leather scabbard is brass-mounted, the ring mounts representing square knots of rope. The drag is formed of two twisted snakes. All brasswork on sword and scabbard is gold-plated, and the weapon is strikingly beautiful. The straight blade is 31 inches long. Over-all length is 36 inches.

Most of those extant are stamped on the back of the blade and underside of counterguard "Mole," who was the English maker; and in addition are also stamped on the ricasso "Courtney & Tennant, Charleston, S.C." (two lines), the dealer-importer. (See 8. Courtney & Tennant.)

Some few of the regulation naval swords do not contain the maker's name at all but are etched on the ricasso "Firmin & Sons, 153 Strand and 13 Conduit St., London." Firmin & Sons were military outfitters, not manufacturers. Their name is frequently to be found on the back of Confederate naval buttons.

Whether bearing the stamp of "Courtney & Tennant" or the etched name of "Firmin & Sons," the intricate chasing on the blade and the casting of the guard appear identical, although of those examined the ones carrying the name of Firmin & Sons are much more deeply etched than the ones ascribed to Courtney & Tennant. It is assumed, but not definitely known, that Robert Mole of Birmingham, England, was the maker of all these weapons regardless of what military outfitter's name appears on the blade or guard.

One other difference is noted and worthy of mention. The blade design on most contains the Confederate Stars and Bars flag, but some are chased with a very handsome flag which, though doubtlessly intended to be Confederate, is evidently the etcher's opinion of how a Confederate naval flag should look. It is identical with the Stars and Bars except that the Confederate battle flag appears as the "union." This error is no worse than the common one of today which consistently depicts the battle flag as rectangular. It was, in fact, always square.

In the Confederate Museum in Richmond, in addition to Colonel Morgan's sword, is a similar one which belonged to Captain French Forrest, Commandant of the Norfolk Navy Yard, afterward the Commander of the James River Squadron. Both bear the marking "Firmin & Sons." Colonel Morgan's has the Stars and Bars flag while Captain Forrest's has the flag with the battle flag union.

The same museum has two other swords of this type from Courtney & Tennant. One was carried by Captain James C. Bulloch, C.S.N., and the other by Lodge Colton of the *C.S.S. Shenandoah*.

The belt buckle depicted is regulation C.S. Navy, and will be noted to bear also the C.S. Navy coat-of-arms, a fouled anchor superimposed on crossed cannons, the surrounding wreath of cotton and tobacco leaves. This particular buckle was worn by Commander John McIntosh Kell at the time he was Executive Officer of the *C.S.S. Alabama*, under Raphael Semmes. After the war Kell became Adjutant General for the State of Georgia. Belt buckles such as these are extremely rare. One in the Confederate Museum, Richmond, has the letters "C.S.N." under the coat-of-arms, as usually found on most Confederate naval buttons.

Another sword which came to the Confederacy through the house of Firmin & Sons is the one that was presented to "Captain Raphael Semmes, C.S.N., by officers of the Royal Navy and other friends in

England as a testimonial of their admiration of the gallantry with which he maintained the honour of his country's flag and the fame of the ALABAMA in the engagement off Cherbourg, with a chainplated ship of superior power, armament, and crew, June 19, 1864."

Jay P. Altmayer in his *American Presentation Swords* describes this as "one of the most outstanding historical Civil War items known.—The quality of workmanship, exclusive of its historical significance and its importance in design, all rank it as a superb piece." Mr. Altmayer's appraisal is fully endorsed.

The sword was formerly on display at the public library in the City of Mobile, Ala., in its original mahogany box lined with blue velvet.

Gold, silver, jeweled and enameled, it is hard to imagine a more exquisite piece, except only the one carried by General Robert E. Lee.

13. Georgia State Arsenal & Armory, Milledgeville, Ga.

(BAYONETS)

AT THE time of the Civil War, the capital of the State of Georgia was located at Milledgeville. Also located there, on the grounds now occupied by the Georgia Normal and Industrial College, was the State Penitentiary. Early in the war this was converted by Governor Joseph E. Brown into a State armory and it continued to operate in this capacity until burned by Wilson's raiders in 1865. Governor Brown in reporting to his State Legislature in early 1862 advised that the works was turning out 125 "good arms per month." He failed to mention the type of arms but it is assumed they were muskets and rifles. The first musket made at Milledgeville is said to have contained a silver plate on which was inscribed: "Presented to his Excellency, J. E. Brown, Governor of Georgia."

In addition to the manufacture of shoulder arms the Georgia State Armory also did considerable repair of all types of arms, and served generally as a clearinghouse for all State-owned ordnance. *Confederate Records for the State of Georgia* makes frequent reference to the Armory and its activities. There is no indication that revolvers, knives, bowies or pikes were actually made there, although all of these items were received at this point and inspected by Peter Jones, Master Armorer, formerly connected with the U.S. Armory and Arsenal at Harpers Ferry, Va. Over Jones was Lachlan H. McIntosh, Chief of Ordnance for the State of Georgia. T. M. Bradford was MSK (Military Storekeeper).

In his message to the Georgia General Assembly on December 12, 1862, Governor Brown made note that Georgia had, at the request of President Jefferson Davis, furnished the Confederate States a total of 829 pikes and 321 knives and had since issued to Colonels William Phillip and Jack Brown 960 knives "for the use of the brave troops under their command in Confederate service." Also, a "Colonel Griffin in command at Augusta had been furnished 400 pikes."

These and other such items were inspected by Peter Jones, as were the bayonets which were made at the Armory. The bayonets were of two different kinds and were evidently made for two types of rifles or muskets. Both are sabre bayonets.

Figure 35

One has a 27-inch over-all, 22-inch curved blade, single fuller on either side, tapering at the point end and coming to a deep rounded stop at the hilt end. It has an iron guard and butt with checkered wooden grips riveted to the tang of the blade. It is stamped on the ricasso with "Ga. Armory" and the date. What appears to be a serial number can be found stamped on the wooden grip. In appearance it greatly re-

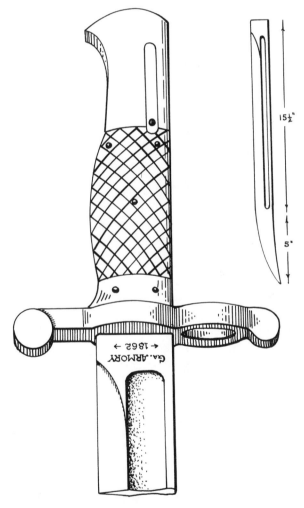

Fig. 35. Georgia Armory, sabre bayonet with wooden grip (B)

sembles the French bayonet of the Franco-Prussian War. The bayonet pictured is in the Battle Abbey collection in Richmond, Va., Item #216, and bears the serial number "127."

Figure 36

The other type of bayonet has a 22-inch yataghan blade, also stamped "Ga. Armory" and the date on the ricasso. The guard, however, is of brass and very similar to the Mississippi rifle bayonet guard. Serial number "16" is stamped on the back of the grip and "3" on the hilt. The scabbard is of black leather, with brass mouthpiece and tip, fastened with copper rivets. This bayonet is also included in Battle Abbey, Item #215.

It is not known why some bayonets were made with iron and wood hilts and others of brass.

If any swords or sabres were made at the Armory, available records are silent on this fact.

After the destruction of the Armory by Wilson's raiders in 1865, a joint committee was formed to examine the condition of the Penitentiary and Armory. The report is as follows (*Senate Journal*, March 1, 1865, page 77):

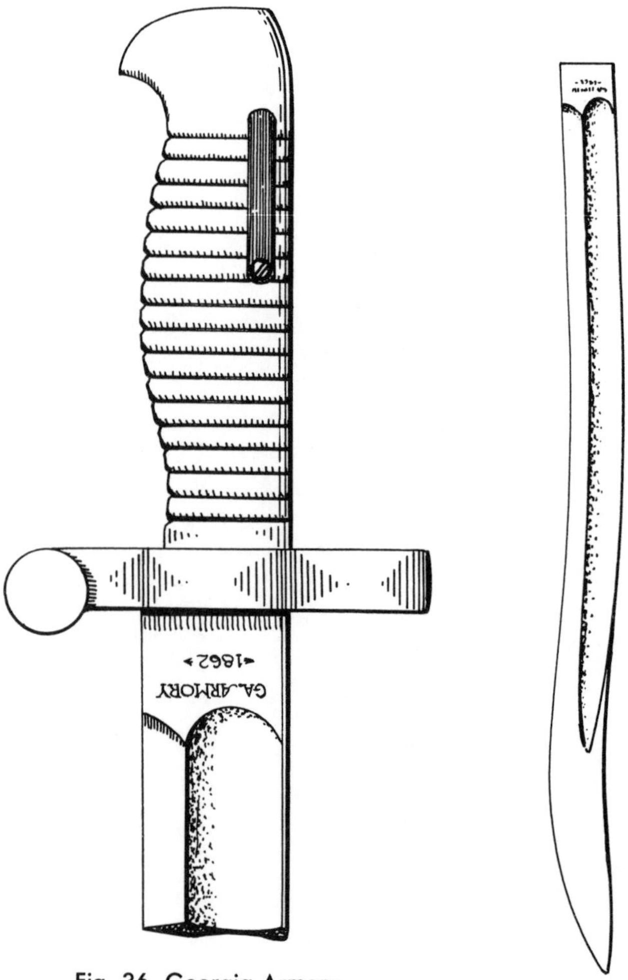

Mr. President:—The committee appointed by a joint resolution of the General Assembly of the State of Georgia to examine the Penitentiary and report upon the policy of rebuilding or abolishing the Penitentiary, beg leave to make the following report:

There are confined in the Penitentiary, and convicted ready to be sent 20 convicts and for the proper employment of these, as well as those who may hereafter be convicted under the present law, it will be necessary to repair the cell building, the woodshop building, the blacksmith building, the tanyard building and the barracks. The outside walls of the Penitentiary, as well as those of all the other buildings are uninjured except the north side of the wood shop building, which has fallen down; about a fourth of the roof on the tanyard building has been replaced. The walls and cells in

Fig. 36. Georgia Armory, sabre bayonet with brass grip (B)

the cell building are without injury. It will require an expenditure of $10,000 to put on the roof and the flooring as the passages where it is burnt. It will take $10,000 to repair the wood shop. It will take $4,000 to repair the blacksmith shop. The walls of the barracks are good, and it will cost $3,000 to put on a roof and furnish window facings and shutters. It will require $1,500 to finish repairs on the tanyard building.

The Committee recommend the repairing of said buildings which will probably answer all the wants of the Penitentiary for the present and for the next two years. The engine can be repaired in two weeks by two workmen and will probably cost $1,000 for that purpose and repairing the engine house. The committee are glad to be able to report that the card machine material etc. were safely removed and will soon be ready to be put to work in the . . . room building. The tanyard is in successful operation, and the present and energetic Principal Keeper hopes to be able from its successful management, to pay the expense of the institution and pay off the debts contracted for supplies, which were destroyed. When the repairs have been made herein recommended, it is thought it will fully supply all the necessities for the next two years.

The committee further recommend that the Governor be authorized to dispose of all the iron, steel, brick and surplus articles appertaining to the Penitentiary and not at this time needed by repairs at public or private sale and apply the proceeds of said sale towards the repairing of the institution.

The committee further report that they have examined into the condition of the State Armory and find on hand 65,000 pounds of bar iron and a large lot of tools and files in good condition. They further find that a portion of the machinery has been so much damaged by burning as to render it unfit for use without replacing many parts of it with new machinery and great outlay of expense.

There is however, a portion of the machinery which was not damaged, except some breakage in its removal from the Penitentiary, and can be put in working order for the repair of arms, and the committee would recommend that the same be put into operation and continued at present for the repair of arms, and not the construction of same. The committee after having fully looked into the condition of the institution, number of convicts now confined in there (15) and others sentenced, but not received (5) and the stock of material on hand in the tanyard and other branches of mechanical labor, formerly carried on there, and the sum necessary to be expended in the repair of the cell building, work shop and engine, would recommend that the institution be continued until further circumstances and considerations may dictate a change in our policy of punishment for crime.

14. Samuel Griswold, Griswoldville, Ga.
(PIKES)

DURING the days of the Civil War there lay about 10 miles east of Macon a little village called Griswoldville, which was at that time a stop on the Central of Georgia Railroad. This village was founded by Samuel Griswold, who came to Georgia from Connecticut in 1814.

As do most Northerners who come South, Samuel Griswold formed a deep loyalty toward his adopted State, taking its customs and traditions as his own. At Griswoldville he erected a large machine and cotton gin shop and began the manufacture of cotton gins which bore his name. His Yankee ingenuity and industry had their usual reward and he prospered, owning property of some 5,000 acres and many slaves.

Born December 29, 1790, Samuel Griswold was an old man at the start of the Civil War in 1861—if we judge age by years alone. He was not too old, however, to respond immediately to the call from his adopted State's Governor for pikes with which to arm State troops against Northern aggression. He was one of the first to turn his machine shop into an armory and by April 3, 1862, turned 16 pikes over to the State Ordnance Department, located at the State capital, which was then Milledgeville, Ga.

The initial lot was supplemented by an additional 90 on April 15, 100 on the 22, 300 May 17, 97 on

May 27 and 201 on June 2, for a grand total of 804 pikes. For these, he received $5 per pike. Meanwhile Mr. Griswold was setting up his machine shops for the purpose of making revolvers, entering into a contract with the Confederate Government for 100 revolvers per month. The 3,600 brass-framed revolvers received over a three year period attest to the integrity of at least one Yankee, for Samuel Griswold was one of the few arms contractors who did exactly what he said he would do.

The story of the Griswold & Gunnison revolvers is too familiar a story to repeat here. Those interested can refer to *The Confederate Brass-Framed Colt & Whitney*, published in 1954. The only material information that can be added since this date is: it has been established that A. W. Gunnison was manager and foreman of the Griswold Cotton Gin Works for many years prior to the war, and that reproductions of this revolver are now being made in Italy and imported to this country, where without question many of them after slight doctoring will be sold as "genuine." It is a shame that in our quest for the dollar such practices are tolerated.

Figure 37

The only edged weapons made by Griswold were the pikes. As far as is known, all of these were of the clover-leaf design, the pike head being composed of three blades, the center one some 10 inches in length, peach-leaf-shaped with diamond cross section. The side blades extend at right angles from the main blade and are 3½ inches from center to point. These heads were mounted on a 6-foot staff, having a round knob on the bottom. Wrought-iron straps run from an iron collar encircling the blade down the staff for some 24 inches. They are stamped variously "Griswold" or "S. Griswold."

While visiting the site of the revolver factory at

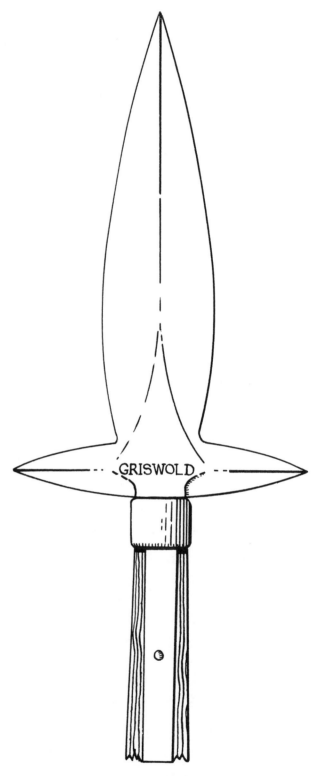

Fig. 37. Samuel Griswold, clover-leaf pike (B)

Griswoldville, Ga., some years ago, the writer was given a rusty head from a clover-leaf pike by a gentleman living nearby, who had picked it up himself from the debris of the destroyed Griswold & Gunnison revolver works.

After the war a number of these pikes were purchased by Francis Bannerman, owner of a large war surplus store in New York, whose annual catalogue has for many years been the "bible" of gun collectors. At the time items such as these could scarcely be given away. To make them more salable Bannerman painted the staffs red, gilded the heads and mounted a number, fan-shaped, on a board. In the process, the ends of the staffs were cut off at the proper angle so as to fit the succeeding pike placed on the board. This information is given to account for the large number of pikes which are today found with short staffs painted red, the ends of which are sawed off at an angle and whose heads have been gilded.

15. Louis Haiman & Brother, Columbus, Ga.

(SWORDS, BAYONETS AND CUTLASSES)

THROUGH the years L. Haiman & Brother have become known as the largest sword manufacturers in the Confederacy. If this be so, it seems odd that so few of their weapons still exist. Undoubtedly in the future some swords now termed "maker unidentified" will be established as the product of this establishment.

Louis Haiman and his brother Elias came to this country from Colma, Prussia, in the early 1800s and settled in Columbus, Ga., which was then a small village. Here they opened a small tinshop. Their business was successful and they became substantial citizens. Entirely loyal to their adopted land, with the war they turned their tinsmithy into an armory and did everything in their power to assist the Confederacy.

In my files is a letter from David Wolfson, a relation and a former operative of Haiman's, written in 1924:

> Haiman made swords, sabres and revolvers. We employed over 500 people. The first sabres we made were for Clanton's Regiment of cavalry from Alabama. We also made swords for officers. We had two people from Virginia who were experts in the manufacture of Colt's pistols. They built machinery to make several parts of these pistols and we made quite a number of revolvers in the exact imitation of the Colt. The demand for work was so large that we had to annex leather works to make the boxes and straps to carry the cartridges and also opened a foundry to make cooking utensils for the Army. The proprietors of the establishment were Louis and Elias Haiman. Louis looked after the business here in Columbus while Elias went to Europe and sent material over here through the blockade. The works were carried on until the close of the war when the Federals came in and destroyed the works.

The Haiman sword factory occupied the upper part of the building whose lower floor was tenanted by the Columbus Iron Works, at Dillingham and Short streets on the banks of the river. The pistol factory occupied the old Muscogee Iron Works Building and the foundry was just behind it, and here were cast the small brasses for gun and sword mounts.

DeBow's *Review*, May-August, 1862, in referring to Louis Haiman, commented that the establishment planned to make Mississippi rifles and were installing machinery capable of turning out 5 rifles per day. According to this source, the firm was then making swords at the rate of 100 per week.

The first sword made by Haiman was presented to Colonel Peyton H. Colquitt, who was afterward killed at Chickamauga. It is said to have been one of the handsomest in all the Southern Army, being inlaid in gold.

Under the caption "War! War! War!," Haiman advertised in the Columbus *Times*, September 2, 1861:

Made to order: Brass Buckles and Plates, for belts and Cartridge Boxes, and Mountings for bayonet Scabbards. All tin and sheet Iron Furniture for Camp Stoves. Officers' and Sergeant Swords finished in the best style. Cavalry Sabres, etc. We also put bayonets to double barrel Shot Guns and Rifles.

On November 17, 1861, the following advertisement appeared in the same paper:

Swords! Swords! The best quality of swords are now made and for sale at the "Confederate States Sword Factory", Columbus, Ga. by L. Haiman & Bro. who have large contracts for the Confederate Govt. They will furnish officers swords with belt for $25 or for $22 where as many as four are ordered in one lot. Every sword is tested according to rules laid down in the manual of War.

Chapter IV, Volume 135, of the *Captured Rebel Records* in the National Archives contains a letter written by L. Haiman to Captain Richard Cuyler, then "Chief of Ordnance, Military District of Savannah." This letter, dated October 22, 1861, gives the following prices on swords: officer's plain—$25; officer's with figured blades and gilted mountings—$35–$50; cavalry sabres 36 inches long with basket hilt of brass, metal scabbard and black leather belt, shoulder strap and tassel to the guard—$23; artillery sabres, 32-inch blade, with single strap guard, metal scabbard, black leather belt without shoulder strap and tassel—$20; artillery swords, 19-inch blades, leather scabbards brass-mounted, black leather belt, heavy brass handle—$14.

Same source, Volume 12, contains a letter dated May 2, 1862, from M. H. Wright, "Ordnance Officer, C.S.A., Atlanta Arsenal," addressed to the "Proprietors of the Sword Factory, Columbus, Ga.," inquiring:

Will you please do me the favor to let me know if you are now engaged in manufacturing sabres: what your facilities are: and inform what terms you can furnish 8,000 articles of the cavalry sabres? Have you any contract with the State, or CSA? I desire to learn as soon as possible whether I can get any sabres from you without interferring with any State or CS contracts.

Sunday, April 16, 1865, General Upton's troops (U.S.A.) of Wilson's cavalry corps captured Columbus. Haiman's property was confiscated and turned into a Federal arsenal.

General Wilson, the commander of the army of occupation, proposed to restore to Haiman his property if he would take the oath of allegiance to Federal authority. This Haiman refused to do and with the departure of the Union troops his factory was razed to the ground.

September, 1866, found "L. Haiman & Bro." proprietors of the Phoenix Foundry and Machine Shop, which was "now in successful operation and prepared to make Grist and saw mills and all kinds of mill work to order. We keep constantly on hand; sugar kettles, from 10 to 100 gallons; ovens, spiders, wash pots, plows, etc. All kinds of iron and brass castings made to order. Country produce taken in exchange for work at market prices." (Columbus *Sun.*)

Later, Haiman became associated with Joseph T. Blount, who when the war started was a cadet at West Point. He entered Confederate service as a lieutenant of the Dearing Georgia Artillery, rising to the rank of colonel. The firm of Blount & Haiman & Co., also known as the Southern Agricultural Works, was located on Oglethorpe Street and specialized in chilled plows. The association continued until January 12, 1876, at which time it was formally dissolved by the death of Mr. Blount (Christmas Day, 1875), at the age of 35. After this, Haiman removed to Atlanta, Ga., continuing the same type of business. He operated in that city until 1878, the year of his death.

Figure 38

Several exceptionally handsome swords by L. Haiman & Bro. are to be found in the Confederate Museum, Richmond, Va. One carried by General

60

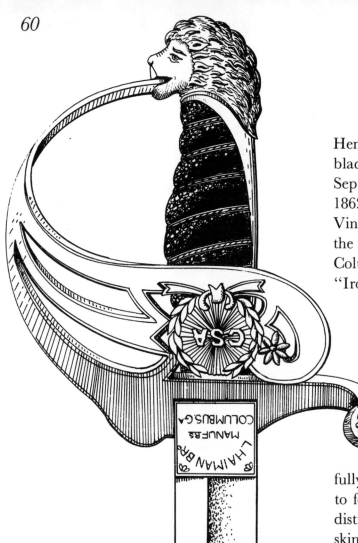

Fig. 38. L. Haiman & Bro.,
presentation sword (B+)

Henry D. Clayton has a beautifully etched straight blade 34 inches long. It is inscribed: "Chicamauga, Sept. 19, 20, 1863; Murfreesboro, Dec. 30th & 31st, 1862; Pensacola, Nov. 22nd & 23rd, 1861; Deo Vindice; Virtus Nobilitat." The reverse ricasso bears the firm's name etched in a semicircle over "Manufrs., Columbus, Ga." The back of the blade is etched "Iron-proof." The gold-plated brass guard is beauti-

fully executed, two branches joining the counterguard to form a laurel wreath inside of which in Haiman's distinctive angular lettering is "C.S.A." The shark-skin grip is wound with 7 turns of 3 twisted gilt wires. The pommel and backstrap form a lion's head. The scabbard is of polished iron with brass mounts.

A sword of similar design is also in the Confederate Museum. This is one which was carried by General Archibald Gracie. The guards of the two swords are the same except that the General's initials, "A.G.," appear in the laurel wreath rather than "C.S.A." The grip is of leather. The blade is etched: "C.S.A., Gen. Archibald Gracie, presented by Lieut. E. B. Cherry." The firm's name is to be found etched within an oval midway of the blade. Both swords have a single stopped fuller on either side.

Figure 39

A naval sword by Haiman is also in the Confederate Museum. It is the one worn by Captain E. V. White, C.S.N., Engineer of the *C.S.S. Virginia* (better known as the *Merrimac*) during her famous fight with the *Monitor*. The straight, single-edged blade is 30¼ inches long, with a single unstopped fuller on either side. It is richly etched with floral designs, stand of arms, etc., and a large "C.S.A." One side of the blade contains the firm's name and address. The gold-plated brass guard bears the raised letters "C.S." in Haiman's distinctive style of angular lettering on the turned-down counterguard. The pommel is decorated on the forward edge with a laurel spray. The grip is of leather, wound with twisted gilt wire. The scabbard is of metal with brass mounts.

An identical sword, Item #187, is included in the Battle Abbey collection.

Figure 40

In the Battle Abbey collection, their Item #176, is a sabre generally conforming to the old U.S. Dragoon, Model 1833. The blade is slightly curved, 34 inches

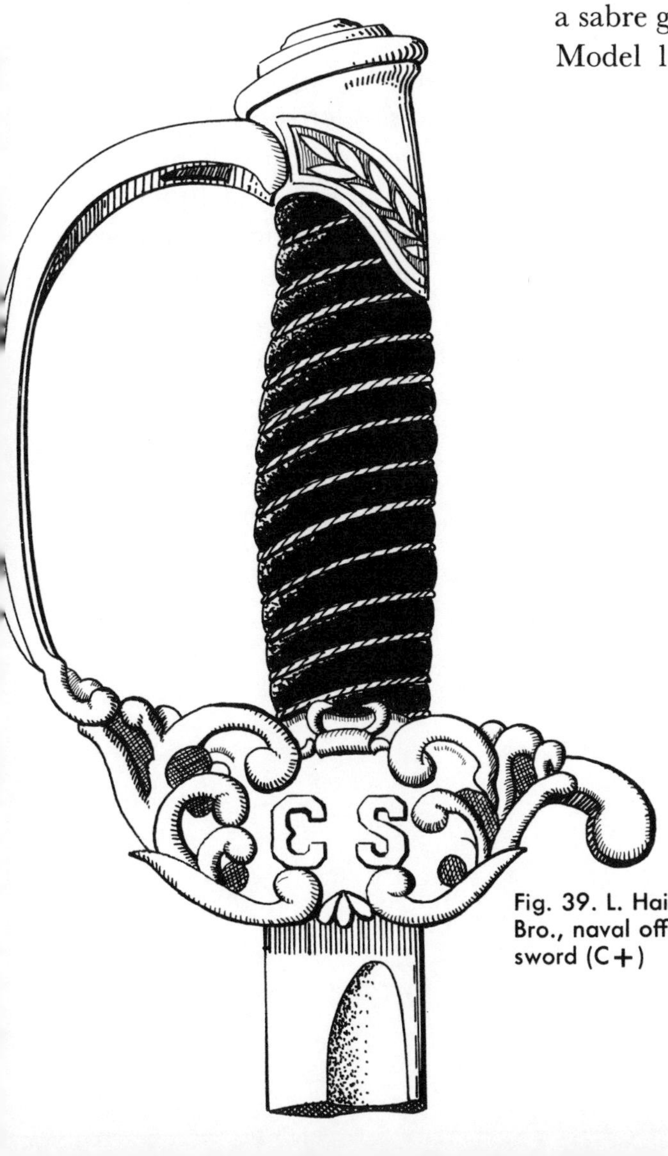

Fig. 39. L. Haiman & Bro., naval officer's sword (C+)

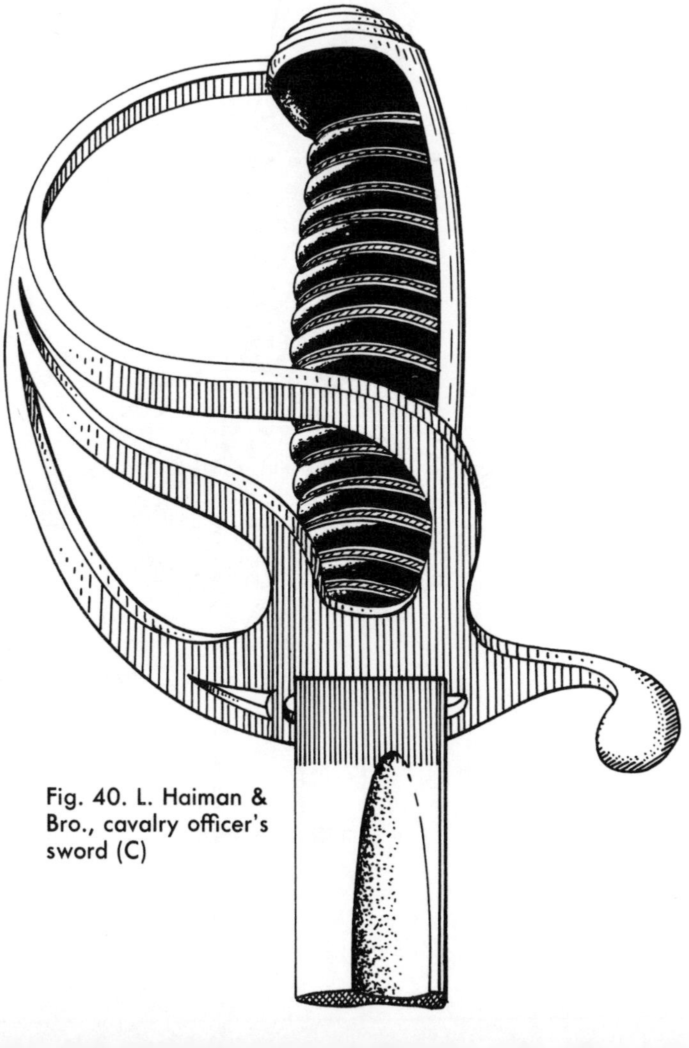

Fig. 40. L. Haiman & Bro., cavalry officer's sword (C)

long, with a single unstopped fuller on either side. One side is etched with stands of arms, a cross and "C.S.A." The other side has three panels of etchings, the middle one "Capt. E. G. Dawson, presented by L. Haiman & Bro.," the other two panels a floral design and stand of arms. The gold-plated brass guard is of the half-basket variety with knuckle bow and two branches. The pommel is of the bird's-head type with extending backstrap and ferrule at the base of the grip. The scabbard is metal with ornamented brass mounts. It was worn by Major Edgar G. Dawson of the Terrell Light Artillery of Georgia.

Figure 41

Another Haiman sword worn by Major Dawson, also in Battle Abbey (Item #177), is of foot officer's type but crude in design. The counterguard is not cast with the usual roses between the branches but instead has a vine. The pommel cap is undecorated and the knuckle bow has no slot for sabre knot. The grip is leather-covered and wound with twisted brass wire. The weapon has an over-all length of 40 inches, with a 32-inch slightly curved blade, single unstopped fuller on either side. One side is etched with scroll, cannon, tents, "C.S." and "Capt. E. G. Dawson" in Old English letters. The other side has Confederate flags, and "Terrell Artillery." On the back of the blade appears: "etched by C. S. Spear, Columbus, Ga.," and stamped near the guard on the flat blade back is "L. Haiman & Bro." The scabbard is leather, brass-mounted.

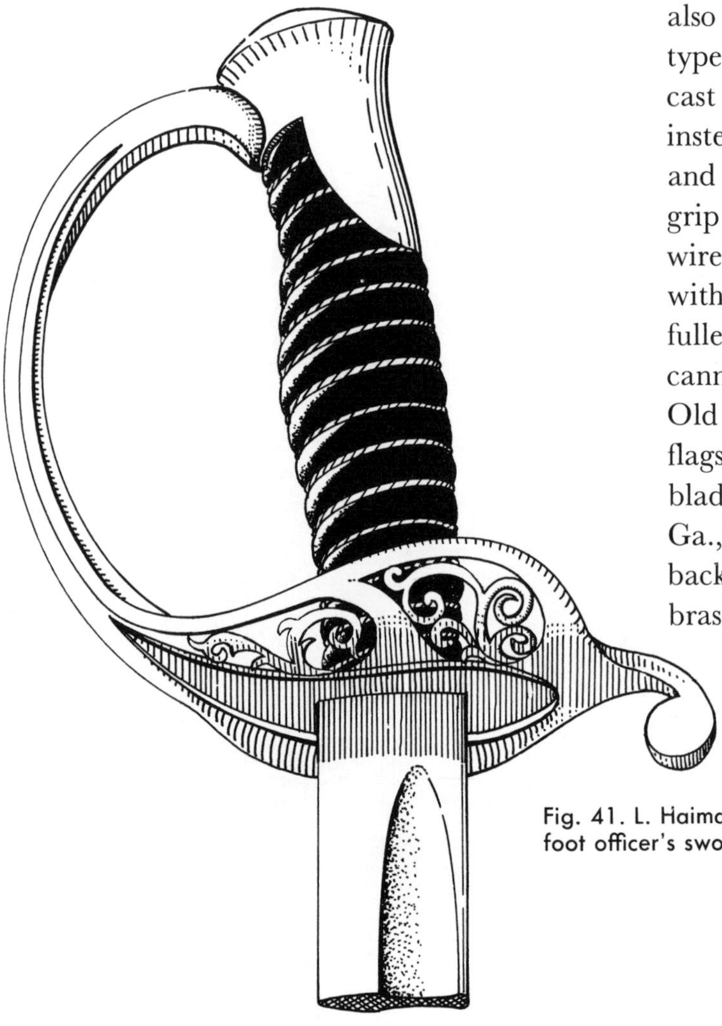

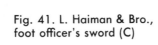

Fig. 41. L. Haiman & Bro., foot officer's sword (C)

Fig. 42. Halfmann & Taylor, cavalry officer's sword (C)

16. Halfmann & Taylor, Montgomery, Ala.

(SWORDS)

Figure 42

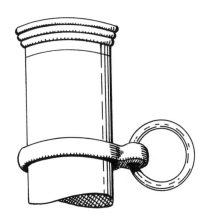

THE PICTURED sabre is of English make, imported to the Confederacy by the firm of Halfmann & Taylor, military outfitters, not manufacturers. The slender blade is 33 inches long, diamond point, with single stopped fuller on either side. Each side is etched with the usual scrollwork and an eagle with shield bearing the letters "C.S.A." surmounted by 11 stars. The ricasso is etched "Halfmann & Taylor, Montgomery, Alabama & London." Near the ricasso on the obverse side is inserted the customary brass disk found on English pieces stamped in raised letters "Proved."

The grip is covered with fishskin and wound with 7 turns of 3 wires (one twisted). The guard is of thin pierced sheet steel, the knuckle bow widening to form a counterguard and quillon terminating in a curled disk. The counterguard is divided into four branches by openwork, two of them joining on the obverse side to form an oval disk on which appears an eagle whose breast contains the letters "C.S.A." (letters formed by a series of punches). The eagle is surmounted by 11 stars (one star for each State in the Confederacy). The knuckle bow joins a button-type pommel and backstrap, also of steel. The scabbard is all of metal. A sabre of this type is to be found in the Battle Abbey collection in Richmond, Item #169.

Some swords of this type are found with the name "Isaac & Campbell Co." etched on the ricasso. (See 19. Isaac, Campbell & Co.)

If Halfmann & Taylor imported swords other than the type described above none have been brought to my attention. The firm's name is most frequently found on the reverse of fancy script "I" (Infantry) Confederate buttons of English make and imported to this country through the blockade. Some are stamped "Halfmann & Taylor, Montgomery," while others bear "Halfmann & Taylor, Montgomery, Alb." (Note misspelling of the abbreviation of Alabama.)

17.   C. Hammond (Address Unknown)

(SWORDS)

Figure 43

AVAILABLE Confederate and Union records make no mention of a "C. Hammond" and yet his name is to be found stamped on a number of very good imitations

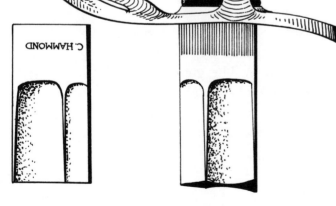

Fig. 43. C. Hammond, cavalry sabre (D)

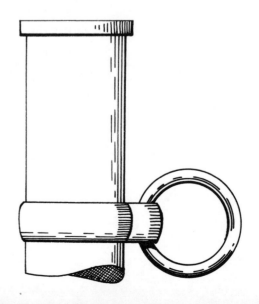

of the U.S. Cavalry Sabre, Model 1840. As in the U.S. model, the flat-backed blade is curved, with two fullers on either side, the large one stopped. The blade is 35 inches long and the maker's name, "C. Hammond," is stamped on the reverse ricasso. The guard is of brass, the knuckle bow being triangular in cross section, and joined by two oval branches which in turn join an oval counterguard. The pommel is standard for cavalry. Only in the grip is there an obvious departure from the U.S. model, it being of about the same diameter at bottom, top and middle, instead of large at the bottom tapering to top as is found in the Model 1840, or swelled in the middle as is the Model 1860.

Most bear a "serial" number stamped on the underside of the counterguard, although this is not true in all cases. The scabbards are entirely of metal, somewhat crudely made, of the "wrap-around" variety, the edge being brazed.

If swords other than those of the type above described were made by this firm they have yet to appear. Beyond the facts that C. Hammond did make sabres with his name stamped thereon, and that these sabres are believed to be Confederate and that most of those extant were discovered in Virginia, nothing is known of the maker or his weapons.

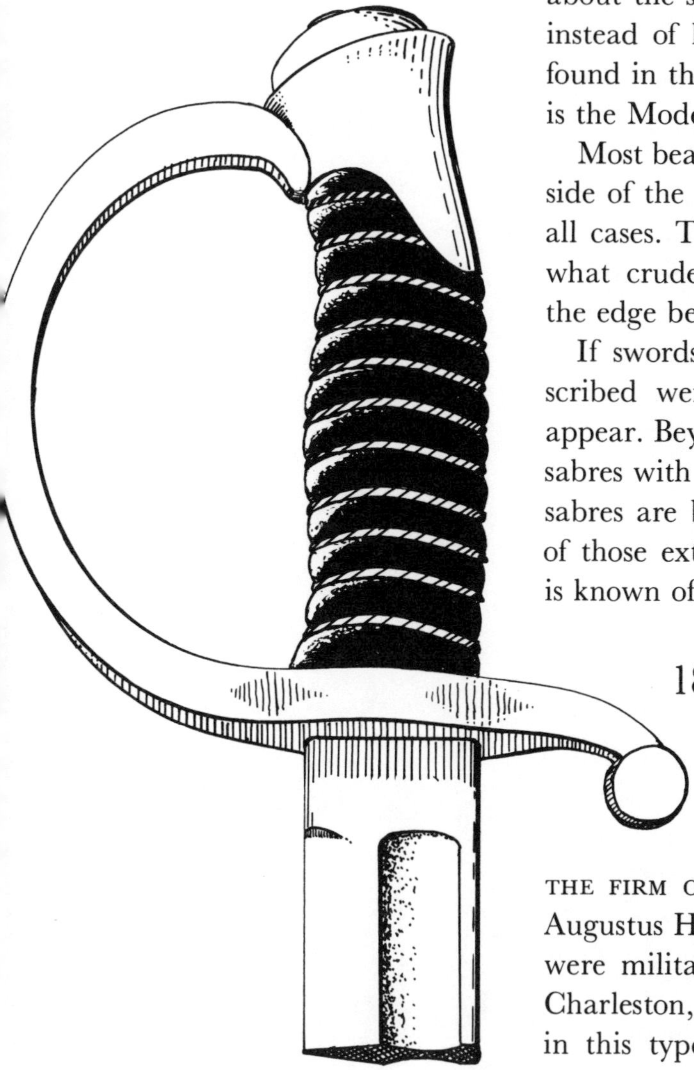

18.   Hayden & Whilden, Charleston, S.C.

(SWORDS)

Figure 44

THE FIRM OF Hayden & Whilden was composed of Augustus H. Hayden and William G. Whilden. They were military outfitters located at 250 King Street, Charleston, S.C. Mr. Hayden had long been engaged in this type of business, first operating as a junior

Fig. 44. Hayden & Whilden, artillery sabre (D+)

partner of Eyland & Hayden from about 1833 to 1835, when at the death of the senior partner the business changed to Gregg & Hayden, under which style it did business until about 1850, when it became Hayden & Whilden.

The predecessors of this firm supplied many fine swords to the South Carolina militia, most of them being imported, and of the eagle-head pommel variety with ivory grips. One particularly handsome sword had a knuckle bow fashioned to represent a palmetto tree around which was encircled a snake. The back of the blade was engraved: "Imported by Eyland & Hayden, Charleston, S.C." Single-shot percussion pistols are also to be found bearing this firm's name.

Weapons made by (or for) Hayden & Whilden are not common. The one in the Battle Abbey collection in Richmond (Item #166) is an artillery sabre with very curved blade, single stopped fuller on either side, 31½ inches long. It is stamped on the reverse ricasso "Hayden & Whilden, Charleston." The guard is of the standard "D" artillery type, undecorated brass. The pommel cap, also of brass and undecorated, is of modified Phrygian pattern.

19. Isaac, Campbell & Co. (Isaac & Co.), London, England

(SWORDS)

NOT ALL FACETS of the Civil War reflect credit upon those involved and this is a sorry chapter, which a more charitable person than I would simply refer to as "war profiteering." My own reference is unprintable. Fully explored by anyone with a strong stomach and who could stand the smell, the activities of Isaac, Campbell & Co. would make interesting if distasteful reading.

Those more interested in the subject can piece together this firm's shoddy dealings and supreme love of money from the *Official Records of the War of the Rebellion*, Series IV, Volumes 1, 2 and 3, or in *King Cotton Diplomacy*.

At the outbreak of the war Saul Isaac and his uncle, Benjamin Hart, purchased the old and respected military outfitting firm of S. Campbell & Co., 71 Jermyn Street, London, England. From this address they supplied the South with all types of military arms and equipment. Considering that the principals of the firm both came from New York it is highly questionable whether they held any great love for the South or the Confederacy. There can be no question, however, as to their love of money and surely the nose of each must have had a dollar mark stamped on its end. Overcome at times with magnanimity, they sometimes charged only twice what an item was worth, but more often, when their true character showed through, they felt obliged to get all the traffic would bear. After all, for their own brother these wolves couldn't have done more.

Caleb Huse, purchasing agent for the Confederate Army abroad, early fell under the spell of the company and through them vast quantities of arms and supplies were purchased in blood money for those men fighting for all they held dear. To date, Major Huse's own position in relation to this business has not been made really clear, although seemingly he was cleared of ugly charges in this connection.

Isaac, Campbell & Co. were in existence only during the war. Their contracts were only with the South. Therefore, all Civil War items bearing this name can be considered Confederate. Quantities of buttons, knapsacks, etc., etc. are to be found containing the unillustrious name of these bloodsuckers. We are concerned, however, only with edged weapons.

In the Smithsonian Institution, Washington, D.C.,

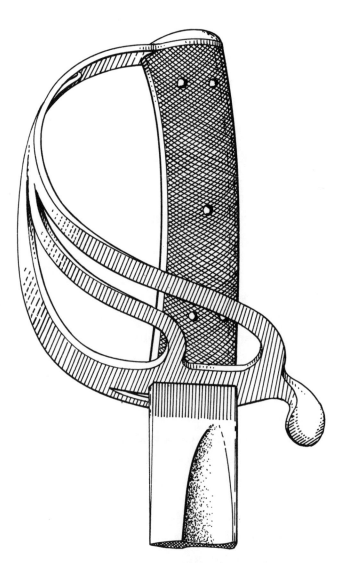

Fig. 45. Isaac & Campbell, cavalry sword (D)

is the sabre carried by Captain William Wheeler, C.S.A. It has a 33-inch straight blade with diamond point, single unstopped fuller on either side. It is etched (each side) with an eagle bearing "C.S.A." upon its breast and surmounted by eleven stars (one for each seceding State). Inscribed on the ricasso is "C. Campbell & Co., 71 Jermyn St., London." The guard is formed by a thin steel plate which widens into a broad counterguard divided into four branches by openwork, and in a portion of this is an oval on which is a bugle surrounded by a crown. The grip is of fish-skin and the pommel and backstrap are of iron.

Here we have a case of an old sword made to sell by S. Campbell & Co. to the British infantry, but which was dressed up by the addition of 11 stars, "C.S.A." and an eagle etched upon the blade. One can only guess at the difference in price.

Elsewhere in this book is a short description of Halfmann & Taylor, Montgomery, Ala. A close scrutiny of the swords and buttons sold by this firm leads one to conclude they were originally purchased through Isaac, Campbell & Co. It is also possible that those weapons stamped with the import stamp of "Courtney & Tennant, Charleston, S.C." were sold this company by the subject firm. However, let the reader make no mistake as to the sincere loyalty and patriotism of the South Carolina concern.

Figure 45

The most common sword sold by Isaac, Campbell & Co. was the English cavalry sabre, Model 1853. The 34½-inch blade was almost straight, with an unstopped fuller on either side. The flat iron knuckle bow is joined by two branches at the flat oval counterguard, which terminates in a quillon ending in a flat disk. The grips, once thought to be gutta-percha, are of leather, riveted to the tang of the blade with five rivets. The scabbard is of iron. The flat back of the blades are stamped "Isaac & Co." It is very similar to those brass-guard sabres made by Mole, and identical to some few iron-hilted blades bearing the stamp "Courtney & Tennant, Charleston, S.C." on the ricasso (obverse) and "C.S.A." (die-struck) on the reverse.

Unmarked sabres of this type can no more be called Confederate than can Enfield rifles.

20. E. J. Johnston & Co., Macon, Ga.
(ALL TYPES OF EDGED WEAPONS)

ACCORDING TO DeBow's *Review* of March-April, 1862, the firm of E. J. Johnston & Co. of Macon, Ga., were turning out 40 infantry swords, 40 naval cutlasses, 40 artillery sabres and 40 cavalry sabres per week. This then was a sizable operation. To date none of Johnston's naval cutlasses, artillery or cavalry sabres have been identified as such but several of his infantry officer swords and foot artillery swords survive to give credit to his establishment.

There is a marked similarity between the weapons of William J. McElroy & Co. (see) and those made by E. J. Johnston, in both style and method of manufacture, suggesting a definite tie-in between the two firms. Remembering that both operated in Macon, which was then a small town, it would not have been unusual if the two compared notes and possibly performed several phases jointly. For example, both produced swords whose blades contain *stopped* fullers, this being an unusual feature in Confederate edged weapons. The hilt castings, also, suggest a common source.

Also in Macon was one B. P. Freeman. A news item in November, 1861, commented upon a sword made without machinery by this individual which, "in solidarity, shape and finish is not excelled in Yankeedom or elsewhere." Freeman is stated to have worked for both McElroy and Johnston and did some of the blade etching for both firms. A Mr. F. Herzog is also understood to have performed the same services.

Figure 46

Sketched is a handsome weapon made by E. J. Johnston. The blade is 32 inches long, straight and with a diamond point. Etched on the obverse side in large letters is "E. J. Johnston Co., Macon, Ga." (two lines), a floral design and large "C.S.A." The reverse contains floral designs and "Presented to Lieut. Col. John W. Mallet, by the grateful citizens of Macon in remembrance of July 29—Aug. 1, 1864" (four lines). Lieutenant Colonel Mallet, Superintendent of Con-

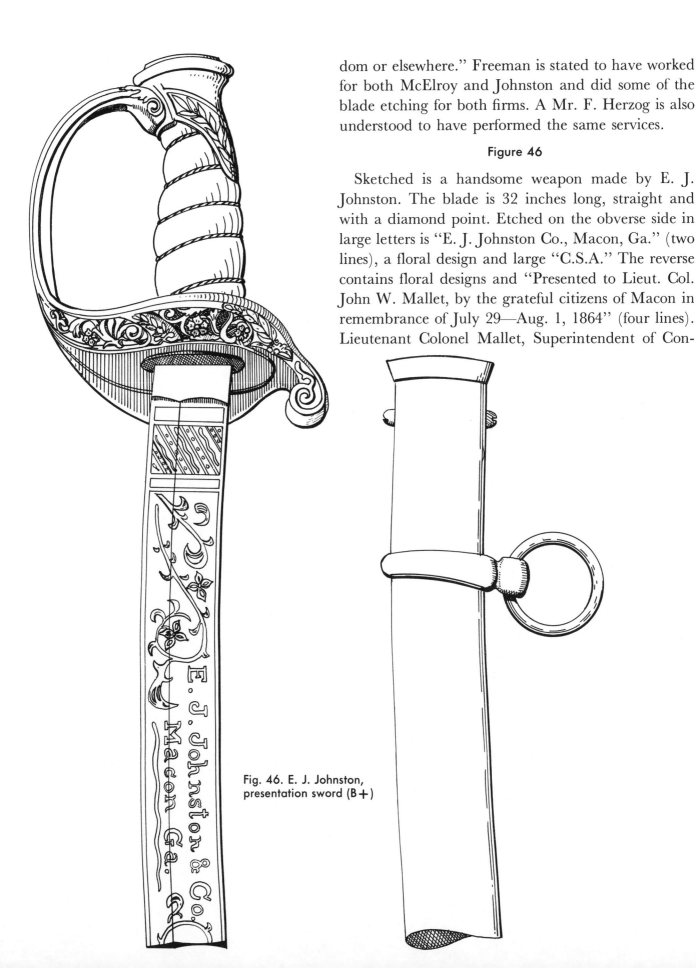

Fig. 46. E. J. Johnston, presentation sword (B+)

federate Ordnance Laboratories, was stationed at Macon during a good bit of the war, and at the time that city was attacked by a large raiding party under the command of Major General Stoneman, U.S.A., in July, 1864, Mallet commanded two infantry companies from the Macon Arsenal. Stoneman was beaten off with considerable loss and doubtlessly it was in this connection that Colonel Mallet was presented the sword in question.

The guard of this sword is of brass, standard foot officer's type, as is the pommel. The grip is of leather, wound with twisted brass wire. The scabbard which came with this sword is of iron but does not appear to be original.

A similar sword is one "Presented by Co. B. of the Macon Volunteers to Lt. A. G. Butts." This also bears the name of E. J. Johnston & Co., Macon, Ga. but has only a 30-inch blade and undecorated pommel cap.

Figure 47

Still another foot officer's sword of this same general pattern is in the Smithsonian Institution, Washington, D.C. It has a 30-inch straight blade, slightly rounded back, with stopped single fuller on either side. It is etched with floral designs, a large "C.S." on one side of the blade and the maker's name and address on the other. The grip is of leather, wound with 13 turns of single-strand brass wire. Pommel is decorated with a laurel leaf design. The scabbard is leather with all brass mounts.

It is noted that the etching on the swords made by Johnston and McElroy is consistently found to be quite deep, differing in this respect from those produced by Boyle & Gamble of Richmond, Va., whose etching is so light as to be more in the form of a "wash."

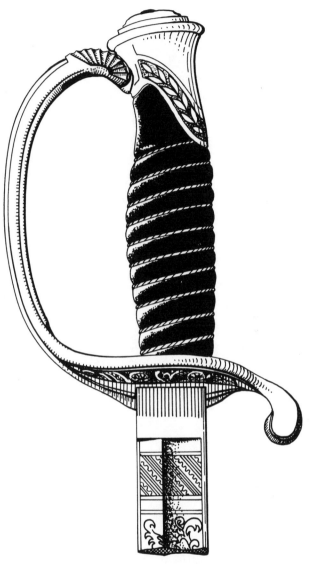

Fig. 47. E. J. Johnston, foot officer's sword (C)

Figure 48

A few foot artillery swords made by Johnston are still with us. These all appear to be identical, having a 19-inch double-edged wasp-blade that has a triangular fuller near the ricasso and an unstopped fuller directly beneath but not joining. The cross-guard quillons end in an undecorated disk. The grip is serrated in parallel grooves. The ball pommel is undecorated. Die-stamped in the guard in very small letters is "E. J. Johnston, Macon, Ga."

On August 2, 1862, it is noted in *Captured Rebel Records*, Vol. 6, Chapter IV, 250 artillery swords were received from Johnston for the Choctaw Artillery at $12 per sword. These were probably of the type above described.

21. Kraft, Goldschmidt & Kraft (K. G. & K.), Columbia, S.C.

(SWORDS AND BOWIES)

ON DECEMBER 17, 1860, the South Carolina Secession Convention met in the First Baptist Church, Columbia, S.C., and by December 20 ratified an ordinance "To dissolve the union between the State of South Carolina and other States united with her under the compact entitled 'The Constitution of the United States of America.'"

Capital of the State of South Carolina, Columbia was, by today's standards, still a village, having a population of under 5,000. As all male citizens between the ages of 18 and 45 were obligated to the militia, it was quite a military town. Columbia boasted of the following volunteer companies: Governor's Guards, Richland Rifles, Emmet Guards (made up mostly of Irishmen), Carolina Blues, Columbia Grays, Chicora Rifles, Harper Rifles, Columbia Artillery, Columbia

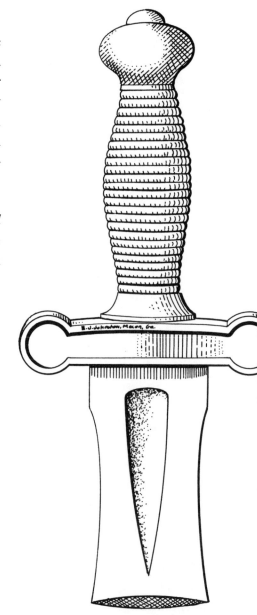

Fig. 48. E. J. Johnston, foot artillery sword (D+)

Zouaves and the Congaree Cavalry. In addition to
those named, there was the militia for those who for
some reason could not get into the volunteer companies. All of these organizations did not see service
during the war, but the first companies to respond to
the call were the Columbia Grays, the Columbia
Artillery, the Richland Rifles and the Governor's
Guards.

In a town with such a military background it would
have been unusual had there not been a number of
persons engaged in supplying arms, uniforms and
accouterments.

The most handsome of all Confederate swords to
come out of South Carolina were made in Columbia
by the firm of Kraft, Goldschmidt & Kraft. Principals
were H. F. Kraft, a former jeweler, and his brother
Peter W. Kraft, a gunsmith listed in the 1860 City
Directory as operating from 181 Richardson Street.
The third partner, Goldschmidt, is unknown.

The Richmond *Dispatch* of January 3, 1861, contains the following advertisement of Peter Kraft:
"Bowie knives, fine English, French and German
double guns, Colts, Smith & Wessons, Allen and
Wheellocks and Adams English repeaters. Double
barrel guns, rifles and pistols made to order. Mounted
men solicited to buy from our stock at 184 Main
Street."

According to *Old and New Columbia*, published 1929:

On the corner where the Black Drug Store is in the
Keenan building was a sword factory run by Kraft, Goldschmidt and Kraft. They made cavalry and straight swords,
the latter being sharp on both sides. They were forged out
in the blacksmith shop and ground to an edge on a large
grindstone about six feet in diameter. On one occasion one
of these stones exploded and half of it went through the
roof, but fortunately no one was hurt. On the Sumter
street corner of the block was a brass foundry where the
guards for the swords and the trimmings for the scabbards

were cast. Old man Peter Kind and his son Yawcob, were the moulders.

The above is not the only reference to double-edged blades being made in Columbia, for in *Hampton and His Cavalry* is found the following: "At Columbia were made the heavy, long, straight, double edged swords, very serviceable and Crusader-like, with cross-hilts."

Figure 49

Probably the above accounts refer to the sketched sabre, of which four are in the Confederate Museum in Richmond. Superficially these appear like French Napoleonic dragoons, with long straight double-edged blades (38 inches long). The brass knuckle bow is joined by three branches. The oval counterguard has no quillon. Grip is of sharkskin, wound with 9 turns of single- and double-strand brass wire. The pommel cap is decorated on the obverse forward edge with laurel leaves and on the reverse with oak leaves and acorns. This feature, incidentally, is a peculiarity of Kraft, Goldschmidt & Kraft. The inside of the guard is equipped with a thumbstrap. The scabbard is of metal with large brass throat, ring mounts and drag. Over-all length is 45 inches!

All four of these swords are associated with General Wade Hampton, C.S.A., of Columbia, S.C. Two were his personal property and used by him during the war. One was given by Hampton to General Bradley T. Johnston of Maryland, and the other to General M. C. Butler, C.S.A. All four swords are identical. The blades all date back to the early 1800s, but the guards, grips, scabbards and pommels are unmistakably the work of the subject firm.

In the Smithsonian Institution, Washington, D.C. (not on exhibit), is a sword similar to the above. The blade is identical but the grip, guard and pommel are of the typical two-branched cavalry variety. The scabbard identifies it as being a Kraft, Goldschmidt &

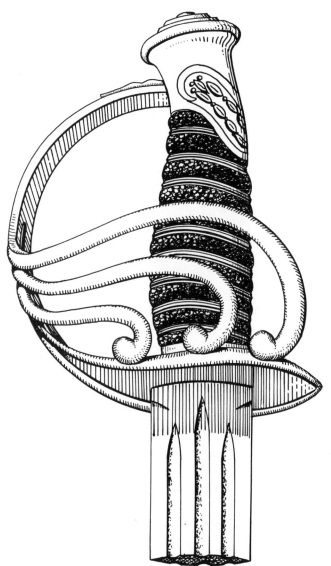

Fig. 49. Kraft, Goldschmidt & Kraft, cavalry sword (E+)

Kraft weapon, it being the same as on the four swords with the Hampton connection, which in turn are identical with the one following.

Figure 50

The best known of the K. G. & K. swords is the field or staff officer's, with 32-inch straight single-edged blade, 1¼ inches wide, with a wide shallow single unstopped fuller on either side extending up almost to the guard. The cutting edge is knife type, it being "stopped" prior to reaching the hilt. The etching on all blades appears standard, consisting of cotton bolls, cannon balls, large "C.S.," pikes, cannon, shield, stars and floral designs. Etching is not deep, only frosted. One side of the ricasso is etched in large letters "K. G. & K.," and the other side "Columbia, S.C." The counterguard of brass is cast in a design of oak leaves with an oak wreath encircling "C.S." The knuckle bow ends in the shape of a monster's head where it attaches to the pommel. The pommel cap is decorated on one side (obverse) with laurel leaves, and with oak leaves on the reverse. A Roman numeral is always found under the leather washer between blade and guard. The leather-wrapped grip is wound

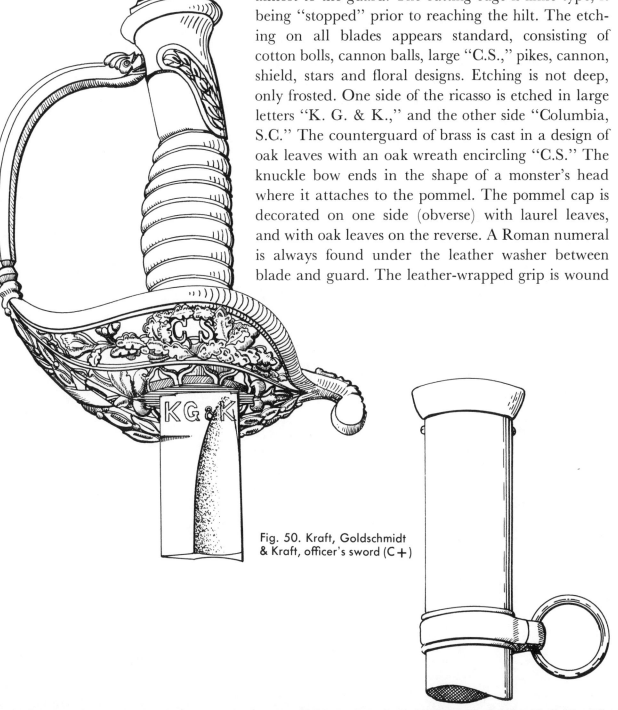

Fig. 50. Kraft, Goldschmidt & Kraft, officer's sword (C+)

with thin, untwisted copper wire. There is a brass collar at junction of grip and guard. As already stated, the scabbard is of metal, painted black with brass mounts, the top mount being very pronounced.

The Battle Abbey collection in Richmond contains two swords as above described (Items #147 and #150), and in addition, another sword which is very handsome. It has a slightly curved blade 36 inches long, finely etched with "C.S." in a wreath, floral designs, etc., with the name "Kraft, Goldschmidt & Kraft, Columbia, S.C." included as a portion of the etchings. The heavy guard is of brass, ornamented with an eagle, a wreath and large stand of colors. The pommel is formed by a lion's head. The grip is of leather, wire wound with a single-strand, thumbstrap at the base. Scabbard is of iron with brass mounts, the two carrying ring mounts being decorated with the head of a helmeted warrior.

This beautiful sabre was carried by General William L. Jackson, cousin of the famous "Stonewall" at the time he was colonel of the 19th Virginia Cavalry. He later commanded Jenkins Brigade of Cavalry, C.S.A.

22. Leech & Rigdon (Memphis Novelty Works), Memphis, Tenn.

(SWORDS, BOWIES AND BAYONETS)

ON SEPTEMBER 18, 1861, there appeared in the Memphis *Appeal* the following advertisement:

Memphis Novelty Works, Thomas Leech & Co., Corner Main and McCall Sts., Memphis, Tenn. Established primarily for the Manufacture of Army cutlery and brass castings of all kinds. We are now prepared to receive and fill orders for the following, viz; Infantry swords, cavalry swords and sabres, artillery cutlasses and knives. Bowie knives of every description, bayonets for shotguns and rifles. Stirrups and spurs of the latest and most approved patterns.

Bullet moulds of all kinds. Brass mountings for saddlery. Special attention paid to the repairs of printing presses. Light machinery and machine blacksmithing generally. We have engaged the services of competent workmen and will warrant our work to give complete satisfaction. All orders will meet with prompt attention. We will pay a high price for all the old copper and brass you can send in.

A week previous to this Leech had advertised for 10,000 pounds of old zinc, copper and brass for "military purposes." Both advertisements indicate an establishment of some size.

The 1857 Memphis City Directory lists Thomas Leech as a cotton broker at 35 Front Row. In the 1859 Directory he is listed as both a cotton broker and a "dealer in guns." This latter business he conducted on Elliott Street between Hernando and DeSoto. At this period he is not known to have made any firearms. He was a dealer only.

In the fall of 1861 or early in 1862, Leech was joined by Charles H. Rigdon of St. Louis, Mo. Rigdon was a scale-maker and machinist and upon his connection the firm began the manufacture of imitation Colt .36-caliber revolvers.

Confederate authorities anticipated the fall of Memphis, Tenn., and set up an armory at Columbus, Miss., to which point everyone engaged in arms-making removed when Memphis fell to the Federals in May, 1862. Leech and Rigdon were among the many who continued their activities at Columbus.

As early as May 1, 1862, the firm advertised in the *Appeal*:

Swords! Swords! Swords! A large lot of fine infantry and field officer's swords just received from our manufactory in Columbus, Miss., and for sale at the Memphis Novelty Works, corner Main and McCall St. Seven or eight brass finishers wanted immediately at the Novelty Works, Leech & Rigdon.

A week later:

Notice, Swords! Swords! A few more infantry and field officers' swords which will be sold cheap if application be made today at the Novelty Works. All persons having swords left here for repairs are hereby notified to call for them today, as we are going to start for Columbus, Miss., Friday morning. Leech & Rigdon.

In late 1862 Columbus was threatened by the Federals and the entire activity removed. Most followed the commanding officer, Colonel Hunt, to Selma, Ala., but Leech & Rigdon chose Greensboro, Ga. At this point it is believed that their sword-making ceased and that all energies were devoted to revolver making. Those interested in the revolvers made by this firm can turn to *The Original Confederate Colt.* Our present concern is with swords only.

During the time Leech & Rigdon were in Memphis, Tenn., and Columbus, Miss., they turned out a quantity of edged weapons of all varieties. Most familiar is the foot officer's sword, this being similar to the U.S. foot officer's swords of the time, but with the letters "C.S." (in raised letters within an oval) cast on the reverse top of the counterguard. The oval has a spray of laurel leaves on either side. The pommel cap is also decorated with laurel leaves. The grip is leather, wound with twisted brass wire. The blade is 30 inches long with a slightly rounded back and bears an unstopped fuller on either side. The scabbard is of leather with all-brass mounts. These swords are found with etched or unetched blades.

Figure 51

The field officer's swords made by Leech & Rigdon are identical with the foot officer's, the only difference being the addition of an extra branch which follows the counterguard and coils snake-like around the knuckle bow, as shown in the accompanying sketch.

This particular sword is sheathed in a leather scabbard, sewed at the top. On the top brass mount is

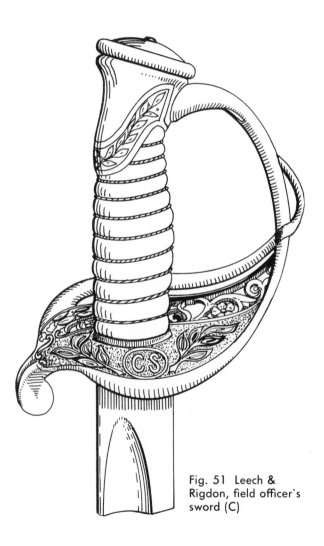

Fig. 51 Leech & Rigdon, field officer's sword (C)

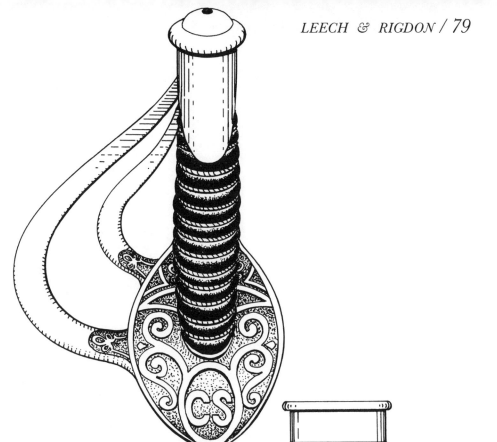

scratched: "R. L. R., 44 Rgmt. N.C. Vols." Leech & Rigdon's field officer's swords are not common.

Figure 52

The cavalry officer's sabres are similar to the above in that they have the distinctive "C.S." in an oval, but it is on the top rear of the counterguard. The two branches are vaguely decorated. The knuckle guard is not, nor is the pommel cap. The grip is leather-covered and wound with twisted brass wire. The blade is 30 inches long with a decided curve and a single un-stopped fuller on either side. The scabbard is of metal with ornamented brass mounts. Such a sabre was carried by Colonel Harvey Walker of the 3rd Regiment of Tennessee. Colonel Walker formed a company of men at Lynnville, Tenn., and was killed at Marietta, Ga. Some etching still remains on the blade. Another sabre of this type can be seen in the Georgia Room of the Confederate Museum in Richmond, Va. It was worn by Colonel George Washington Raines, having been presented to him by the "Memphis Novelty Works."

Fig. 52. Leech & Rigdon, cavalry officer's sabre (C+)

Figure 53

An unusual sabre which is believed to have been made by Leech & Rigdon was recently uncovered. The double-edged blade is straight, 32 inches long and 1¾ inches wide, roughly diamond in cross section. The guard, pommel and backstrap are of brass, poorly cast. Branches are flat with rounded edges. The scabbard is of tin with the brass carrying rings brazed to it.

A sword similar to the above is in the Battle Abbey collection (Item #143). It has a straight double-edged blade 36 inches in length with a leather wire-wound grip and the standard two-branched cavalry guard and pommel. The top of the brass guard is stamped "Memphis Novelty Works, Thos. Leech & Co." The metal scabbard has brass bands and tip.

Identically stamped is a cavalry sabre with similar hilt and guard, but single-edged with a single unstopped fuller on either side and with a flat back. It is unornamented and was evidently intended for an enlisted man, as was the one previously described.

Figure 54

A very interesting cavalry sabre of the two-branch knuckle-bow variety very much like those made by Thomas, Griswold & Co., with ornamented branches on top of the counterguard, is one which turned up in Nashville. It is etched on the back of the flat blade in script: "Manufactured by Thos. Leech & Co., Novelty Works, Memphis, Tennessee, C.S." The reverse of the single fullered unstopped blade is etched: "Presented to Major Jas. L. Brown."

Recently there appeared a fine foot officer's sword that had come "raw" from an antique shop. Had it been seen in the shop the average collector would not

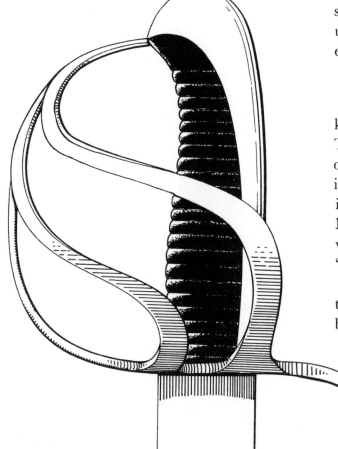

Fig. 53. Leech & Rigdon, double-edged cavalry sword (E+)

have looked at it twice. It gave every indication of being a standard "Yankee." The guard was finely cast with customary rose pattern, the pommel was nicely decorated and the grip was of sharkskin, wound with twisted gilt wire. The blade was stopped with two fullers on either side. The scabbard was of leather, brass-mounted. Although somewhat rusty, it was otherwise in good condition, but had it been offered me for $25 I would have refused until noting the blade to be finely etched with "Leech & Rigdon, Memphis, Tenn." and a large "C.S." in Old English letters, in addition to the usual floral designs, stands of arms, etc. The $200 I offered the owner was refused.

Some of the swords with finely etched blades are noted to be signed "C. H. Rigdon, Etcher."

A short sword made by the subject firm is in the hands of a private collector. It is stamped simply, "Novelty Works." It has a wide double-edged 18-inch blade with a single unstopped fuller running down either side. The cross guard is of brass, "S"-shaped. The grip and pommel are those of the regulation foot officer's, but as the pommel was never slotted or pierced to receive the end of the knuckle bow it must have been made for this particular piece and not put together by someone wishing to utilize spare parts. The grip is covered with oilcloth and wound with double-strand wire. The ridges in the grip are formed by a wrapping of heavy cord under the oilcloth. Pommel cap is undecorated.

As the firm advertised "bowie-knives of every description, bayonets for shotguns and rifles," it is presumed that such were made, but to date, none have appeared that can be identified as products of Leech & Rigdon.

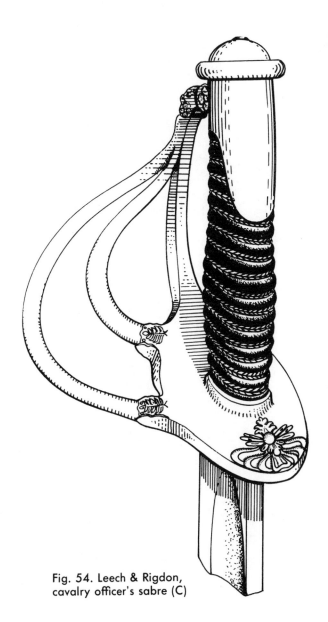

Fig. 54. Leech & Rigdon, cavalry officer's sabre (C)

23.   William J. McElroy & Co.,
Macon, Ga.

(ALL TYPES OF EDGED WEAPONS)

AN EYEWITNESS ACCOUNT of an operation always carries more weight than a secondhand observation. In my files is a letter from Bridges Smith, who, at the time of its writing in May, 1922, was the Judge of the Bibb County (Ga.) Juvenile Court, Macon, but who in the 1860s was an operative of the C.S. Macon Arsenal. Says Judge Smith:

In 1861 when the new Confederate Government saw the necessity of beginning at once the manufacture of army equipment, it depended largely upon patriotism, which was not lacking in a town like Macon, for co-operation. D. C. Hodgkins & Sons, turned over their gunsmith shop, and then began the making of pistols and conversion of old weapons into, at that time, more modern guns. At first these were made of the Colt pattern by Hodgkins, but later were made by the government of the same general Colt model, but by mechanics brought here from Harpers Ferry, and I understand the model was altered in some way. From 1861 to 1865, I was detailed to make ammunition for shotguns, muskets and rifles, but none for small arms, and therefore had little opportunity of seeing the manufacture of pistols.

W. J. McElroy & Co., tinsmiths turned over their large factory for the purpose of making canteens, and later by reason of having some skilled men in their employ, began to make swords. In the course of time, this shop was turning out some of the finest weapons of this class, beautifully ornamented by the then process of dipping the blade in melted wax and chasing the designs with a steel pointed instrument, and then pouring acid all over and letting it "eat" into the blade. This may have been very crude compared to modern methods, but we used to regard the product as almost perfection.

At any rate, I am satisfied that these were the first swords made and worn by the officers of the Confederate Army. This factory continued until the war ended and the swords were made into plowshares, as the saying is. The government had no sword-making establishment of its own in Macon.

The first cartridges made here, and about the first made in the South, were of the "buck & ball" variety for shotguns; composed of one large (about the size of a boy's marble) leaden ball and 3 buckshot, a thimblefull of powder, all in a container of brown wrapping paper and tied with small twine, the powder end being folded in a way that would hold its position. This is the cartridge that brought the command: "Chaw Cartridge," following after the command "Load." The soldier bit off the folded end and poured the powder in the barrel of the gun, and then put the buck and ball with their paper wrapper in, the paper serving as the wadding, and then rammed it down with the ramrod. He then put on his percussion cap and was ready for the command "Fire!"

You can see how much time was wasted in the earlier stages of the war, when you think of the metal cartridges that came later, especially with the opposing army. Another cartridge was that of the slug for rifles. At first these were moulded, and I think of them when I read about the dum-dum bullet, both being of soft lead. Later, through the ingenuity of a Michigan man, a civil engineer, and by the way, a major of my battalion, these balls or slugs were made as hard as iron. He had lead wire, about the size of your little finger made in coils, and invented a machine to cut it in proper lengths, and made to fall into a recess the shape and size of the slug, where by powerful pressure it was compressed into hardness.

Brown paper was also used for making these rifle cartridges until a vessel loaded with a quality of paper something of the appearance and texture of what we call "bondpaper" used for stationary, ran the blockade at Wilmington, and then we made decent looking cartridges. After the rifle cartridge was made, the slug end was dipped in wax. All cartridges were put in packages of ten, with a small package containing 13 percussion caps.

In 1865, the Confederate government had just completed large and handsome buildings, one for a laboratory in which to make ammunition, and the other for an armory in which to make small arms. Before they could be turned over by the contractors, General Wilson, U.S.A., had the audacity to walk in with his cavalry and demanded the

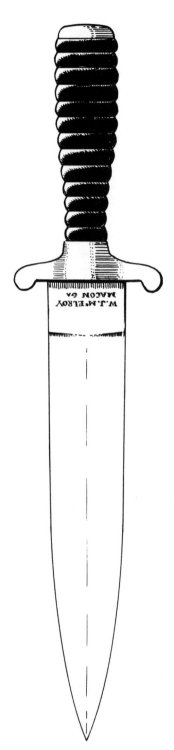

Fig. 55. Wm. J. McElroy,
bowie knife (B)

surrender of the city, and the people at that time just didn't have the heart to refuse him. After that, I lost interest in the manufacture of cartridges and weapons.

I believe that modern-day collectors are inclined to agree with Judge Smith in considering the weapons turned out by McElroy as being "almost perfection." At any rate the products of this manufactory are eagerly sought and commercially command a good healthy figure.

Figure 55

McElroy early started his war effort by delivering 210 pikes to the State Arsenal and Armory at Milledgeville on April 19, 1861. So far as is known, none have been identified. Along with the pikes McElroy made bowie knives, and fortunately, these are marked. At least two different types have survived the years. The first is of double-edged variety with a spear-type blade, 12 inches in length. Stamped on the ricasso is "W. J. McElroy, Macon, Ga." in two lines. The grip is of walnut, spirally serrated, and a bronze cap on the top. The cross guard is of bronze, the quillons terminating in flat disks. The hilts contain both a serial number and a Roman numeral. The scabbards are of leather with a hanging belt loop stitched to the top. Such a bowie may be seen at the Battle Abbey, Richmond, Va. (Item #208).

Another McElroy bowie is single-edged with 8-inch blade. It is etched on the ricasso "Wm. J. McElroy, Macon, Ga." in two lines. It has only a rudimentary false edge. The grip is of one-piece walnut, unserrated. The "pommel" and cross guard are identical with those on the bowie above described. Both are well-made and serviceable weapons.

Of the man McElroy, very little is known. The 1860 Census for Bibb County, Ga., reveals him as being 37 years of age, and a person who was born in New York. His wife was named Esther, and they had four children. His real estate was valued at $5,500 and his personal property at $17,550. He is classed only as a "merchant."

DeBow's *Review* of March-April, 1862, reflects that the subject firm made all types of swords, and according to this source his output was: "20 infantry swords, bowie knives, naval cutlasses, sergeant's swords, sword belts, straps for same, belt clasps and mountings for same per week. Also about 50 brass cavalry spurs per week. Also made tin canteens and bayonets."

McElroy also made "Frame" belt buckles.

Figure 56

One of the foot officer's swords made by McElroy is here pictured. As do the weapons made by Johnston, this one has a stopped blade and single fuller. It is 28½ inches long, etched with floral designs, a "C.S." within a curlicue and the name "Wm. J. McElroy & Co., Macon, Ga." This etching is deep. The counterguard has open spaces between the branches instead of the rose design customarily found. The pommel has only a rudimentary decoration and is crudely made. The scabbard is of leather with all-brass mounts. It is stitched on the top.

Figure 57

A very fine artillery sabre made by McElroy is one which was carried by Major John A. A. West of Augusta, Ga. Major West was Chief of Ordnance on the staff of General Richard Taylor, C.S.A. His sabre is similar to the U.S. Light Artillery Model 1840, having a very curved 32-inch blade, single stopped fuller, flat back. The obverse is deeply etched: "Wm. J. McElroy & Co., Macon, Ga." (two lines), with floral designs and "C.S." The reverse proclaims in large letters: "We Fight For Southern Rights." The grip is leather-covered, wound with twisted brass wire. The guard is of brass of the "D" variety. The pommel is that of a typical artillery sabre. The scabbard is of iron with brass ring mounts.

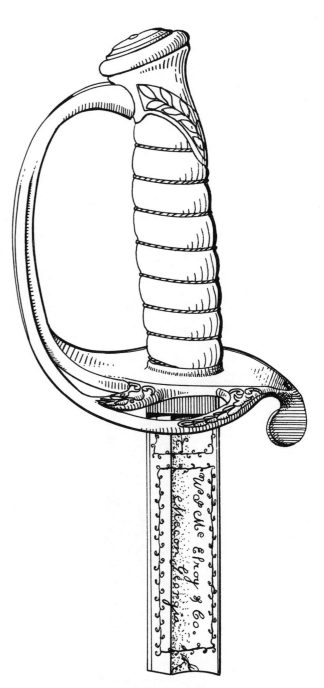

Fig. 56. Wm. J. McElroy, foot officer's sword (C)

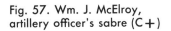

Fig. 57. Wm. J. McElroy, artillery officer's sabre (C+)

The cavalry sabres made by McElroy conform closely to those made by the U.S. Government, but while the fuller in the blade is stopped, there is only a single fuller on either side. The guard and pommel are of standard cavalry design, the latter being stamped around its top "W. J. McElroy, Ga."

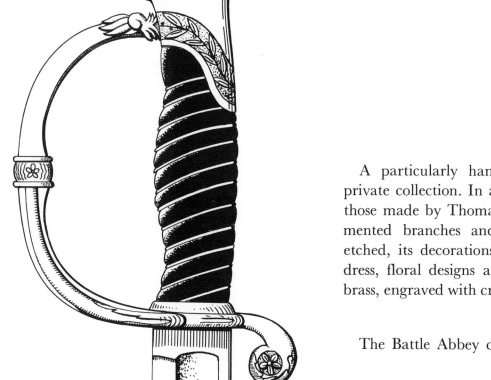

A particularly handsome cavalry sabre is in a private collection. In appearance it is very much like those made by Thomas, Griswold & Co., with ornamented branches and guard. The blade is finely etched, its decorations include the firm's name, address, floral designs and "C.S." The scabbard is of brass, engraved with crossed Confederate flags, etc.

Figure 58

The Battle Abbey collection includes a fine sword

Fig. 58. McElroy & Herington, foot officer's sword (C+)

(Item #142), with one side of its etched blade showing it to have been made by "W. J. McElroy, Herington & Co., Macon, Ga." (The Herington mentioned was connected with the Macon Arsenal.) The other side of the blade, in addition to a large "C.S." and crossed Stars and Bars Confederate flag, is etched: "W. R. Thomas, Co. F., 57th Regt., Ga. Vols." The blade of this weapon has two fullers on either side, such as are found on Union swords. The guard is of brass, with only one branch extending to the knuckle bow. Counterguard and pommel cap are decorated. The grip is of dark bone with wire grooves. The scabbard is of black leather with decorated brass mounts.

This sword is a direct copy of a French model, and without the blade etchings would most certainly be identifiable only as "French."

24. Nashville Plow Works (Sharp & Hamilton), Nashville, Tenn.

(SWORDS)

PRIOR TO THE war the Messrs. Sharp & Hamilton operated a farming implement establishment under the trade name of Nashville Plow Works. Prompt to grasp that plows would have but little demand, with the first tocsin of war, the proprietors quickly converted their establishment into an armory, thereby literally reversing the Bibical injunction, and began turning plowshares into sabres.

A *Record of Stores Purchased, Received and Issued at Nashville, Tenn., and Atlanta, Ga. Arsenals* (*Captured Rebel Records*, Vol. 19, Chapter IV) for the month of October, 1861, lists receipts from "Sharp & Hamilton" (Nashville Plow Works) as follows: October 4, 81 sabres at $851.50; October 10, 100 sabres at $1,050.00; October 14, 19 sabres at $199.50; October 16, 65 sabres at $682.50; and October 23, 34 sabres at

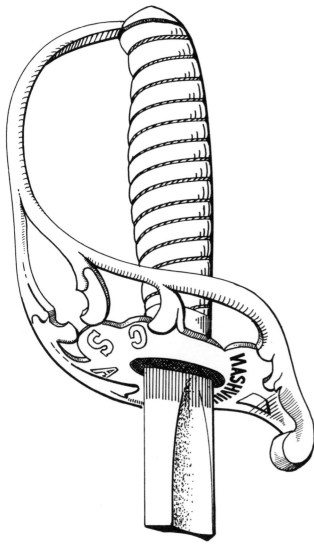

Fig. 59. Nashville Plow Works, officer's cavalry sabre (C)

$357.00. If I can still count correctly, this is a total of 299 sabres for the month of October, 1861, for which the firm received $3,140.50.

Figure 59

If Sharp & Hamilton manufactured edged weapons other than sabres, the records do not so indicate. These sabres are most distinctive, bearing in their cast-brass guards both the firm's name (Nashville Plow Works) and "C.S.A." in large block letters (a collector's idea of how all arms should be marked). That all of the guards were not cast from the same mold is shown by some being stippled, some buffed smooth with minor variations in the design itself. The sabre pictured is somewhat unusual in that the initial "N" of "Nashville" is inverted and the entire firm name is considerably smaller than usually found. It also differs from most in that the twisted wire wrapping the grip extends from pommel to the iron collar at the grip. On most, this extends only two-thirds up from the guard.

The Nashville Plow Works continued operations until April 1, 1862, when the city was taken by Federal troops. Many citizens were then arrested, including Mayor Cheatham, and both the Messrs. Sharp and Hamilton. The charge against all three was—treason! The operations of the Nashville Plow Works were thus brought to an abrupt conclusion.

The Nashville *Banner*, of April 1, 1862, contains a two-paragraph news item as follows:

"Last Saturday, Messrs. Brennan were arrested by Col. Matthews, provost-marshall, and paroled until ten o'clock yesterday morning, when they were again paroled till noon today. Sunday, R. B. Cheatham, Esq., Mayor of the city was arrested, and paroled till twelve yesterday. He appeared at that hour, and his parole was extended till twelve today. Yesterday Messrs. Sharp & Hamilton, of the Nashville Plough Manufactory, were also arrested, and put under bonds of three thousand dollars for their appearance. The charge against these gentlemen is treason.

The Messrs. Brennan, iron-founders, are said to have manufactured cannon, shells, and balls for the Confederate States, and upon this, we believe, the charge against them is founded. Aiding and abetting the enemy, that is, the Confederate States—is the basis of the charge against the Mayor. Messrs. Sharp & Hamilton, it is reported, instead of turning "swords into plough-shares," converted plough-shares into swords and knives for the Confederates, and thus made themselves amenable to the charge of treason against the United States.

It is not hard to see on which side of the fence the Nashville *Banner* found the greenest grass growing.

Judging from the number of specimens still extant, the firm of Sharp & Hamilton managed to turn out a large quantity of sabres before apprehension by Federal authorities, and they are eagerly sought after by today's collector. Generally, most conform to type, having a somewhat curved blade 36 inches long with a flat back and a single unstopped fuller on either side. As already stated, the brass guards contain both the name "Nashville Plow Works" and "C.S.A." The pommel and backstrap are of one-piece brass. It is interesting to note that the makers of the College Hill Arsenal sabres, whose guards are very similar, fashioned their pommel and backstrap of iron. The grip is of leather, wound with twisted brass wire. An iron ferrule, or collar, bronze-welded at the seam, is at the base of the grip. The scabbards are always of iron with brass ring mounts, throat and drag. The throat, incidentally, is oversized and the carrying rings are iron and quite small.

In the August issue of the *Confederate Veteran*, 1909, there appeared the following:

E. T. Cressey writes from Sioux Falls, S. Dak.: "A cavalry sabre came into my possession in the battle of Mill Springs, Ky., January 19, 1862, which has these words cast in the hilt; 'Nashville Plow Works, C.S.A.' Crudely scratched with a sharp point are the initials 'A.T.M.R.' (on the back of the belt plate). Attached to the weapon are the belt and shoulder strap of leather; on the belt is a regular

USA brass-plated clasp for fastening. All these are in good order. I have had these for forty-seven years and shall be delighted to return them to the proper claimant. I have no desire to keep them any longer. A brief notice in the *Veteran* might enable you to find relatives of the brave fighter who wore them. You had no cowards in that war . . .!"

The above sabre was "properly" returned and is in the hands of "relatives," being a portion of the Battle Abbey collection (Item #140). The original owner is unknown.

Another sword of this type is stated to have been carried by Orderly Sergeant Jonens, of the 63rd North Carolina.

Firmly entrenched in a private collection in Texas is a variation of the above-described swords, for although it has an identical blade it is stamped on one side of the ricasso "Sharp & Hamilton" and on the other side "Nashville, Tenn." The "D"-type guard consists of a heavy strip of cast brass at right angles to the blade. The quillon ends on a disk-knob similar to those of the standard Nashville Plow Works. The pommel and backstrap are of brass and of one piece.

25. The Palmetto Armory (Wm. Glaze & Co.), Columbia, S.C.

(SWORDS)

A DECADE BEFORE the Civil War, South Carolina came to the reasonable conclusion that armed conflict between North and South was not only possible, but probable. To prepare herself the State entered into a contract with William Glaze of Columbia, S.C., and Benjamin Flagg of Millbury, Mass., on April 15, 1851. The contract provided that Glaze and Flagg were to supply the State with the following: 6,000 muskets, 1,000 rifles, 2,000 pistols, 1,000 cavalry sabres and

1,000 artillery swords. It was further stipulated that all arms were to be made within the confines of the State. South Carolina was to pay "$6.50 for swords and sabres with equipment." This presumably meant scabbards, and belts. It is also presumed that the muskets and rifles were to be supplied with bayonets, although this is not mentioned in the contract.

The above arms were made at the Palmetto Armory in Columbia, S.C., with machinery imported from Millbury, Mass., where the armory of Asa Waters had been purchased and added to that of B. Flagg & Co.

Previous to the arms contract the Palmetto Armory had operated as the "Palmetto Iron Works" and had been engaged in the manufacture of all types of ornamental ironwork. William Glaze was the proprietor of the establishment located on the northeast corner of Laurel and Lincoln streets, facing what is now the Governor's Mansion.

All of the firearms are dated "1852" on the lockplate, and most of them "1853" on the barrel. It is obvious then that these were the two years required in completing their manufacture.

The contract called for "arms of the pattern now in use in the Army of the United States," and accordingly the pistols and muskets were of the type known as U.S. Model 1842. The rifles were U.S. Model 1841. At the time, the U.S. Cavalry carried what is known as the Heavy Cavalry Sabre, Model 1840, this having been adopted by the War Department for the Army's three regiments of dragoons. It was a close copy of the French light cavalry model of 1822.

Figure 60

The blade is curved, flat-backed, with a single edge and a rudimentary false edge. There are two fullers: a broad one running from about 10 inches from the point to the ricasso where it is stopped, and a shorter, narrower fuller at the back of the blade, starting some

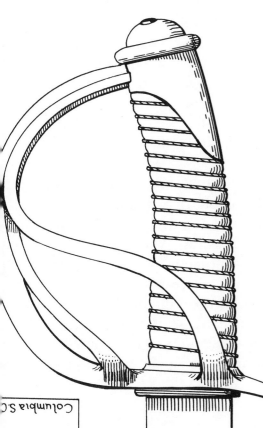

Columbia S.C.

Fig. 60. Palmetto Armory, cavalry sabre (D +)

10 inches from the ricasso and continuing for about 16 inches, tapering off at either end.

The cavalry sabres made under the Palmetto contract conform to the above, having a 35½-inch blade as described. The guard is of the half-basket type with a knuckle bow and two branches on the obverse side joining an oval counterguard. The pommel is of the Phrygian helmet pattern. Guard and pommel are of brass. The grip is cone-shaped (larger end at the blade), of wood around which light cord was wrapped. It was then covered with leather and wound with twisted brass wire which followed the diagonal indentations made by the cord.

Stamped on the reverse of the ricasso is "Columbia, S.C." Some few are stamped "Wm. Glaze & Co." on the obverse of the ricasso. As far as can be determined all weapons bear the "Columbia" stamping. Those that do not are simply unmarked heavy cavalry sabres of the Model 1840.

There have recently appeared a few sabres crudely stamped "Columbia, S.C., Wm. Glaze & Co." on one side of the ricasso and "C.S.A." on the other. Such marking is not standard and before buying one, caution is suggested. The author can see no reason why "C.S.A." would be stamped on a Palmetto sword, it being the property of the State of South Carolina.

The scabbards for Palmetto sabres are of all-iron.

As in the case of the pistols, rifles and muskets, the sabres are well made, and compare favorably with those accepted by the U.S. Army. Whether these arms can be referred to as "Confederate" is something of a question. They were made ten years before the Confederacy was formed. However, they were made in the South for the definite purpose of defensive action against Northern aggression, and it is believed that all were issued to South Carolina troops at the start of the war. Numerous ones have been found in Virginia, indicating that many saw service away from home. Considering that only 1,000 were originally made, these sabres are not uncommon today.

Not at all common are the "1,000 artillery swords." None have ever been identified. Note is made that the contract calls for "swords" not "sabres," so it is presumed that they would be of the foot artillery type and not the light artillery Model 1840.

A specimen of the Palmetto cavalry sabre may be seen in the Battle Abbey collection in Richmond, Va. (Item #151). One stamped both "Columbia, S.C." and "Wm. Glaze & Co." is in the Charleston, S.C., Museum.

(The original Palmetto contract is in the hands of the South Carolina Historical Commission, Columbia, S.C. A rather complete account of the Armory appeared in the *Texas Gun Collector's Magazine*, January and February, 1955.)

26. H. Stevens, Georgia
(PIKES)
Figure 61

H. STEVENS was one of the many who responded promptly to Governor Brown's appeal for pikes to arm the State troops against Northern aggression. *Confederate Records of Georgia*, page 352, reflects that this manufacturer supplied the State with 194 pikes on May 10, 1861, 215 on May 30, 199 on September 29 and 47 on October 1. Mr. Stevens received $5 for each pike accepted at Milledgeville, Ga., then capital of the State, and site of the Arsenal and Armory.

The pikes made by Stevens are identical in shape with those supplied by S. Griswold, of Griswoldville, Ga., a description of which has been given under the portion of this book devoted to Samuel Griswold. Like

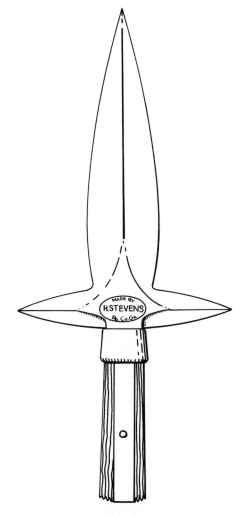

Fig. 61. H. Stevens, cloverleaf pike (C)

those of S. Griswold, the Stevens pikes were bought up by Francis Bannerman of New York, their staffs painted red and the heads gilded.

There seems to be some question as to the location from which Stevens operated, this arising from the manner in which his weapons are stamped. Some are stamped with his name and "R.C., Ga." Others appear to be stamped with his name and "Po. Co., Ga." It is believed that Stevens was located at Augusta, Ga., this city being in Richmond County. Thus, "R.C., Ga." would stand for "Richmond County, Ga." Those that seem to read "Po. Co., Ga." are believed the result of a poor die.

27.   Thomas, Griswold & Co. (T. G. & Co.), New Orleans, La.
(ALL TYPES OF EDGED WEAPONS)

A PROLIFIC MANUFACTURER of edged weapons was the firm of Thomas, Griswold & Co., of New Orleans. This business came into being as an outgrowth of Hyde & Goodrich, whose name as "Agents of the United States South" is occasionally found stamped on imported English Tranter revolvers, and on the backs of Mississippi "Star" buttons. Hyde & Goodrich, military outfitters, operated until August 23, 1861, when the following announcement appeared in the New Orleans *Daily Delta:*

> The copartnership heretofore existing between A. L. Hyde, William M. Goodrich, Henry Thomas Jr. and A. B. Griswold, under the style and firm of Hyde & Goodrich, is this day dissolved by limitation, and the withdrawal of A. L. Hyde. The business will be continued with the same capital, and by the same partners who have conducted it for the last 15 years. The style of the new firm will be; Thomas, Griswold & Co. Messrs. A. L. Abbott and Henry Ginder are also interested in the business house.

Shortly afterward the above the firm printed a

"Lancer's Manual," the back page of which was devoted to advertising that Thomas, Griswold & Co. were "Importers of guns, pistols, bowie-knives, caps and cartridges, military and sporting goods. Manufacturers of Enfield rifles, cavalry and artillery sabres, line and field officers swords and lances." Further note was made that "Our lances are made strictly upon the model of those used in the French service, with staffs of the best mountain ash, and well tempered steel blades."

Whether Thomas, Griswold & Co. ever made Enfield rifles is a matter of some conjecture, and to date no lances have appeared which came from this manufactory. However, they did make swords, some of the best in the South and which compare favorably with those made in the North. As New Orleans fell to the Federals in April, 1862, the output of this company must have been terrific for so many examples of their work to be still extant. Operating from the corner of Canal and Royal streets, they produced practically every type of edged weapon imaginable. Today's collector can give particular thanks to this company for stamping most of their arms with either full name or initials, thus making identification positive and not just by guess or hunch.

Figure 62

The best-known swords of Thomas, Griswold & Co. are the naval cutlasses patterned after the U.S. Model 1841. The grip is of brass cast in imitation of fish scales. The ball pommel bears an American eagle and shield (eagle clutching arrows and thunderbolt) on the obverse. The reverse is plain. The guard is heavy, beaded on the edge with a wide counterguard ending in a flat-disked finial. The knuckle bow has a round perforation near the pommel similar to a slot for a sabre knot. Its purpose is not known, but possibly it is for a lanyard. The blade is double-edged, 21½

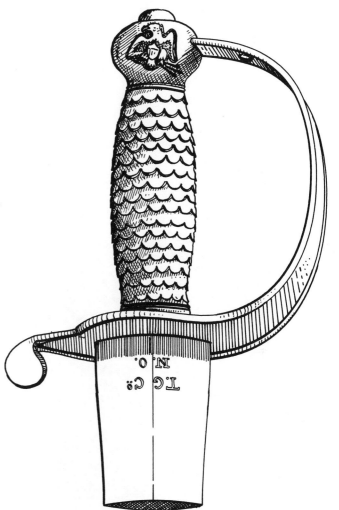

Fig. 62. Thomas, Griswold & Co., naval cutlass (D+)

inches long, 1¾ inches wide at the guard, slimming down to about 1 inch near the middle, then widening to its original width before tapering to point. Cross section is diamond-shaped and there is no fuller. Stamped on the reverse ricasso is "T. G. & Co., N.O." (Thomas, Griswold & Co., New Orleans). Over-all length is 27 inches. The scabbard is of leather with brass throat and toe, the former with a stud for frog. It is to be noted that the grip does not have the three rivets through the tang of the blade that are usually found on the U.S. counterpart.

In a private collection is an unusual variation of the above. The blades are identical in shape and dimensions but this one bears the full firm name, "Thomas, Griswold & Co., New Orleans." The guard and grip are of the standard two-branched cavalry variety. The pommel cap is of regular artillery sabre design. The entire is not unlike the navy cutlasses imported by Courtney & Tennant, but be this a naval cutlass or foot artillery sword is not known.

Figure 63

Another well-known sword by this company is the cavalry officer's patterned after the U.S. Officer's Model 1840, which in turn was a direct steal from a French model of twenty years previous. The blade has a distinct curve, is 34 inches in length, with a flat back and a single stopped fuller on either side. It is 1⅛ inches wide with a false edge extending back about 8 inches from the point. Stamped on the reverse ricasso in a semicircle is "Thomas, Griswold & Co.," and immediately below in a straight line, "New Orleans." The guard is of brass, two branches joining knuckle guard, both branches ornamented at the

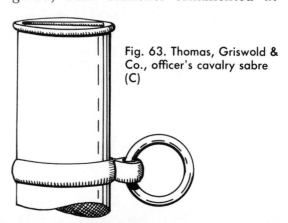

Fig. 63. Thomas, Griswold & Co., officer's cavalry sabre (C)

junction. The back top of the counterguard also bears a floral design in high relief. The grip is leather-covered and wound with twisted wire. The forward edge of the pommel cap bears a laurel leaf design. The scabbard is entirely of brass.

A sabre such as described is in the Battle Abbey collection in Richmond (Item #184). As already stated, Thomas Leech of the Memphis Novelty Works and William J. McElroy of Macon, Ga., made sabres which were similar, but in both cases the pommels are undecorated.

Figure 64

Thomas, Griswold & Co. also made foot officer's swords which in general conform to the U.S. Model 1850. These have the usual rose pattern in the brass counterguard. The pommel cap is decorated with laurel leaf design along the forward edge. The grip is of brown leather, wound with 14 turns of twisted brass wire. The blade is 1 inch wide, 30 inches long, with a flat back and a single shallow stopped fuller on either side. Some bear the full firm name on the ricasso as described in the previous cavalry sabre, while others are marked simply "T. G. & Co., N.O." The scabbards are also of two types, one all of bronze (brass), the other leather with brass mounts. The specimen depicted has a leather scabbard, stitched on the bottom. The blade is etched in its center with the ornamental letters, "C.S.A."

In the Confederate Museum, Richmond, Va., is a sword of the type just described, it having been carried by General W. M. L. Jackson, C.S.A. The top mount of the brass scabbard is engraved: "Col. W. M. L. Jackson, from the 31st Reg. Va. Vol., 1861." Another sword made by T. G. & Co., and also of the same type, is one worn by General Richard Taylor, C.S.A. It too has an all-brass scabbard.

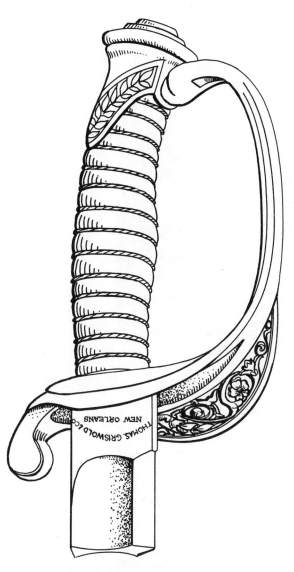

Fig. 64. Thomas, Griswold & Co., foot officer's sword (C)

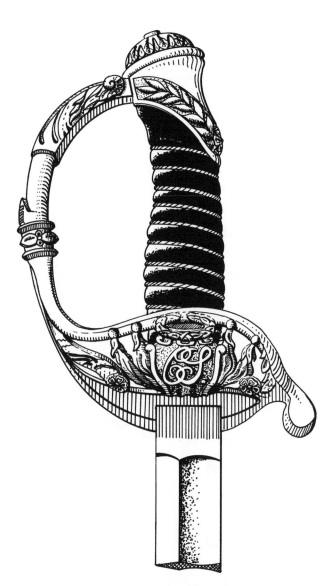

Fig. 65. Thomas, Griswold & Co., foot officer's sword (C)

Figure 65

A very ornamental foot or staff officer's sword is the one pictured. It has a 30-inch slightly curved blade, 1 inch wide. The reverse ricasso is stamped "Thomas Griswold & Co." (in a semicircle) over "New Orleans." The blade bears no further marks, stamps or etchings.

The brass guard bears the large letters "C.S." in script, flanked by a stand of arms. Knuckle bow and pommel are profusely ornamented. The grip is of leather, wound with 12 turns of twisted brass wire.

Nothing is known of the sword's background.

Figure 66

One of the most unusual Confederate swords encountered is a presentation piece with the blade handsomely etched with the inscription: "Presented to Captain J. F. Girault, New Orleans, Oct. 16, 1861. *Fortis et Probus*." Stamped on the ricasso is the full firm name and address. The guard is formed by three twisted snakes, the quillon finial ending in a snake head. The grip is of serrated ivory, while the backstrap and pommel form an eagle's head. All metal on the guard is silver-plated. The scabbard is of leather with gold-plated engraved mounts. The entire piece is a thing of great beauty.

Figure 67

Another fine presentation sword by this firm is in the Confederate Museum in Richmond. It is one which was given to General Sterling Price, C.S.A., by the women of New Orleans in early 1862 after the Battle of Lexington, Mo. The sword is stated to have cost $1,000, this amount being raised by public subscription. No contributions over $1 were accepted so that a large number could participate in the gift.

The sword is so designed as to bear the motifs and coats-of-arms of the States of Louisiana and Missouri, the scabbard being of pure gold with ornamented

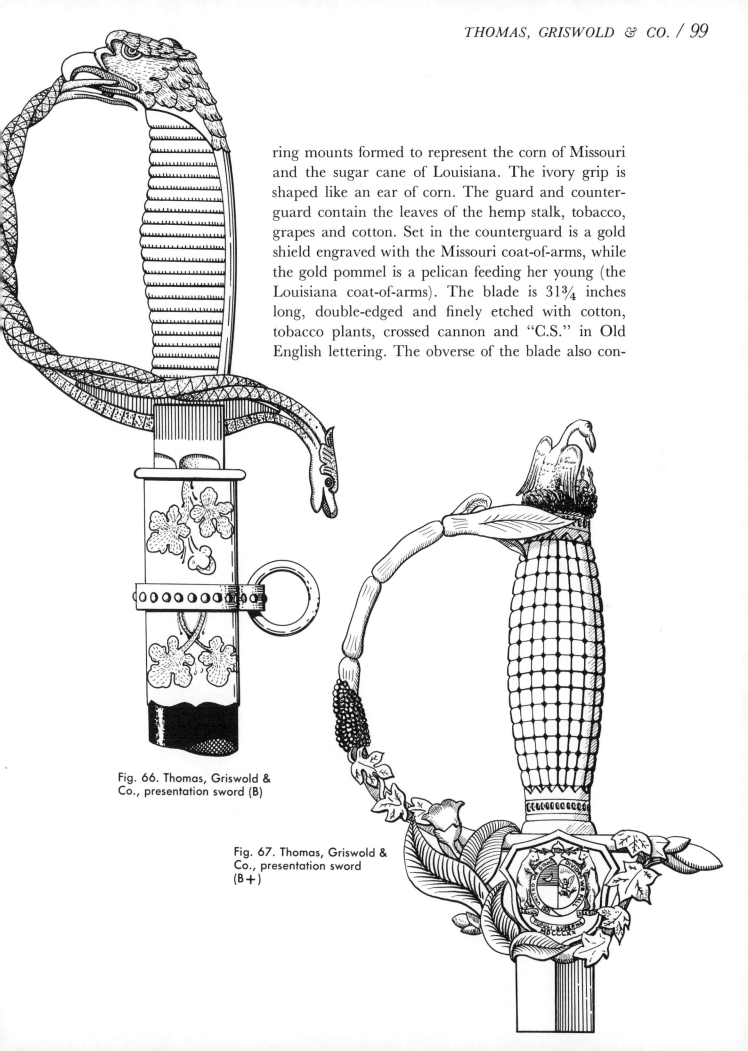

ring mounts formed to represent the corn of Missouri and the sugar cane of Louisiana. The ivory grip is shaped like an ear of corn. The guard and counterguard contain the leaves of the hemp stalk, tobacco, grapes and cotton. Set in the counterguard is a gold shield engraved with the Missouri coat-of-arms, while the gold pommel is a pelican feeding her young (the Louisiana coat-of-arms). The blade is 31¾ inches long, double-edged and finely etched with cotton, tobacco plants, crossed cannon and "C.S." in Old English lettering. The obverse of the blade also con-

Fig. 66. Thomas, Griswold & Co., presentation sword (B)

Fig. 67. Thomas, Griswold & Co., presentation sword (B✛)

tains the motto: "*Ense et Virtute per aspera ad alta.*"
The maker's name is stamped on the reverse ricasso.
Sword and scabbard are enclosed in a golden plush-
lined wooden box.

28. The Tredegar Iron Works, Richmond, Va.
(SWORDS?)

THE ONLY REASON to include the Tredegar Iron Works
in a book on edged weapons is because at least two
swords were made by this establishment. Generally
speaking, however, this firm did not make side arms.

The Tredegar Iron Works, Joseph R. and Charles
J. Anderson, proprietors, was located just west of the
Virginia Armory between the James River and the
Kanawaha Canal. It was surmounted on the north
by Gamble's Hill, a favorite Sunday promenade by
Richmonders of the 1850s and '60s. Situated so close
to the Virginia Armory, it was often considered to be
a portion of these works and Union spies at times
referred to the "rolling mills" at the Armory which
according to them were turning out large cannon,
etc. Actually they meant the Tredegar foundry, which
had the only large rolling mill in the South at the
time of the war, and here were made the armor plates
that sheathed the *Merrimac* (*C.S.S. Virginia*). Here also
were made numbers of the Williams breech-loading
cannon, as well as the large guns which were stamped
"T.F., J.R.A." (Tredegar Foundry, Joseph R. Anderson) on the trunions.

There are consistent reports of small arms being
manufactured here but the records, which are suffi-
ciently complete, do not bear this out. Workmen the
world over like to experiment and undoubtedly
"pilot models" of all types of arms were produced at
Tredegar on various workmen's time and company's

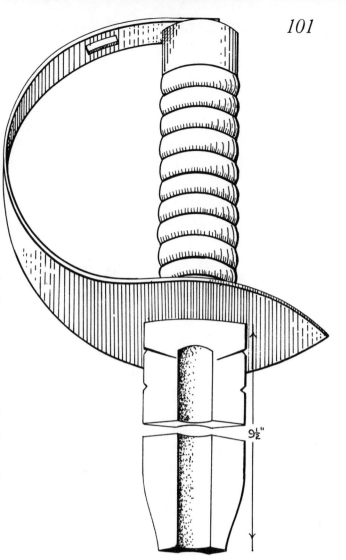

machinery and stock, but other than such minor deviations the company was simply not geared for "small stuff."

Figure 68

The Virginia Room in the Confederate Museum, Richmond, Va., contains a sword which was presented to General Charles J. Anderson, C.S.A., one of the owners of the plant, and is said to have been made at the Iron Works. This is entirely possible, although it appears to be of more ancient vintage than the Civil War.

The straight double-edged blade of colichemarde type (wide at guard for several inches, then suddenly narrowing and finally tapering to the point) is 28¾ inches long with a semi-stopped fuller on either side. The knife edges are stopped about an inch short of the guard, which is of sheet steel extending at the counterguard for 2 inches on either side of the grip. The knuckle bow is slotted for sabre knot. The grip is of turned wood with ten parallel grooves and has never been covered with leather nor wound with wire. A metal cap serves as pommel. The piece is totally without marks.

A very similar sword is known to exist, bearing the same type of blade of identical dimensions. The guard is similar but the obverse of the counterguard is pierced with two curved slots, 3 and 2 inches long respectively. On the underside of the counterguard appear the Roman numerals "XXVIII" and "III." At one time this sword must have had a wooden grip

Fig. 68. Tredegar Iron Works, officer's sword (E+)

but someplace along the way this has been replaced by a metal tube. As in the sword first described, this one also has a slot for sabre knot in the knuckle bow near its junction with the grip. Scabbards for these swords were of leather with a stud for frog.

29. The Virginia Armory (The Virginia Manufactory), Richmond, Va.

(SWORDS)

SINCE COLONIAL TIMES and up to the Civil War, the State of Virginia had its own standing army and facilities for the manufacture of arms. In 1798 the Virginia Assembly authorized the establishment of an armory at Richmond. Prior to this there had been an arms-making plant at Westham, near Richmond. This was destroyed by Benedict Arnold at the time of his invasion of Virginia in 1781. As a young man, the author remembers the ruins of Westham very well.

The Armory was completed in 1802 and was a very impressive structure. A contemporary writer describes it as having a long handsome front, surmounted in the center by a cupola and with two wings on either end. To the rear were the barracks which connected the two wings, and the ensuing square was used as a parade ground. The "Public Guard" was housed in the Armory, which became known variously as the Richmond State Armory, the Virginia Armory, the Virginia Manufactory, or simply "The Armory." The 1859 Richmond City Directory gives its location as "End of Fifth St. between Canal and River." Overlooking it to the north was Gamble's Hill, a popular promenade on Sunday afternoons, and to the west were the Tredegar Iron Works, so close as to lead many to believe they were a portion of the Armory itself. The Armory faced on the Kanawaha Canal and on its southern border was the James

River, referred to by Richmonders as "the muddy Jeems."

All types of arms were manufactured at the Armory and its anticipated output was 16 stands per day or 4,000 per year. In 1806, a typical year, it turned out: 1,265 muskets with bayonets, 205 muskets without bayonets, 579 pistols, 852 cavalry swords, 444 polished iron scabbards, 164 artillery swords, 158 sword tips and 84 rifles.

The manufacture of arms continued until 1822. Thereafter the buildings continued to house the "Public Guard" and also served as an arsenal. In 1845 serious consideration was given to the use of the establishment as a military school similar to the Virginia Military Institute (VMI) at Lexington, but such plans fell through. Northern war clouds prompted its rehabilitation, however, and an act of January 21, 1860, authorized the appointment of a committee to supervise its restoration as a manufactory of arms. On August 17 of the same year, a contract was entered into with the Tredegar Iron Works to "prepare the Armory for the fabrication and repair of arms."

Fully refurbished and with the addition of the Harpers Ferry machinery captured by the State troops in April, 1861, the Armory was turned over to the Confederate Government in September the same year and continued operations during the entire war, being the principal armory of the South.

During the evacuation of Richmond the Armory was set on fire and destroyed, although until very recent years portions of its walls still stood, blackened and charred, reminding the citizens of Richmond of what happens to those who lose a war.

There is no indication that any type of edged weapons was made at this establishment during the war years, although such were constantly in store. It is noted that on October 1, 1863, there were listed as being on hand "120 lances and 120 bowie-knives." The source of these weapons is not indicated.

For many years the identity of the Virginia sabres was not established, mainly because they had erroneously been classified as "Hessian." This fairy tale was accepted almost generally until as late as 1947, when there appeared in the *Bulletin of the Society of American Sword Collectors* (Vol. 1, October, 1947) an article by Richard D. Steuart which removed all doubts as to their origin. Since then one hears no talk of "Hessian" sabres and they are now referred to by their proper names of Virginia Manufactory sabres.

As originally issued most of these sabres were truly monsters! Their scimitar-curved blades were 40½ inches and the over-all of the weapon was 46 inches! The blades had two fullers on either side, one broad and shallow (in the middle of the blade) and the other deep and narrow near the back. Both were unstopped.

Figure 69

The early cavalry models had a wide sheet-iron guard with slotted perforations, as shown in the accompanying sketch. This guard joined a flat-topped iron pommel and backstrap. The wooden grips were covered with leather and variously wound with heavy iron, brass or copper wire. Sometimes light twisted brass wire was used in as many as three separate strands. Later research will probably reveal that these differences applied either to the year of manufacture or possibly to the rank of the person for whom the

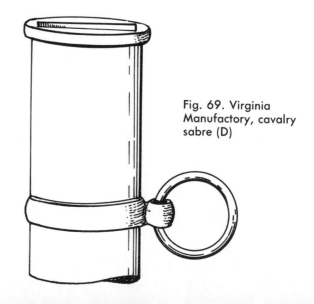

Fig. 69. Virginia Manufactory, cavalry sabre (D)

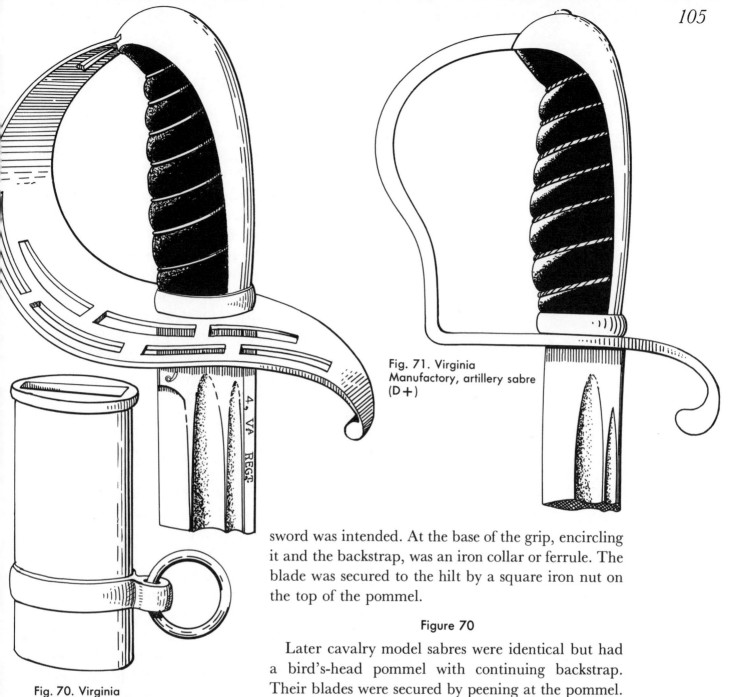

Fig. 71. Virginia Manufactory, artillery sabre (D+)

Fig. 70. Virginia Manufactory, artillery sabre (D)

sword was intended. At the base of the grip, encircling it and the backstrap, was an iron collar or ferrule. The blade was secured to the hilt by a square iron nut on the top of the pommel.

Figure 70

Later cavalry model sabres were identical but had a bird's-head pommel with continuing backstrap. Their blades were secured by peening at the pommel. The scabbards for these as well as the early models were of heavy iron with a stud for attachment to a frog. They had no drags.

Figure 71

The artillery models are essentially the same as above except they were made with a 30-inch blade and a knuckle guard of the reverse-"P" type, pierced near the pommel for a sabre knot. The scabbards for these are the same as for the cavalry sabres.

The blades of many of these sabres are stamped on the back variously: "1st," "2nd," "3rd" or "4th Va. Regt." In the early days Virginia was divided into four military districts. So far as cavalry and artillery were concerned the noted markings pertain to the geographical location rather than the numerical designation of the infantry regiment to which cavalry or artillery was attached. The stampings were placed on the blade in accordance with an act of January 28, 1800, whereby all arms issued to the militia were to be "marked with the number of the regiment, and/or the county."

At the time of the war Virginia had in storage in Richmond and at the Lexington Arsenal an untold number of these sabres, 3,350 being in the hands of militia on April 17, 1861, the day Virginia seceded from the Union. Subsequently, General Charles Dimmock, Virginia Chief of Ordnance, reported to the State Legislature that up to October 1, 1863, "7,863 sabres had been issued to the troops, majority of which were Virginia [sabres]."

The troopers to whom these weapons were issued found their 46-inch length both awkward and unnecessary and a number were cut down to 36 inches. Commenting on this the Columbia *South Carolinian* of January 3, 1861, states: "A quantity of old sabres owned by the State of Virginia, 500 in Richmond and 1,000 in Lexington have been shortened and rescabbarded, and are now of modern design. Ames of Springfield, has pronounced them to be of the best material." The rescabbarded swords consistently carried an iron sheath with brass mounts, throat and drag of iron. In addition to having their blades shortened, many were also slenderized as well.

A number of Virginia sabres have been found whose blades appear to have been made originally

35 inches and without extreme curve, but otherwise conforming to those already described. There is considerable controversy over these among collectors, but it is the writer's considered opinion that they are cavalry sabres made after 1816, by which time it had been discovered that a 40½-inch scimitar blade was unnecessary.

Figure 72

In the Virginia Room of the Confederate Museum is displayed a handsome and rather well-made sword which was carried by Lieutenant Maxwell T. Clarke, C.S.N., during the last three years of the war. This weapon must have been acquired by Lieutenant Clarke prior to his entering the navy as it is distinctly a foot officer's sword. The attached tag indicates that it was made by the Virginia Armory during the Civil War. If actually made there, which the writer doubts, it must be unique.

The almost straight blade is 1 inch wide, 30 inches long, unstopped fuller on either side. It is very lightly etched with floral designs, crossed cannons and lances, and on the ricasso are the small letters "C.S.A." arranged within a triangle. The counterguard has open spaces between the branches, much as do those of the McElroy swords. Knuckle bow is pierced for a sword knot. Pommel is undecorated. Grip is of black leather, wound with 10 turns of brass wire. The scabbard is of leather with brass mounts.

The sword itself gives no clue as to its origin.

30. W. Walsoneid, Solingen, Germany
(SWORDS)

SOLINGEN IS TO GERMANY what Sheffield is to England, and Springfield to the United States—the seat of many manufacturers engaged in the making of various edged weapons.

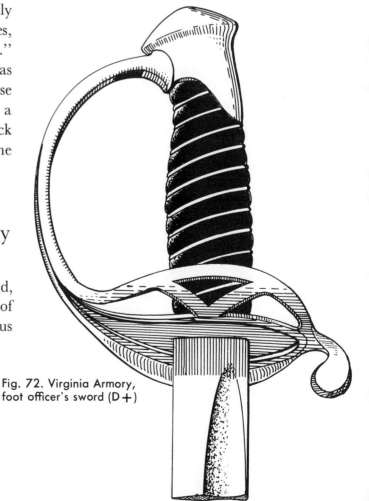

Fig. 72. Virginia Armory, foot officer's sword (D+)

During the Civil War many thousands of sabres, swords and bayonets were shipped to America from foreign sources, which included many made in Germany. Unfortunately, most of these items were stamped only with the maker's name and place of manufacture, and it is impossible to determine which went to the Federal Army and which to the Confederacy, or indeed whether an item was used in our Civil War at all and not imported later. Thus, as a general rule, collectors are wise to consider foreign-made swords merely as such, and not as a "type used by the Confederacy," or some similar meaningless term.

Only a comparatively few foreign edged weapons can definitely be considered "Confederate." Those English pieces bearing the name "Isaacs & Co." fall into this category, as do those "Mole" sabres with the heavy sheet-brass type of cavalry guard.

Some imported edged weapons show by the blade or guard design that they were intended exclusively for the South and of these there can be no question except those stamped simply "C.S.A.," for let us remember that a set of die stamps cost very little compared to the enhanced value of a weapon bearing these three magic letters. In the category of the unquestionably Confederate are those exquisite naval officer's swords with chased blades, Confederate naval coat-of-arms, etc., made by Mole, or those swords imported by Halfmann & Taylor with "C.S.A." as a portion of the blade etchings.

Figure 73

Also Confederate is the noncommissioned officer's sword by W. Walsoneid of Solingen, Germany. The straight blade is 32 inches long, $\frac{7}{8}$ of an inch wide and has a single stopped fuller on either side. The guard and grip are of brass, the grip containing

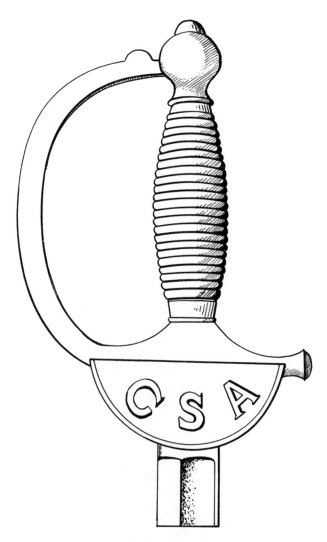

Fig. 73. W. Walsoneid, noncommissioned officer's sword (C)

parallel ridges. The knuckle bow is flat and joins a ball-type pommel on one end and a turn-down counterguard on the other. The latter bears the large raised letters "C.S.A." The scabbard is of leather, brass-mounted at drag and throat, the last having a stud for frog. Over-all length is 38¼ inches. It is finely made. It is stamped on the ricasso "W. Walsoneid, Solingen." A sword of this type is to be seen in the Battle Abbey collection in Richmond (Item #160).

Whether Walsoneid made other swords that can truly be called Confederate is not known, but a number of his weapons (cavalry sabres) can be documented as having been carried by Confederate soldiers.

31. J. C. Wilson, Houston, Texas
(SWORDS)
Figure 74

BEYOND THE FACT that J. C. Wilson of Houston, Texas, made Confederate swords little can be added. His name does not appear in available records. It does, however, on the ricasso of the sketched foot officer's sword, being etched thereon. The blade is slightly curved, 33 inches in length, with a brass guard and pommel. Over-all length is 38¾ inches. The scabbard is of black leather with brass mounts.

So far as is known, only two swords exist as a monument to J. C. Wilson of Houston, Texas. Two swords seem a meager testimonial to commemorate one who undoubtedly lived, loved and died, and yet many persons do not even have this. At least, Mr. Wilson will be remembered as long as Confederate swords are collected.

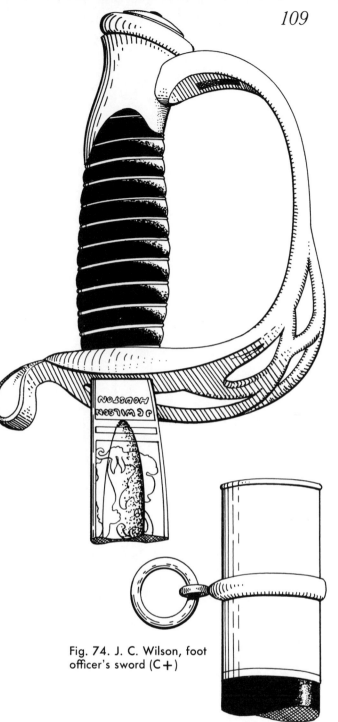

Fig. 74. J. C. Wilson, foot officer's sword (C+)

32. Ross Winan, Baltimore, Md.
(PIKES)

THE PART that Ross Winan played in the Civil War is a small one and almost forgotten. Other men have done considerably less and have been long remembered. Had fate been kind to Winan and the Confederacy, we might now be celebrating a birthday that would today require considerable research to establish.

On the nineteenth of April, 1861, two days after the secession of Virginia from the Union, a regiment of Massachusetts Volunteers attempted to pass through the city of Baltimore on their way south to coerce by force the Southern States back into the Union. At that time, Baltimore and Maryland were very pro-Southern in feeling and the regiment was mobbed in their passage through the city, the citizens properly resenting the illegal passage of troops. It was on this occasion that the first blood of the Civil War flowed.

Baltimore and the State of Maryland were thoroughly aroused (for the moment) and sought and received military aid and assistance from her sister State, Virginia. Responsive as always to injustice or coercion, Virginia immediately supplied Maryland with a number of arms, which as events proved, would have been put to real use only had they remained south of the Potomac River, real dividing line between North and South.

Figure 75

The Police Marshal of Baltimore at the time was a man named Kane. At his instigation and following the wave of indignation at having been "invaded" by Northern troops, Ross Winan, proprietor of the Winan's Works, was contracted to supply the city with the cheapest form of arms—pikes. Winan immediately set about fulfilling his contract and made several thousand of these weapons. They were crude

Fig. 75. Ross Winan, pike (D)

affairs, made in haste, and scarcely any two of them were exactly alike, although all had a double-edged wrought-iron head roughly shaped like a peach leaf with a long tang. The tang was driven into an 8-foot staff and held secure by a thick ferrule of wrought iron. In cross section the pikes were roughly diamond-shaped.

The several thousand that were made were delivered to the city and some very few were distributed among the citizens just before Baltimore was seized by Federal authorities. Under Federal guns, Baltimore, except for a few of the more hearty, soon lost its "pro-Southern" feeling, and thought the Yankees were just the nicest kind of people. It was not hard to ascertain from such spineless citizenry that Winan's surplus pikes had been stored in a warehouse on the southeast corner of Gay and Second streets. Local accounts advise that 3,500 pikes and 2,900 muskets (given these brave people by Virginia) were seized and carted off to Fort McHenry, headquarters of the army of occupation.

The Richmond *Dispatch* of May 28, 1861, stated: "General Butler's troops on the 20th instant marched to Greenmount cemetery and dug up 4,000 muskets and 3,000 pikes buried there and conveyed them to Fort McHenry in a convoy of 40 wagons."

Had the balance of the South had the intestinal fortitude of the citizens of Baltimore, Maryland, the American Civil War might at the outside have lasted 60 days! There can be no question, however, of the patriotism of a number of Marylanders who fought valiantly for those beliefs they held dear—to name a few: Steuart, Johnson, Semmes, Gilmor, Brown and Albaugh. These and many others sacrificed everything, while the bulk of the populace vacillated, rationalized their timidity, and finally capitulated entirely and embraced, as far as their wavering principles could embrace anything, the ideas and theories of the North. Maryland remains unchanged.

In addition to his pikes, Ross Winan, who was something of a mechanical genius, also invented an armored railroad cannon that was fired by steam. The idea was a revolutionary one. It was offered the South but the price of $5,000 caused many of the farsighted to reject any such scheme that involved such a terrific expenditure. Many of these same farsighted persons are still with us, who approve unlimited loans to so-called "underdeveloped countries" but who balk at expenditures which might possibly keep us ahead of the Russians in a military way. We Americans apparently never learn.

In May, 1861, the model steam cannon of Winan, disguised as agricultural machinery, was shipped to the Confederacy but was captured by the Federals en route.

In the early 1900s there appeared in the Baltimore *News* the following account of the seizure of Baltimore. It is here included to add additional fame to that illustrious warrior—General Benjamin F. (Beast) Butler, U.S.A.: The article is captioned: "How Benjamin F. Butler captured Ross Winan and expected to hang him for treason, and how the same Butler captured Baltimore so quietly that he did not awake a single policeman, is a delectable story of Baltimore in the first year of the Civil War."

This story has almost faded from histories of the city, but it was found in its fullness in an old copy of Butler's autobiography which has been resting undisturbed for years in the Peabody Library.

Butler regarded himself as an outstanding hero for taking Baltimore and occupying Federal Hill. Then fancy the shock of this curt note: "Sir:—Your hazardous occupation of Baltimore was made without my knowledge and of course without my approbation. It is a Godsend that it is without conflict of arms. It is also reported that you have sent a detachment to Frederick; but this is impossible. Not a word have I received from you as to either movement. Let me hear from you."

This was the letter of Gen. Winfield Scott, commander of the Union Army, that was received by Gen. Butler at 8.30 on the morning of May 14, 1861. Butler said that he had been 40 hours in the saddle and that he deserved some sleep so the receipt of this note so early in the morning disturbed him greatly. He never sent a reply to it. "Knowing that I could hold Baltimore as easily as I could my hat," wrote Butler in his autobiography.

. . . Read this from Butler's own story: "A Baltimorean by the name of Ross Winan, a gray-haired old man of more than three score and ten, a bitter rebel and reputed to be worth $15,000,000.00 had made 5,000 pikes of the John Brown pattern to be used by the rebels of Baltimore to oppose the march of United States troops." Butler wanted to capture Winan. "I thought," he wrote, "that if such a man, worth $15,000,000 were hanged for treason it would convince the people of Maryland at least that the expedition we were on was no picnic. I knew that he was going to Frederick to make a secession speech and I believed if we captured him he would be a very proper specimen traitor to be hanged." So Butler sent his troops and captured Winan and took him to Annapolis, but the hanging party did not come off. Winan was a member of the Maryland Legislature.

. . . So returning from his excursion to Frederick to capture Winan, Butler captured Baltimore. The train with the troops "backed down past the Relay House toward Baltimore and just at sunset we were at the Baltimore station." That was on May 13th. "There was substantially nobody at the station," Butler said. The march to Federal Hill was through a violent storm and the citizens did not know what was happening. Butler's boast was that he marched through the settled part of Baltimore and the police knew nothing about it. Upon reaching Federal Hill, Butler took possession of a beer garden there and one of his first acts was to issue this dispatch to the commanding officer at Fort McHenry:

"I have taken possession of Baltimore. My troops are on Federal Hill which I can hold with the aid of my artillery. If I am attacked tonight please open on Monument Square with your mortars. I will keep the hill fully lighted with fires during the night so that you may know where we are and not hit us."

Next day came General Scott's note and as soon as possible Butler was got away from Baltimore. . . . He confesses that in his final talk with General Scott: "I was so wrought up that upon my return to my quarters I threw myself on my lounge and burst into a flood of tears."

In Baltimore the vials of wrath and ridicule were emptied upon Butler, and all through the war period he was derided in this city. A book lampooning him in verse and etchings by the late Dr. A. J. Volck—very well done by the way—was published here. One of the Baltimore histories sarcastically calls Butler's exploit in capturing Baltimore, "The most successful of his military achievements."

PART II

ARMS WHOSE MAKERS HAVE NOT

YET BEEN IDENTIFIED

Introduction

This section has been devoted to edged weapons believed
to be Confederate but whose makers are unknown. No attempt
has been made to portray every unknown sword, sabre,
bowie or bayonet. We have been more concerned with types,
and a very definite attempt has been made to show each type
in the hope that someday the weapon will pass from "unknown" to being the established product of a known or at
present unknown maker.

Wide use of the horse as a means of transportation and
motive power throughout the Southern States required a
blacksmith shop in every town, large-sized plantation, and
practically at every crossroads. Each of these shops was a po-
tential armory, capable of turning out some kind of edged
weapon during the war, and most of them did. The type,
quality and quantity were limited only by the skill (or lack
of skill) of the individual involved. The blacksmith shop was
the main source of skilled or semiskilled labor for Confederate
ordnance.

CONTENTS

A. SWORDS

Listed in the following order: Officer's, Artillery, Cavalry, Foot Artillery and Naval Cutlasses.

AFTER THREE THOUSAND YEARS of honor and glory the sword, except for state occasions, has finally joined the battle-ax and javelin so far as usefulness is concerned. Our American Civil War was the last major conflict in which the edged weapon was actually used for offense and defense. Obsolete the sword may well be now, but it was not in the 1860s. Possibly it is this fact that accounts in large portion for the present-day interest in these weapons of the Confederacy. Effete, but nevertheless entirely romantic, those of us of the current generation who own one can hold in his hands an arm that we know for certain was drawn in anger by a stronger, more virile and courageous race than the United States is presently breeding. The beauty of this weapon, if indeed it possesses any, is secondary, for here we have an arm that was not stored in an arsenal or tucked away in a closet but that was actually grasped and used by a uniformed soldier at a time when, even though divided, our country was proud and vigorous and the Department of State was definitely secondary to the Department of War.

It is occasionally wondered by some of us how many swords were used during the American Civil War. To give a rough answer to this, we submit a report of General Ripley, the Federal Chief of Ordnance, who on June 30, 1862, advised that since the outbreak of the war (roughly a period of one year) the United States had purchased:

	American	European
Officer's swords	1,352	2,107
Noncommissioned swords	6,889	19,951
Musician's swords	2,050	5,363
Cavalry sabres	53,986	138,813
Horse artillery swords	5,250	3,515
Foot artillery swords	300	4,862

The above represents only arms actually purchased by the U.S. Government. It does not include those arms already in the hands of troops or those purchased by the various Northern States to arm their own volunteers and militia.

Similarly, a report by Colonel J. Gorgas, Chief of Confederate Ordnance, on February 3, 1863, that Major Caleb Huse, Confederate purchasing agent in Europe, had bought abroad and shipped to the South 16,178 cavalry sabres, gives no clear picture as to the total number of weapons used, as it does not include those made in the South, nor does it make any mention of other than "cavalry sabres."

Although the two reports given lead us to no actual over-all figures, we nevertheless do get the idea that in both the North and the South somebody was using an awful lot of swords.

In the case of the North it would not be too hard to determine from whence these arms came. Records are still extant and ordnance regulations required the contractor's name to appear on each weapon itself. Not so with the South. The Confederacy was never so firmly established that it could reject a sabre if contractor Joe Blow's name was not neatly stamped upon the ricasso of each blade, and as far as records are concerned, a goodly portion evaporated during those last few weeks when the Confederacy was not just defeated, but badly beaten. Thus, those of us interested in the subject must relie upon various contemporary accounts, not necessarily official, such as newspapers, or even statements of veterans made after the war. As can be understood, both should be accepted with more than a few grains of salt. Another, and more reliable source of information lies in the weapons themselves. Each maker had his own style, finish, decorations, etc., and in many instances even though a sword is not stamped "Joe Blow," by comparison with other weapons that are so stamped, it is simple enough to establish that the unmarked piece did indeed come from the Blow Sabre Factory. However, edged weapons were made at so many points in the South the writer is of the opinion that it would be an impossibility ever to include all manufacturers and to identify their products.

Below are given a few items extracted from newspapers and other sources relating to the Civil War period. These are offered in faint hope that somehow they might give some clue as to those weapons whose makers have not yet been identified.

The steamship *Fingal* cleared from Greenock for Madeira and West Coast with 1,184 rifles and 500 sabres. (Daily Richmond *Examiner*, November 9, 1861.)

Notice—Anyone having swords in their possession of any description will confer a great favor and receive a good price for bringing them to 80 Main Street. Old cavalry swords, navy swords, officers' swords, artillery swords, Knights Templar swords. (Richmond *Dispatch*, June 13, 1861.)

Swords with wooden scabbards were issued to the Fifth Georgia Cavalry, Wheeler's command in the early part of 1865. (*Confederate Veteran*, Vol. XXXII, No. 8, August, 1924, page 300.)

Fourth Kentucky cavalry were issued heavy English sabres which were unpopular. (Musgroves's *Kentucky Cavaliers in Dixie*, page 183.)

Captain Todd at Camp Jackson, Va. was presented a handsome sword by his company, the West Point Guards, in 1862. The sword was made by E. J. Johnston & Co., of Macon, Ga. Todd was killed at Malvern Hill. (*History of Doles-Cook Brigade*, H. W. Thomas, page 85.)

The Louisville *Journal* March 9, 1865—The Confederates captured at Chapman's landing each had a fine Enfield musket and a regular navy cutlass. One of the cutlasses was shown us. Including the handle it is two feet six inches long and the blade is nearly two inches wide. On the handle are the letters "C.S.N." (*Navy Records, War of Rebellion*, Vol. XXVII, page 88.)

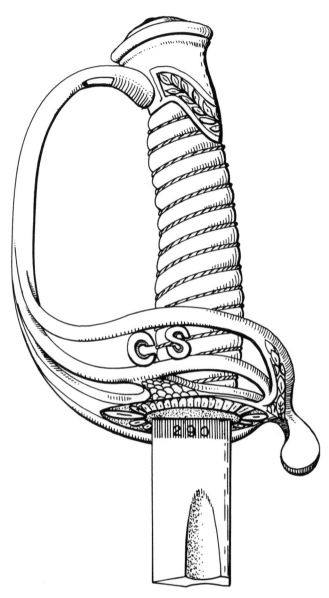

Fig. 76. Field officer's sword, "C.S." between branches (C)

Confederate Field Officer's Sword— Maker Unknown

Figure 76

THE PICTURED SWORD is so handsome and so reasonably common that it seems very odd its maker has yet to be identified. Roughly, it conforms to the U.S. field officer's sword of the period but has open spaces instead of floral decorations between the branches. Branches and counterguard are decorated, as illustrated, in addition to the large letters "C.S." (facing the blade) between the two branches. The pommel cap bears a spray of laurel leaves along the forward edge. The knuckle guard has a slot for a sabre knot. The wooden grip is wrapped with heavy cord, covered with leather and then wound with twisted gilt wire which follows the grooves made by the cord. Guard and pommel are of brass. The flat-backed blade is 32 inches long, each side of which contains a single unstopped fuller. The obverse ricasso is stamped with the number "290," which stamping is repeated on the front of the underside of the counterguard (and doubtlessly would be found on the pommel cap if the weapon were disassembled).

The scabbard of the specimen illustrated is of bright metal with ornamented brass ring mounts, rings, throat and drag. There are no marks or stamps on the scabbard, but other swords of this type are noted to have leather scabbards with brass mounts, each mount bearing the same number as found on the blade and guard.

It may or may not be significant that James Conning of Mobile, Ala., stamped his swords and scabbards similarly.

The author would be happy to know the maker of this sword, specimen of which was carried by General Joe Shelby, C.S.A., who never surrendered his command.

Confederate Field Officer's Sword—
Maker Unknown

Figure 77

THERE IS A marked similarity between this sword and the one that just precedes it. The only major departure is that the "C.S." between the branches in this specimen faces toward the grip rather than the blade. Minor differences consist of an undecorated pommel cap and absence of decoration on the top and underside of the guard. Decoration is apparent on the same portion of the branches as in the other weapon, but are vague and not nearly so pronounced.

As in the other sword, this is stamped with a number (149) on the obverse ricasso, on the underside of the guard at the front of the blade, and on the pommel cap at point of juncture with the knuckle bow. Once again it is noted that James Conning of Mobile, Ala., stamped his swords similarly. The scabbard on this specimen is of leather, seam on the top, brass-mounted. It appears original, although bears no stamping of numbers on the mounts.

The blade on this piece is slightly curved, quite slender and only 29 inches in length, having an unstopped fuller on either side. The back of the blade is flat, as is the one in the preceding sketch.

The Smithsonian Institution possesses a weapon such as described, given by Mrs. Kate N. Foote, widow of Admiral Foote, U.S.N., of Civil War fame. Engraved (not etched) on one side of the blade is:

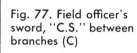

Fig. 77. Field officer's sword, "C.S." between branches (C)

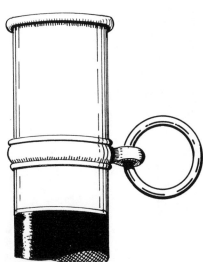

"Lieut. A. Moffitt, 51st. Regt. Tenn. Vols." It is assumed that this is the name of the original owner of the piece and that it was surrendered to Admiral Foote.

Confederate Officer's Sword— Maker Unknown

Figure 78

A BEAUTIFUL SWORD of unknown manufacture is here pictured. It immediately brings to mind those of the same style made by Haiman which contain "C.S.A." in the counterguard rather than a "fort" or "castle," as does this one. However, the style of manufacture does not suggest Haiman, and as the writer has seen at least three swords of this pattern which were not made by Haiman, the natural conclusion is that it is a type rather than a style made by one particular maker. Swords of this type which can be traced back always have a naval background. The background of this particular sword is not known, nor is the significance of the design in the counterguard, although it has been suggested that the fort is a likeness of Fort Sumter, S.C.

The almost straight blade is 29¾ inches long, 1⅛ inches wide, with a modified flat back. Etchings on the blade are of vine design but include a large "C.S." in Old English letters on the center of the obverse side. The guard and pommel are of well-cast brass. The grip is of leather, wound with 11 turns of twisted brass wire. The scabbard is brass, black-leather-covered with brass mounts. There is no clue as to the maker.

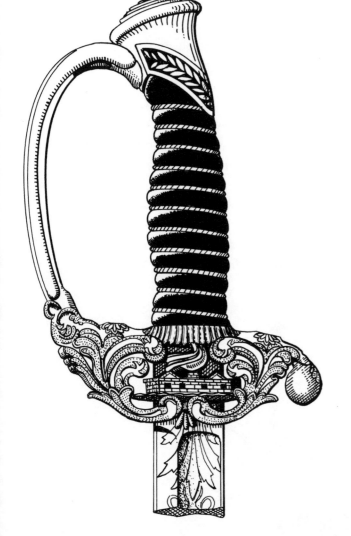
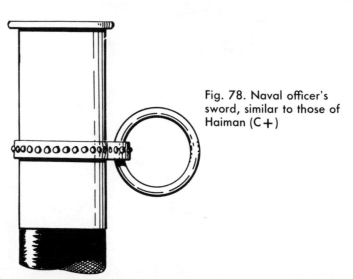

Fig. 78. Naval officer's sword, similar to those of Haiman (C+)

Confederate Foot Officer's Sword—
Maker Unknown
Figure 79

SOMEDAY, someone will be able positively to identify the maker of this unusual sword. As a matter of fact, sooner or later, diligent research will clarify most weapons that are today classified only as "unmarked Confederate officer's sword."

Back in the 1920s I recall so many discussions among serious collectors as to the identity of revolvers which were apparently stamped "Beech & Liggon." Today's collector knows very well that these revolvers are the product of Leech & Rigdon, and now knowing this, one wonders how anyone could have been stupid enough to have ever referred to them as "Beech & Riggon."

The pictured sword was made in Georgia. That similar ones saw service in Virginia is attested to by the fact that the hilt of one was dug up at the Bloody Angle, Spottsylvania Court House, Va. Those thus far viewed by the author are entirely devoid of etching, stampings or any other identifying features. However, the human desire to survive the years is so strong that someday a collector will turn one up that is stamped, etched or engraved "Made by Joe Blow, Atlanta, Ga.," and then everyone will wonder why collectors up until that time were so puzzled as to the maker.

The snake motif in the counterguard of this weapon is not very unusual, remembering that every revolutionary movement in this country has used a snake of some sort as a symbol of "Don't Tread On Me!" Guard and pommel are of brass. In the specimen pictured the pommel is of cavalry type but more often it is of the undecorated officer's variety. The counterguard quillon is heavy and globular. The blade is slightly curved, 31 inches in length, with a modified

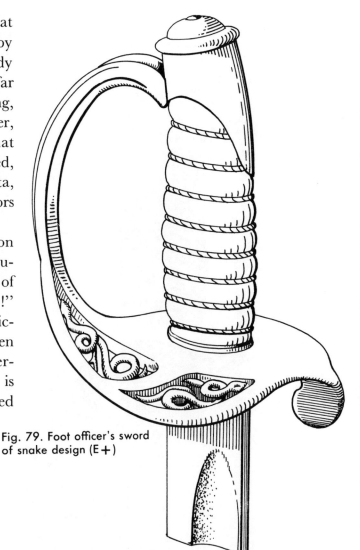

Fig. 79. Foot officer's sword of snake design (E+)

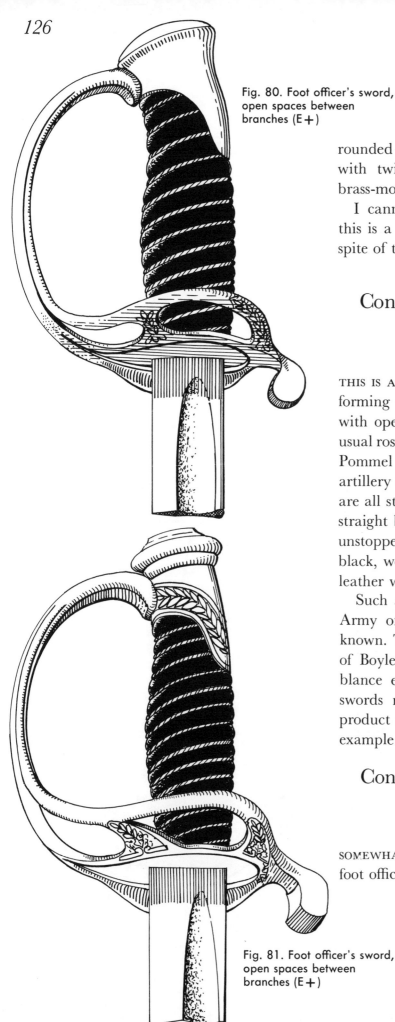

Fig. 80. Foot officer's sword,
open spaces between
branches (E+)

rounded back. The grip is leather-covered, wound with twisted brass wire. The scabbard is leather, brass-mounted.

I cannot resist adding my opinion, which is that this is a product of L. Haiman and Brother—this in spite of the apparent crudeness of the piece.

Confederate Foot Officer's Sword— Maker Unknown

Figure 80

THIS IS A crude and poorly made piece, roughly conforming to the foot officer's sword of the period but with open spaces in the counterguard instead of the usual rose design. The branches are vaguely decorated. Pommel cap is without decoration and is more of the artillery type than officer's. Blade, pommel and guard are all stamped with a two-digit number. The almost straight blade is slender, 30 inches long, with a single unstopped fuller on either side. The leather grip is black, wound with twisted brass wire. Scabbard is of leather with brass mounts, unmarked.

Such arms are known to have been carried in the Army of Northern Virginia, but the maker is unknown. The manner of its marking is similar to those of Boyle, Gamble & MacFee, but there all resemblance ends. There is also a vague similarity with swords made by L. Haiman & Brother, but if a product of this manufactory, it is an extremely poor example of their work.

Confederate Foot Officer's Sword— Maker Unknown

Figure 81

SOMEWHAT SIMILAR to the sword just preceding is this foot officer's sword. It, too, has the open spaces in the

Fig. 81. Foot officer's sword,
open spaces between
branches (E+)

counterguard, but is a much more finely made weapon. The decorations on the underside of the guard and branches, although vague, are much more pronounced than in the other sword, and the pommel cap is of standard officer design with the forward edge decorated with laurel leaves. The knuckle guard is also unpierced for sabre knot. The leather grip is wound with 14 turns of twisted brass wire. The blade is almost 32 inches long, of normal width, with an unstopped single fuller on either side. No marks are apparent on this weapon, which has a leather scabbard with brass mounts. The maker is unknown.

Confederate Sword—Maker Unknown

Figure 82

EXCEPT FOR THE known background of this weapon it would most certainly be in the section devoted to knives and bowies. However, it is a documented fact that the pictured piece was carried by Captain Richard Gatlin, of the Edgecomb Guard of North Carolina. I am sure that Captain Gatlin carried this item only because he was unable to get anything better. This monster in heft and appearance is more of a knife than an officer's sword. The blade is 21½ inches long, with a clipped point and flat back. It is almost 2 inches wide and a full ¼ inch thick. The "D"-type guard is of wrought iron and fastened by means of a nut screwed to the tang of the blade on top of the turned wood grip. The scabbard is every bit as crude as the sword, being made of wood covered with thick leather.

This weapon may be viewed in the North Carolina Room of the Confederate Museum, Richmond, Va. The maker is unknown, but obviously this is no production piece, and judging from its appearance was made at some crossroads smithy.

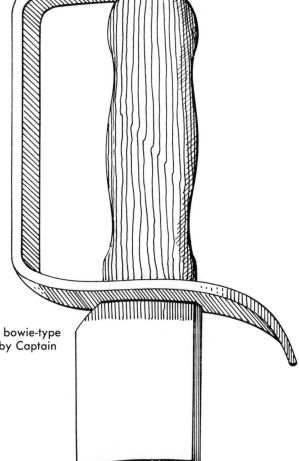

Fig. 82. Crude bowie-type sword carried by Captain Gatlin (E)

Confederate Sword—Maker Unknown

Figure 83

FIRST GLANCE would indicate this sword to be a typical homemade weapon, the product of some local blacksmith shop. However, quite a few have appeared over the years, which would indicate that the maker was on some sort of a production basis.

The almost straight blade is 27 inches long, with flat back, and made without fullers. The guard is of iron with two branches riveted to the knuckle guard and counterguard plate. The turned pine wood grip is painted black, and has never been covered with leather nor wound with wire.

The scabbards to these swords are of wood, painted black. The carrying ring mounts are of copper superimposed over tin mounts. The toe mount is also tin.

Mean in appearance, this sword nevertheless was probably most effective in cut and thrust. Its maker is unknown.

Confederate Foot Officer's Sword— Maker Unknown

Figure 84

THE PICTURED SWORD has no great eye appeal but from a standpoint of rarity it is most desirable. In over forty years of collecting the writer has seen only three. The one in the Battle Abbey collection (Item #185) came from Seattle, Washington, in the early 1900s. How it reached a point so far from the onetime Confederate States would be an interesting story, if it were only known. The other two swords of this type both came from Virginia.

The blade is almost straight, 30 inches long, single unstopped fuller on either side and with rounded back. The guard is of well-cast brass. The counterguard contains a pattern of oak leaves with acorns,

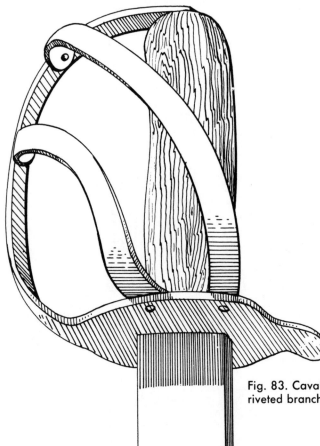

Fig. 83. Cavalry sabre with riveted branches (E)

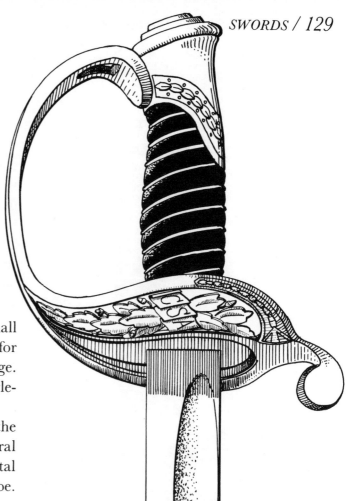

Fig. 84. Foot officer's sword, small "C.S.A." in guard (C)

over which appears a ribbon bearing the very small letters, "C.S.A." The knuckle bow is pierced for sword knot. Pommel cap is decorated on forward edge. Grip is of leather, wound with 12 turns of single-stranded copper wire.

A Roman numeral is found cut in the end of the quillon of all three examined, and this same numeral also appears cut in the brass throat of the metal scabbard, which also has brass ring mounts and toe. These scabbards are lacquered a deep red.

Although a far cry from the specimen whose guard is formed by the cut-out letters "C.S.A." and known to have been made by Froelich at the Confederate States Armory, there is nevertheless a marked similarity in the way both are marked, and in the construction of the scabbards. Possibly this is another example from Froelich's establishment?

Confederate Noncommissioned Officer's Sword—Maker Unknown

Figure 85

FOR SOME REASON or other, noncommissioned officer's swords of the Confederacy are not plentiful. Usually they conform closely to those of the U.S. pattern, but are made with unstopped fullers in the blade and the guards are usually of poor casting.

Pictured is what is assumed to be a noncommis-

Fig. 85. Noncommissioned officer's sword (E)

sioned officer's sword. The wooden grip is leather-covered and wound with single-strand heavy copper wire. The "D"-type knuckle bow is of brass. The pommel cap is similar to those found on the early U.S. Dragoons, only it has no backstrap. A copper ferrule is at the base of grip and guard. The blade is only 26 inches long, almost straight, with a stopped fuller on either side. The only marking is on the blade, a number "959."

The maker is unknown, but there is a similarity between this and the Nashville Plow Work sabres with a similar strap guard, stamped on the ricasso "Sharp & Hamilton" and "Nashville, Tenn."

Confederate Artillery Officer's Sword— Maker Unknown

Figure 86

AN ARTILLERY SABRE such as is pictured was carried by some Confederate officer at the battle of Stone's River (Murfreesboro), Tenn., December, 1862, and January, 1863. The only known specimen is in the Battle Abbey collection (Item #173), having been picked up off the battlefield whereon the Confederate General Roger Hanson lost his life.

This sabre has a very curved blade, 35 inches long, with a single stopped fuller on either side. The grip is of leather, wound with twisted brass wire. The guard is ornamented as shown and in a circular disk centered on the flat knuckle guard are the large letters "C.S." The scabbard is of iron with brass carrying ring mounts. The drag is of iron. The pommel of this sword is more cavalry type than artillery.

The maker is unknown.

Confederate Artillery Officer's Sabre— Maker Unknown

Figure 87

HERE IS A Confederate copy of the U.S. Mounted Artillery Officer's Sabre, Model 1840. The knuckle bow and quillon finial, as well as the pommel cap, are profusely decorated with floral designs. All are of brass, and at one time must have been gold-plated. The pommel cap is peculiar in that it is flat on top rather than dome-shaped. The grip is of brown

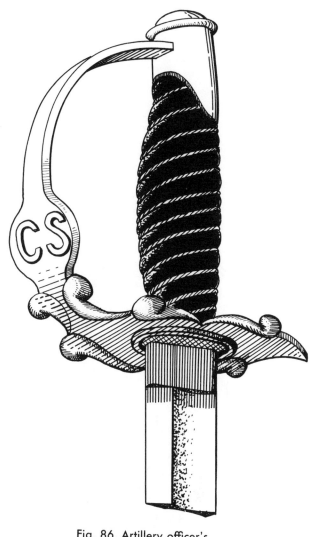

Fig. 86. Artillery officer's sabre with "C.S." in medallion on guard (C+)

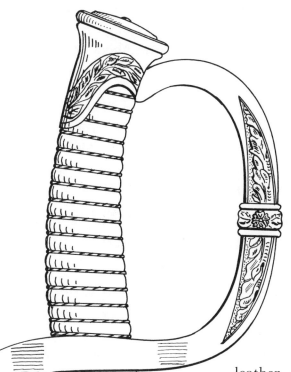

Fig. 87. Artillery officer's sabre, "C.S.A." on blade (C—)

leather, wound with 16 turns of twisted brass wire. Under the knuckle guard is an oval indenture at the blade, so that the unmounted scabbard top will extend about ⅛ of an inch into the guard. Union sabres of this type usually contain a leather washer, but in this case, the aperture is lead-filled.

The flat-backed 31-inch blade has the distinctive curve of the artillery and is profusely and ornately etched. The decorations include a shield, an American eagle bearing a ribbon with "E Pluribus Unum," a Confederate Stars and Bars flag, a multitude of floral designs and a large "C.S.A."

In regards to "E Pluribus Unum" being found on a Confederate weapon, it is noted that this is the motto for the State of Tennessee as well as the United States, and in this case must apply to Tennessee.

Only on swords made by L. Haiman is the etching comparable in quality to that found on this sabre, leading to the suspicion that it is either a product of L. Haiman or of foreign manufacture.

A sabre whose guard is identical with the one in question is included in the Battle Abbey collection in Richmond, Va. (Item #183). The blade is 32 inches in length, elaborately etched, one side bearing the inscription "D'Orleans" and the other side "Artillerie." The scabbard is of metal. This sabre was from the Orleans Artillery Battalion of New Orleans. Thomas, Griswold & Co. made sabres of this type with identical hilts and brass scabbards.

Confederate Artillery Sabre— Maker Unknown

Figure 88

AT FIRST GLANCE this sabre appears to be a standard cavalry model but with the branches cut off and with an artillery-type pommel. Closer examination reveals that the guard never contained branches. There is a small projecting arm on the knuckle guard at the point of juncture with the pommel. Necessity for this is not readily seen. The grip is of leather, crudely wound with twisted brass wire. The blade is very slender, with a deep curve, and is 32 inches long. Each side has an unstopped fuller. A leather washer cushions blade from guard. The scabbard is all metal.

The only apparent mark on this weapon is a Roman numeral "IV" cut in the side of the guard.

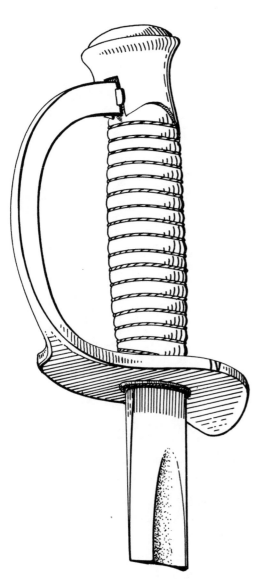

Fig. 88. Artillery sabre with cavalry guard (E)

This is the only sword of this type brought to the writer's attention. There is no clue as to the maker.

Confederate Artillery Sabre— Maker Unknown

Figure 89

CONFEDERATE ARTILLERY SABRES are rare. No reason is known for this, but the fact remains that three or four officer's swords show up for each artillery sabre.

Pictured is an enlisted man's artillery sabre with a 30½-inch curved blade with unstopped tapering fuller on either side. The back of the blade is flat. The "D" guard and pommel are of brass and of standard artillery design. The guard is recessed at the blade to accept the scabbard, which is made without throat mount. Scabbard is of iron, crudely made with brass carrying ring mounts. The grip of this sabre is of wood, covered with oilcloth (black) and wound with 13 turns of single-strand iron wire.

The weapon bears no marks.

Confederate Cavalry Sabre— Maker Unknown

Figure 90

THE SPECIMEN PICTURED is a typical representative of the most usual Confederate sabre encountered, being a close copy of the U.S. Cavalry Model 1840. These are found with innumerable slight variations, but the basic standard remains the same, and so only one sabre of this type has been included in this work.

This particular sabre has a tapering cone grip, leather-covered, wound with a single strand of untwisted iron wire. The two-branched guard and "high-hat" pommel cap are of brass. The curved blade is 35 inches long, with flat back and a single unstopped fuller on either side. Over-all length of weapon is 40½ inches. The scabbard is iron with brass ring mounts. Finishing file marks are evident

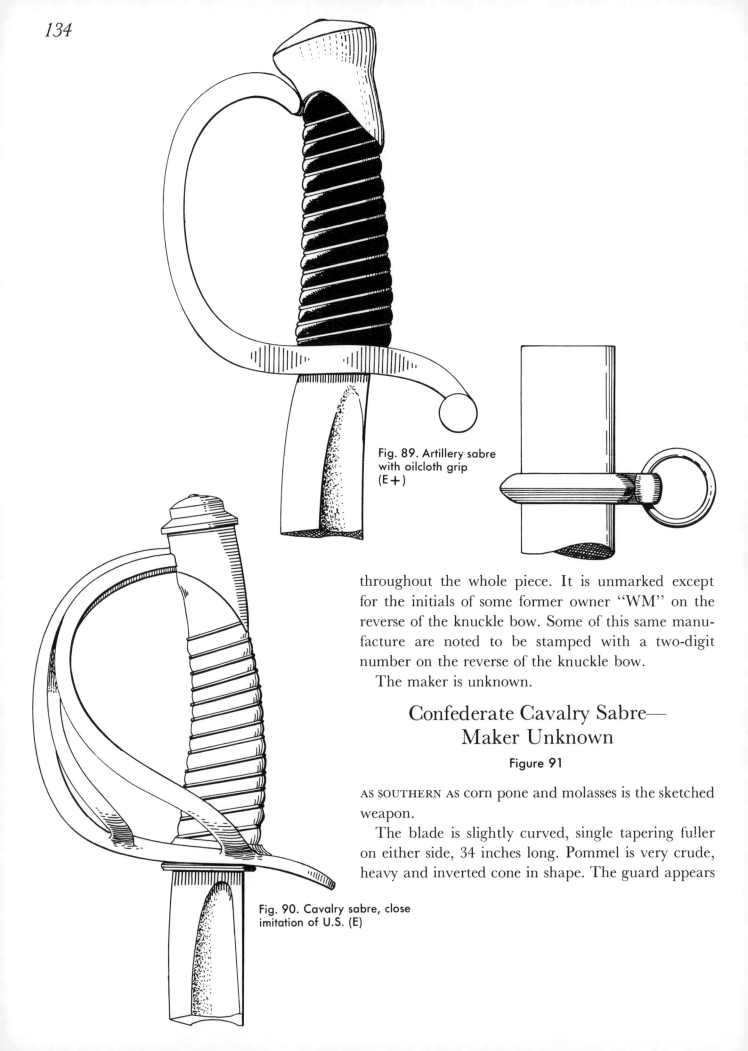

Fig. 89. Artillery sabre
with oilcloth grip
(E+)

throughout the whole piece. It is unmarked except
for the initials of some former owner "WM" on the
reverse of the knuckle bow. Some of this same manufacture are noted to be stamped with a two-digit
number on the reverse of the knuckle bow.

The maker is unknown.

Confederate Cavalry Sabre— Maker Unknown

Figure 91

AS SOUTHERN AS corn pone and molasses is the sketched
weapon.

The blade is slightly curved, single tapering fuller
on either side, 34 inches long. Pommel is very crude,
heavy and inverted cone in shape. The guard appears

Fig. 90. Cavalry sabre, close
imitation of U.S. (E)

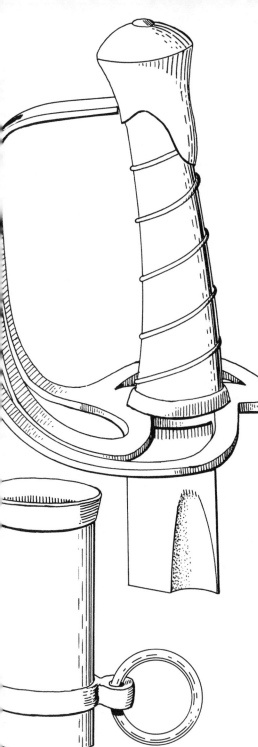

to have been stamped from thick sheet brass, but such is not the case—it was cast. The collar appearing around the base of the grip is an integral part of the guard. File marks are evident on both branches and knuckle bow, which usually has a slot for sabre knot. The scabbard is iron, wrap-around type and brazed at the seam, with brass throat, toe, drag and ring mounts.

The grip is leather-covered and wound with a thick untwisted strand of iron wire. Some have been observed whose wooden grips were never covered with leather, only wound with wire.

Fig. 91. Cavalry sabre, crude pommel and flat branches (E+)

The weapon is unmarked.

Many sabres of this type have been found in Virginia, indicating their association with the Army of Northern Virginia. The one sketched, however, was carried by Captain John Steele of the 11th Alabama Cavalry, which fought under General Nathan Bedford Forrest.

Although not uncommon, it possesses a great deal of "eye appeal" and is most desirable.

Confederate Cavalry Sabre— Maker Unknown

Figure 92

UNTIL THE DISCOVERY of manuscript records in our National Archives showed conclusively that only carbines were manufactured at Tallassee, Ala., it was long believed that sabres of the type depicted were made at that point, and were called "Tallassee sabres." With the discovery that swords were not made at Tallassee the weapon drops back into the category of "maker unknown."

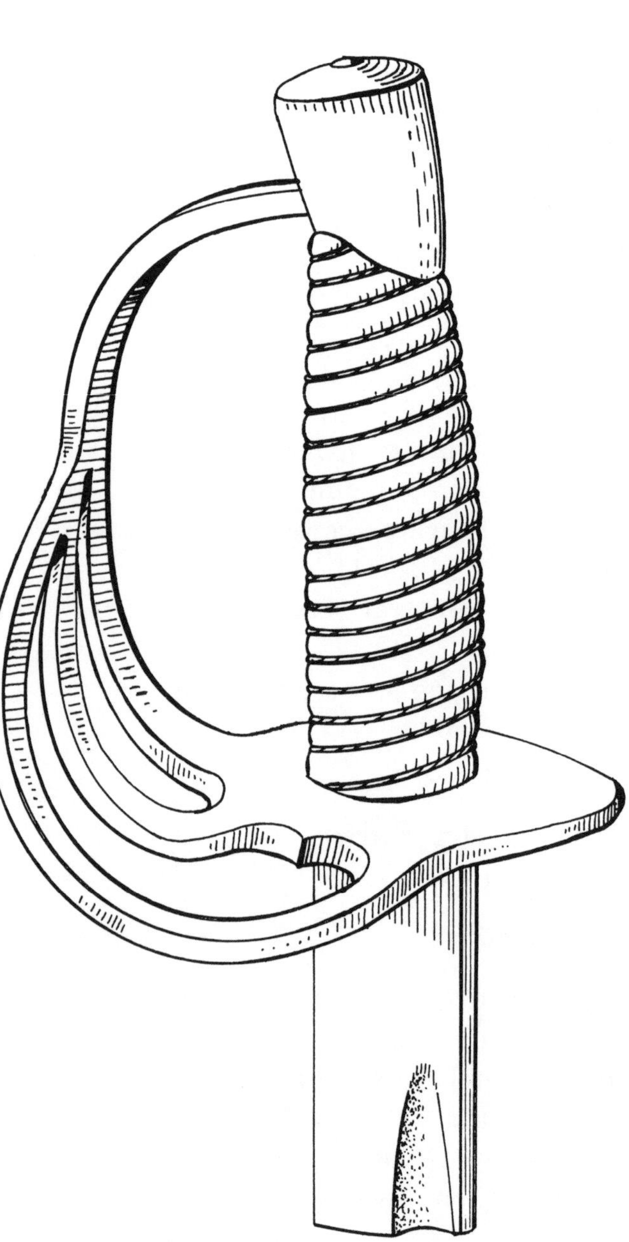

If anything can be typical, then this is a typical Confederate cavalry sabre, and very desirable from a collector's point of view. It embraces most of the features known as "Confederate." The blade is almost straight, 34½ inches long, with a modified flat back and a single tapering fuller on either side. The grip is wrapped with oilcloth and wound with twisted brass wire. The pommel is heavy and "knob-like" in appearance.

Superficial examination would indicate that the guard had been stamped from a sheet of heavy brass, but like the one just preceding this, it has been cast and file marks are apparent on the square sides of the flat branches. There is no slot for sabre knot.

The only marks on the sabre shown consist of three punched "dots" followed by the number "27." This is found on the underside of the counterguard. The blade has a "pancake" weld, indicating how hard-pressed was the South that it had to mend in such a fashion a weapon which as originally issued would have been scorned by most Union troopers.

Scabbard is of metal with all brass mounts, including throat, drag and carrying rings.

Confederate Cavalry Sabre—Maker Unknown

Figure 93

ANOTHER TWO-BRANCHED Confederate cavalry sabre is the one pictured. These swords are not uncommon and must have been made on quite a production basis, although there is not the slightest indication as to where they were made or by whom. Those seen by the author are devoid of markings, unless a series of three or four "dots" punched into the underside of the guard can be called marks. The practically straight

Fig. 92. Crude sabre, crude pommel and flat branches (E+)

blade is 34 inches long, with a single unstopped fuller on either side. The back of the blade is flat. The guard is that of the typical cavalry sabre. The pommel cap appears to be more the "officer" type than cavalry. The grip is of brown leather, wound with 17 turns of twisted brass wire. Scabbard is of iron, brass-mounted. It is a well-made piece.

Confederate Cavalry Sabre— Maker Unknown

Figure 94

HERE IS ANOTHER sabre whose guard appears to have been stamped from sheet brass but which was actually cast. The pommel is heavy and crude. The grip is of oilcloth, wound with a single strand of untwisted iron

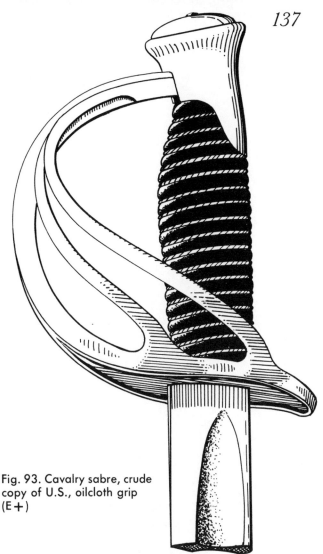

Fig. 93. Cavalry sabre, crude copy of U.S., oilcloth grip (E+)

wire. The blade is almost straight, with a single unstopped fuller on either side. Over-all length is 40½ inches. The blade is 1 inch wide, 35 inches long. The weapon is totally without marks or stamps.

These sabres are not common. The maker is unknown. The particular item pictured came from North Carolina.

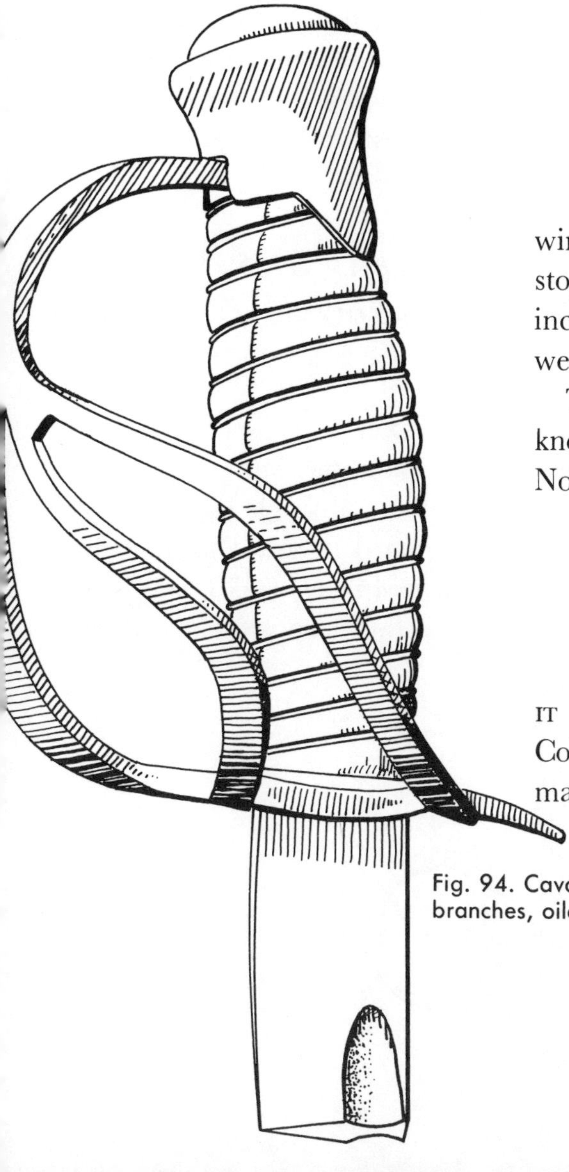

Confederate Cavalry Sabre— Maker Unknown

Figure 95

IT HAS BEEN SAID that these sabres were made in Columbia, S.C. This may well be the case, but the maker remains unknown.

Fig. 94. Cavalry sabre, flat branches, oilcloth grip (E+)

Despite its somewhat crude appearance it is a well-made piece, having a 35-inch straight blade with single unstopped fuller on either side, and flat back. The counterguard is flat, as is the knuckle bow, the flatness of the latter being at right angles to the former. The two branches are rounded. A brass collar is at the juncture of grip and guard. The grip is leather-covered, wound with 13 turns of untwisted iron wire. Pommel cap is plain.

Any number of these sabres have survived the years and all examined have wooden cedar scabbards. Most had iron or tin mounts with brass ring mounts but some observed had iron ring mounts.

One in the Battle Abbey collection, Richmond, Va., (Item #172) was found near the Kelly House on the battlefield of Chicamauga.

The *Confederate Veteran* of August, 1924, makes note that early in 1865 sabres with wooden scabbards were issued to the 5th Georgia Cavalry in Wheeler's command. Whether they were this type of sword we have no way of knowing.

Confederate Cavalry Sword— Maker Unknown

Figure 96

A MONSTER of a cavalry weapon is here pictured. The blade is 36 inches long with only a slight curve. The ricasso is exceptionally long. A single fuller is on either side, stopped. The guard is of flat iron, somewhat similar to the English Mole sabres. There is no pommel, a brass cap serving this purpose. The leather-

Fig. 95. Cavalry sabre with wooden scabbard (E+)

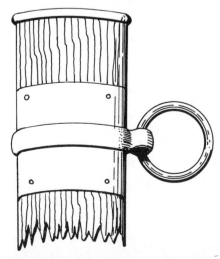

covered grip is wound with 17 turns of single-strand brass wire. Over-all length is 41 inches!

The scabbard is of leather with leather tabs enclosing brass rings rather than the customary ring mounts.

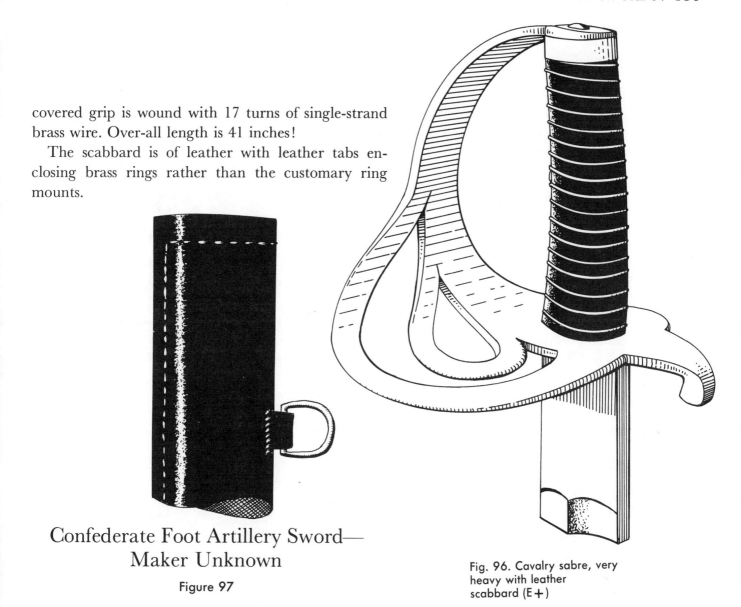

Confederate Foot Artillery Sword— Maker Unknown

Figure 97

Fig. 96. Cavalry sabre, very heavy with leather scabbard (E+)

AN ATTRACTIVE WEAPON is this one with the brass grip and guard (made in one piece) whose quillon terminals are ornamented with the raised letters "C" on one side and "S" on the other. The grip is cast to simulate eagle feathers.

The 19-inch wasp-waisted blade is diamond-shaped in cross section, $1\frac{7}{8}$ wide at the guard and $1\frac{5}{8}$ inches at its middle, again assuming its original width prior to tapering to point.

The illustrated weapon is stamped in several places on the guard "R. Mc.M.," probably the initials of some former owner. Other than this the piece is devoid of markings. Its maker is not known. It is said that this is a coastal artillery short sword. The scabbard is leather with a tin throat and a reinforced leather toe.

Confederate Foot Artillery Sword— Maker Unknown

Figure 98

BECAUSE OF THE STAR in the pommel this has been classified by some as having a Texas background. Others claim it was carried by the Louisiana Tigers, this assumption being based on Lord knows what logic. Here we have a glorified sketch of one of the

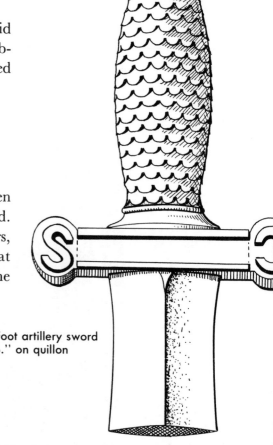

Fig. 97. Foot artillery sword with "C.S." on quillon ends (C)

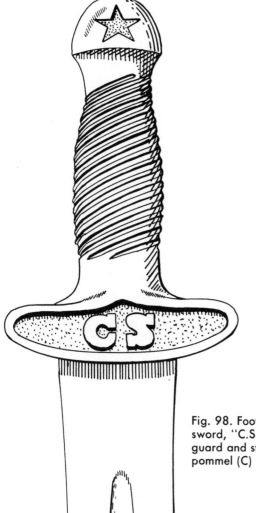

Fig. 98. Foot artillery sword, "C.S." on guard and star in pommel (C)

most common of Confederate relics, and yet its maker remains unknown.

The hilt is of brass, very poorly cast, so much so that the "C.S." in the cross guard can barely be identified as such and the star in the pommel usually lacks an arm or "point." The blade is double-edged, 18½ inches long, wasp-waisted, with an unstopped fuller on either side. No marks appear which would give any indication as to where it was made or by whom. The scabbard is of wood, painted black with tin mounts, also painted black. The top mount contains a button for frog.

Obviously this is a foot artillery sword copied after those used by the Roman gladiators 2,000 years ago. In the days of the Romans, when one man was pitted against another similarly armed, such a weapon was highly effective. In the 1860s, it was issued to foot artillerymen in the hopes that so armed they might disembowel or chop the legs of opposing cavalry that had overridden their supposedly "secure" artillery position. Soldiers of the 1860s found repeating carbines and a 36-inch cavalry blade did much toward dimming the effectiveness of the short sword as a weapon. After one such encounter with the enemy most soldiers relied upon their legs rather than this arm.

The hilt of one of these swords was recently dug up on a battlefield near Fredericksburg, Va., with a small portion of the rusty blade still attached, so there can be no question that some were actually used, but their source remains obscured in darkness. It is for sure that the star in the pommel has no Texas connotation and I am sure that the Louisiana Tigers would have turned up their noses at such a weapon.

Confederate Foot Artillery Sword— Maker Unknown

Figure 99

MANY CONFEDERATE WEAPONS are entirely devoid of markings. Such is the foot artillery sword pictured. It conforms very closely with the French sword of the period, having a brass guard and grip, the latter having parallel grooves. The ball pommel is bare of decoration. The blade is double-edged, usually oval cross section although sometimes found with diamond cross section. It tapers upon leaving the guard, to swell again to its original 2-inch width and then again tapering to the point. Some have fullers, others are made without channeling. The scabbards vary from leather with brass mounts to painted wood with tin mounts.

Because of the close resemblance of this sword to

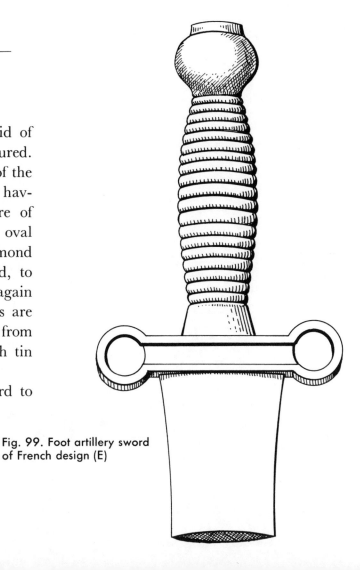

Fig. 99. Foot artillery sword of French design (E)

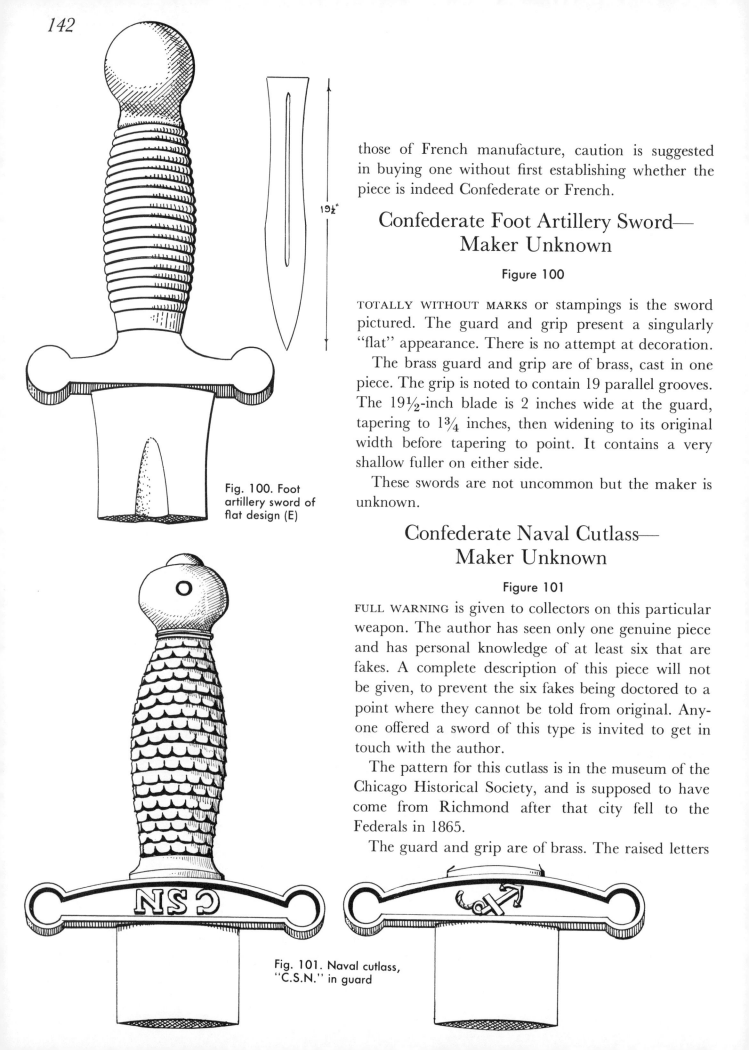

Fig. 100. Foot
artillery sword of
flat design (E)

Fig. 101. Naval cutlass,
"C.S.N." in guard

those of French manufacture, caution is suggested in buying one without first establishing whether the piece is indeed Confederate or French.

Confederate Foot Artillery Sword— Maker Unknown

Figure 100

TOTALLY WITHOUT MARKS or stampings is the sword pictured. The guard and grip present a singularly "flat" appearance. There is no attempt at decoration.

The brass guard and grip are of brass, cast in one piece. The grip is noted to contain 19 parallel grooves. The 19½-inch blade is 2 inches wide at the guard, tapering to 1¾ inches, then widening to its original width before tapering to point. It contains a very shallow fuller on either side.

These swords are not uncommon but the maker is unknown.

Confederate Naval Cutlass— Maker Unknown

Figure 101

FULL WARNING is given to collectors on this particular weapon. The author has seen only one genuine piece and has personal knowledge of at least six that are fakes. A complete description of this piece will not be given, to prevent the six fakes being doctored to a point where they cannot be told from original. Anyone offered a sword of this type is invited to get in touch with the author.

The pattern for this cutlass is in the museum of the Chicago Historical Society, and is supposed to have come from Richmond after that city fell to the Federals in 1865.

The guard and grip are of brass. The raised letters

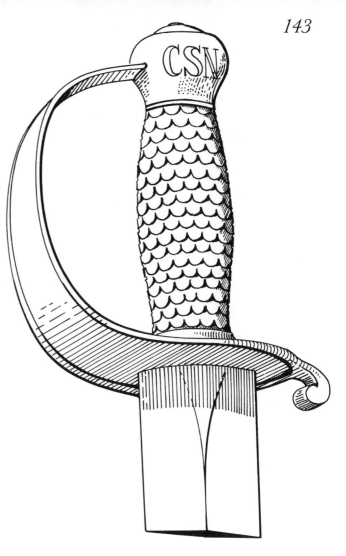

"C.S.N." appear on one side of the cross guard and a raised anchor with line attached appears on the other side. The grip is of simulated fish scales (eagle feathers); the pommel is plain.

An article concerning this sword appeared in the *American Arms Collector* of April, 1958, Volume II, No. 2, Editor's Page, which any would-be purchaser of Confederate belt buckles or swords is advised to read.

Confederate Naval Cutlass— Maker Unknown

Figure 102

GENERALLY SIMILAR to those cutlasses made by Thomas, Griswold & Co. of New Orleans, is the one shown here.

The guard and grip (two pieces) are of brass. The grip is cast to represent fish scales. The pommel bears the indented letters "C.S.N." on the obverse and a fouled anchor on the reverse. The guard has a beaded edge. The quillon end terminates in a flat disk. The knuckle bow end slips through a slot into the pommel and contains a hole through which the tang of the blade passes. This, of course, is not apparent without unseating the blade. If the weapon is unhilted, a small "w" will be found on guard and grip. Its meaning is not known.

The blade is almost 22 inches in length, diamond cross section, of the type that tapers from the guard to about midway, to swell again to its original width of 1⅞ inches.

The scabbards for these weapons were of leather with thin brass toe and top mount which contained a stud for frog. The original frog and belt were of cotton webbing, leather-mounted. The belt had a hook rather than a buckle.

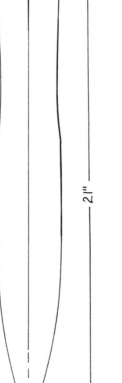

Fig. 102. Naval cutlass, "C.S.N." in pommel and anchor on other side (C+)

21"

These cutlasses are supposed to have been made in Richmond, Va., but their manufacturer is not known.

Confederate Naval Cutlass— Maker Unknown

Figure 103

SOME YEARS AGO cutlasses of the type pictured turned up with great regularity. The source in each case was Norfolk, Va. This was long before the current phase of "faking" and there is no question but that these were original. So many from one geographic point certainly indicates that the weapons were probably made there.

Lacking eye appeal, these cutlasses nevertheless were serviceable weapons. The grip was of turned walnut with a copper washer at the top, to which the tang of the 18½-to 22-inch double-edged blade was peened. Blades were wasp-waisted. The guards are of the "S" type, most of wrought iron but some of cast brass. A brass or iron collar surrounds the grip at its base. Scabbards were of canvas, painted black with a stud for a frog.

Smaller editions of the cutlass have appeared knife-size.

Although the maker is not known, the writer feels confident that they were manufactured in Norfolk, Va., possibly by the Union Car Works of Portsmouth, Va., this city being just across the river from Norfolk. The Union Car Works is known to have made bowie knives, sabre bayonets, etc., for the Confederacy. Their products have never been identified.

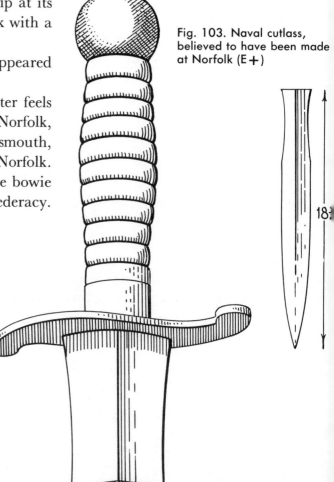

Fig. 103. Naval cutlass, believed to have been made at Norfolk (E+)

B. PIKES AND LANCES

MAN IS AN AMBITIOUS RASCAL, always striving for the impossible, the unattainable. Given the earth he wants the moon. Upon obtaining the moon he will want the sun, and so it goes. Despite this trait of grasping for things beyond his reach, man also has the fortunate quality of adaptability, which enables him to be content with what he has while reaching at the same time for things he cannot have.

Sitting comfortably in this era of push-button war, with a glass of bourbon to sip while awaiting the signal to push the button, we idly wonder how, only one hundred years ago, a Confederate soldier could possibly have been content at being armed with a pike or lance, little better than a sharpened stick, knowing as he did know that he would be opposed by an enemy equipped with the then modern rifle and bayonet. The answer to this question is that the Confederate was not at all happy with such a weapon, but having nothing better he was content with it during the interim before he too could seize with his grimy hands a rifle-musket tipped with a triangular bayonet.

As a matter of historical fact we do not have to go back one hundred years to find the pike or lance as a part of warfare. The Washington *Post* of October 26, 1902, devoted three columns entitled, "Lances Are Used Again in War," to the adoption of the lance by the general staff of the German Army, which "after experimenting for more than two years, and as a result of campaigns in the Philippines and in South Africa, has returned to the lance for arming its cavalry."

Five months after the lance had made its reappearance in the German Army, we note its disappearance from the French Army. The New York *Herald* of February 11, 1903, contained a copyrighted article with dateline "Paris" which began by saying: "Cuirass, lance and helmets, are doomed as far as the French army is concerned. At an early date these relics of ancient times will be abolished."

In 1942 the author was one of many thousands who joined the colors in World War II, hoping in a mild sort of way to "Free the World for Democracy," or maybe it was something else we were fighting for—it was never quite clear, then or now—but at any rate, whatever it was, the ensuing years have pretty well dimmed any idea of its coming to pass. Nevertheless, in 1942 upon being tossed a seabag of uniforms and gear I was surprised at also being given a "relic of ancient times," a helmet. Recalling the *Herald*'s article of 1903, I protested but to no avail. I then inquired for a pike to go with the helmet but apparently the supply officer was just fresh out of these.

At about the time Apprentice Seaman Albaugh was slinging his seabag over his shoulder and placing upon his pointed head the "relic of ancient times," to wit, a helmet; some 3,000 miles to the East, Prime Minister Winston Churchill was declaring that the British would defend vital airfields even if they had to do it with pikes. This amazing statement was taken quite literally by the British War Office, who shortly thereafter announced that piked poles had actually been issued to Home Guard units. Lord Croft, Under-Secretary of War, who received credit for the idea, was quoted as having said, "After members of the Home Guard have attacked with grenades, and mainly at night, the pike is a handy weapon for mopping-up operations." The pike in this instance was a light steel shaft with a short sword attached to its end, having an over-all length of 5 feet 4 inches. All this absurdity was featured in an article in the *New York Times*, February 1942.

Those of us sitting by the push button, sipping our bourbon and awaiting the inevitable World War III, might remember that our gunrooms contain a Georgia pike, in the event our push button fails to operate properly.

This lengthy preface to the subject of Confederate pikes is only to show that this weapon, in the minds of some, does not date back to the days of Chivalry and the Crusades; and further, in the case of the South, it was the only type of arm that could readily and quickly be supplied to the many thousands who came to do their bit for "democracy."

John Brown, who was hanged at Harpers Ferry, Va., in 1859, only because the laws provided for no worse form of death, is hardly a hero to those whose hearts lie south of the Potomac River. His moldy body would probably have turned over many times in his celebrated grave had he known that his idea of arming Negroes with spears was received with acclaim throughout the land he tried so hard to subjugate. I am saying, of course, that his idea of using spears as weapons was acclaimed, not putting them into the hands of the Negroes.

The *National Tribune*, March 19, 1903, contains the following:

Philip Z. Hart, of Lakeport, N.H., although a lad of only 12 years at the time, distinctly remembers a visit that John Brown paid to Unionville, Conn., shortly before the Harpers Ferry affair. Brown had gone East to have manufactured a large number of pikes, and after an unsuccessful effort to get Charles Blair, of Allensville, Conn. to make them, visited Mr. Hart's father at Unionville, Conn., and contracted for 10,000 pikes at 25c each, paying cash on delivery. Brown claimed that the pikes were to be used in arming free-soil settlers in Kansas, who were in danger of attacks from Indians. On the shank of each pike was stamped "C. Hart" (also the serial number— editor).

John Greenleaf Whittier, tears streaming down his long gray beard, wrote of Brown:

John Brown of Ossawatomie, they led him out to die;
And lo! a poor slave-mother with her child pressed nigh.
Then the bold, blue eye grew tender, and the old harsh face grew mild,
As he stooped between the jeering ranks and kissed the negro's child.

No doubt this touching poem caused copious tears to stream down many long gray beards in the North, but with admirable restraint the South managed to remain pretty dry-eyed about the whole affair.

Shortly before Brown attempted his insurrection at Harpers Ferry, the 7th Regiment of New York City escorted the remains of ex-President Monroe from New York to Richmond. After Monroe was properly buried the 7th Regiment remained in Richmond for a few days and were given full hospitality. Their manners, manly bearing and fine gray uniforms attracted considerable attention, all favorable. It was probably at this point that this type and color uniform seized popular Southern fancy and later, somewhat modified, came to be the official Confederate uniform.

A little later the Richmond Grays went to New York at the invitation of the 7th Regiment, and were royally entertained. From this fraternization it came about that when the Grays went to Harpers Ferry to capture Brown, they also captured a number of the iron pikes with which Brown planned to arm the Negroes. These were sent to the New York 7th Regiment as souvenirs. (It is stated that 483 spears and 175 broken handles were captured.)

These pikes, made by Hart on special order for Brown, were made under the following specifications: "The blade to be double-edged and to average 9 inches in length, 2 inches in width at the base, tapering to a point; to be made of tool steel, with cast malleable iron ferrule and guard, attached to a 6-foot ash pole with screw, fastening spears to the pole; the spears packed in boxes, the poles in bundles." Brown claimed this method of packing was for convenience in shipping and quick assembly. He did not also mention that packed in such manner their true character would be concealed in transportation.

The above information is given, not to identify a Confederate weapon, but in order to identify a weapon that is not Confederate. It is said, however, that many of these spears or pikes, after capture from Brown, were stored at the Harpers Ferry Arsenal, later to be sent South and finally finding their way into the hands of a Texas regiment. With the defeat of the Confederacy they were stored in the Arsenal at Mount Vernon, Ala., later destroyed by fire; and still later, their remains, as old metal, were sent to the rolling mill at the Rock Island Arsenal. Obviously, only a few still remain, but why anyone would want an item with such a background is beyond me—not, of course, that I am in any way biased.

For a number of years the writer has made a hobby of collecting news items which pertain to various Confederate weapons. Those relating to pikes he has found particularly interesting, and they reflect the fact that even before hostilities began in April, 1861, the South anticipated the war and was arming accordingly. The story of the Confederate pike is pretty well covered in the newspaper accounts which follow.

We learn that the gun factory at Huntersville, Pocahontas county, Va., is turning out the best quality of Sharp's rifles. The County Court ordered the fabrication of four to five thousand lances for home defense. (Lynchburg *Republican*, January 6, 1862.)

Mayor Baugh of Memphis, Tenn., has had 64 Irish pikes made there for a company just organized. They are about ten feet long with a bayonet head for thrusting and a hook for cutting. These and double-barreled shotguns will be an efficient armament. (Richmond *Examiner*, June 11, 1861.)

Undoubtedly this account refers to what we now term "bridle cutters," which at that time were believed to be particularly effective against cavalry. The idea was to use the bridle hook to "pull in" a horse weighing several thousand pounds so that the rider could then be transfixed with the spear-type head of the pike. What the rider of the horse, armed with a carbine, sabre and revolver, might be doing in the meantime seems a question that occurred to only a few, but after one hundred years the answer seem reasonably plain even to one who has no more sense than a gun collector.

Having had the "Irish Pike," we now turn to another nationality, described by the Richmond *Examiner* on August 10, 1861:

It is proposed to arm some companies with the Polish scythes. A scythe fastened to the end of an 8 or 10 foot staff. Shells and Bowie-knives are being made at Spartanburg. The appropriation of $5,000 to build a Winan's gun is an outrage. Private businessmen saw its defects and would not be interested. It was tried years ago at West Point and a steam plant in the field is impossible. A shot in the boiler would be fatal to all.

We wonder what those wise men of 1861 who objected to spending $5,000 for the development of a revolutionary type weapon (described under "Winan," Part I) would have to say about the money being spent for military development in 1960!

With the second year of the war and the increasing scarcity of arms, Colonel J. Gorgas, Chief of Confederate Ordnance, stated:

In the winter of 61–62 while McClellan was preparing his great army near Alexandria, we resorted to the making of pikes for the infantry and lances for the cavalry and many thousands of the former were made at various arsenals, but were little used. I remember a formidable weapon, which was invented at that time, in the shape of a stout wooden sheath containing a two-edged straight sword some two feet long. The sheath or truncheon could be leveled and the sword, liberated from the compression of a strong spring, by touching a trigger, leaped out with sufficient force to transfix an opponent. (*Southern Historical Society Papers*, Vol. 12, page 74.) (See also "Rev. Dr. Graves," Part III.)

On January 1, 1862, the Richmond *Examiner* commented upon an address by General William Harvey Richardson at Memphis, Tenn., wherein he is quoted as saying:

A battle line must be established with batteries heavy and light; muskets; minie, Enfield, Mississippi and sporting rifles, by shotguns, swords and bayonets, by lancers, bowie-knife and pikemen. Let us turn to the Roman sabre and the bowie-knife placed on 10-foot poles. The head should be 15 inches long, sharp on both sides and point or one edge and point and one-third or one-half the other edge; secured by bands and rivets to a six or ten foot pole.

Same source, January 28, 1862: "The coast defense regiments will be armed with Alabama pikes, manufactured under appropriation of the State Legislature. This weapon has a keen, two-edged steel head like a Bowie-knife blade near 18 inches long with a sickle-like hook, very sharp, bending back from near the socket." As we recall, the *Examiner* referred to this same type of pike as an "Irish Pike" on June 11, 1861.

On February 9, 1862, General J. E. Johnston wrote to Adjutant General Samuel Cooper:

We should have a much larger cavalry force. The greatest objection, or rather difficulty, in increasing it, is said to be the want of proper arms. This can easily be removed by equipping a large body of lancers. These weapons can be furnished easily and soon, and would be formidable—much more so than sabres—in the hands of new troops, especially against the enemy's artillery. The shafts should be about ten feet long and the heads 7 or 8 inches. Those furnished to us are—many of them of heavy wood and too short, the heads too thin and unnecessarily broad. Ash, is the best wood.(Johnston's *Narrative*, page 479.)

The day following Johnston's letter, Acts of C. S. Congress, Vol. I, page 778, contains a resolution instructing the Committee on Military Affairs to inquire into the propriety of arming troops with pikes, lances, spears or shotguns.

General Joseph E. Johnston might have been in favor of pikes, but his namesake, Albert Sidney Johnston, apparently had little use for them:

At Bowling Green a distinguished Tennessee politician called upon Johnston and requested him to make a contract with parties in Nashville for the manufacture of spears, with a bill-hook or sickle attached to the head with which foot soldiers could attack cavalry, the sickle to be used in cutting the bridle reins and pulling the troopers from their horses. General Johnston asked: "What would the troopers be doing with their pistols while the spearsmen were trying to cut their bridle reins?" (*Life of General A. S. Johnston,* W. P. Johnston, page 389).

The General appears to be one of the few who took a realistic view of the whole affair.

On February 20, 1862, the *Examiner* reported on an Act to organize a battalion to be armed with revolvers and pikes. Up until this time, the great State of Georgia had been silent on the question of pikes, but on this same date, her Governor, Joseph E. Brown, issued a "Proclamation" which he addressed to "The Mechanics of Georgia" as follows:

The late reverses which have attended our armies show the absolute necessity of renewed energy and determination on our part. We are left to choose between freedom at the end of a desperate and heroic struggle, and submission to tyranny, followed by the most abject slavery to which a patriotic and generous people was ever exposed.

Surely we cannot hesitate. Independence or death should be the watchword and reply of every freedman's son of the South. Our enemies have vastly superior numbers and the greater advantage in the quality and quantity of their army. Including those, however, which have been and will be imported in spite of the blockade, we have enough guns in the Confederacy to arm a very large force, but not enough for all the troops.

What shall be done in the emergency? I answer, use the "Georgia Pike," with six-foot staff and the side-knife, eighteen-inch blade, weighing about three pounds. Let every army have a large reserve, armed with a good pike and a large heavy side-knife, to be brought upon the field with a shout for victory when the contending forces are much exhausted, or when the time comes for the charge of bayonets.

When the advancing column comes within reach of the balls let them move in double-quick time and rush with terrible impetuosity into the lines of the enemy. Hand to hand the pike has vastly the advantage of the bayonet, which is itself but a crooked pike with shorter staff, and must retreat before it. When the retreat commences let the pursuit be rapid, and if the enemy throw down their guns and are likely to outrun us, if need be, throw down the pike and keep close at their heels with the knife until each has hewed down at least one of his adversaries.

Had five thousand reserves been thus armed and brought to the charge at the proper time, who can say that the victory would not have been ours at Fort Donelson.

But it is probably important that I state here the use to be made of that which I wish you to manufacture. I have already a considerable number of these pikes and knives but I desire within the next month ten thousand more of each. I must have them and I appeal to you, as one of the most patriotic classes of our fellow-citizens, to make them for me immediately.

Each workman who has the means of turning them out in large numbers will be supplied with a proper pattern by application at the Ordnance Office at Milledgeville.

In ancient times that nation, it is said, usually extended its conquests furtherest whose arms were shortest. Long range guns sometimes fail to fire, and waste a hundred balls to one that takes effect, but the short range pike and the terrible knife, when brought within proper range (as they can be in almost a moment) and wielded by a stalwart patriot's arm, never fail to fire and never waste a single load. I am, very respectfully, your fellow citizen.

Had the South won the war, Governor Brown's proclamation would now rank with those of Winston Churchill's. Even so, it brought considerable results. Ten thousand pikes were not forthcoming in the following month as the Governor requested, but from the time of his proclamation in February until September 16 of the same year, 1862, 7,099 were received at the State Arsenal at Milledgeville. These were inspected by Peter Brown, Master Armorer, who, reportedly, rejected many. (*Confederate Records of Georgia*, page 345.)

Although the Governor mentioned that a "proper pattern" would be supplied, judging by the number of varieties, each maker of pikes made them according to his own ideas on the subject. Roughly, there were three models: one had three blades, a large central one, and two smaller, leaf-shaped blades at the sides. This was known as the "clover-leaf" pike (see "Samuel Griswold" or "H. Stevens," Part I). A second type had a straight blade and a hook with a sharp edge, known as the "bridle-cutter." The third type had a straight double-edged blade about 13 inches in length. There were many, many variations of all three types.

Regardless of the style, none of these pikes were successfully received by the troops, and when the 31st Georgia Regiment was armed with them, their issuance almost caused a revolt. (*Confederate Veteran*, Vol. 24, No. 1, page 21, and Vol. 31, No. 9, page 337.)

Early in 1862, with the air of proclaiming the ultimate nuclear weapon, a Mobile, Ala., newspaper announced:

A NEW WEAPON—THE ALABAMA PIKE! The State of Alabama is arming her troops for coast service with a very effective weapon. The Mobile correspondent of the Memphis *Appeal* thus describes it: "We are arming our men with a weapon new in this war, and in modern warfare generally, but a most effective weapon, as it will compel the Southern soldier to his best fighting points and throw the Northerner on his worst, to wit: hand-to-hand fighting. This weapon being the pike, a large number having been, and still being, manufactured under an appropriation of the State Legislature. The

Alabama Pike consists of a keen, two-edged steel head, like a large bowie-knife blade, near a foot and a half long, with a sickle-like hook, very sharp, bending back from near the socket. This is intended for cutting the bridles of cavalrymen, or pulling them off their horses, or catching hold of the enemy when they are running away. This head is mounted on a shaft of tough wood about eight feet long. A gleaming row of these fearful implements of slaughter gleaming down upon them at the *pas de charge*, would strike the terror of ten thousand deaths to the apprehensive souls of Butler's Yankees."

When we first heard of this weapon designed to strike terror in ten thousand Yankees, it was under the name of "Irish Pikes." Later it became a "Polish Scythe." Evidently it is now an "Alabama Pike." Here then is a weapon that can apparently be all things to all people.

February 25, 1862, the Acts of C.S. Congress, Vol. V, page 26, reflect a Resolution to arm 20 regiments with pikes. The nationality, or State designation, of these proposed pikes is not mentioned. Two days later, the *Examiner* of Richmond states:

There is a factory in this city near the paper mill engaged in making pikes with which to arm a portion of our forces. This weapon is furnished at a cost not exceeding $5.00 each. The specimen we have seen is a formidable infantry weapon, about eight feet in length, including the spear head. The staff is made of ash. We would suggest by way of improvement to this weapon that the shape of the spear head is too broad and flat. A narrow, triangular shape like that of the bayonet with enough to transfix the body of a man would be much more effective and formidable. A lighter weapon than the specimen we have seen would be needed for cavalry.

Governor Brown's initial appeal to the mechanics of Georgia for pikes was directed toward patriotism alone. This was followed on March 12 by the statement that the State would pay $5 for every pike accepted, the shaft to be of ash, white oak or hickory, with heads of well-tempered steel. Knives with tipped scabbards, belt and clasp would be received at $4.50 each. (*Confederate Records of Georgia*, page 350.)

Under date of March 23, 1862, no less a personage than General "Stonewall" Jackson gave his endorsement to the pike by saying: "We must, under divine blessing, rely upon the bayonet when firearms cannot be procured. Let me have a substitute to make the arm six or more inches longer than the musket with bayonet on, so that when we teach our troops to rely on the bayonet they may feel that they have the superiority of arm resulting from length." (*Confederate Veteran*, September, 1917, page 415.)

The following day a bill was introduced in the Confederate Senate which "provided for the organization of troops to be armed with pikes or other available arms when firearms cannot be procured."

The Richmond *Examiner* of April 5, 1862, contained a long article urging the concentration of lancers and pikemen and special drill therefor.

On March 31, 1862, in a letter to Colonel S. B. French, General Jackson reiterated his remarks of the twenty-third and enlarged upon them: "Let us have a substitute [arm] so as to make the arm six inches longer than the musket with bayonet fixed. I would not mix the firearm and substitute in the same company. I hope 1,000 pikes will be furnished." (*Official Records of the War of the Rebellion*, Vol. XII, Part 3, page 141.)

General Robert E. Lee endorsed the above by writing Colonel Gorgas on April 9, 1862: ". . . 1,000 pikes should be sent to General Jackson if practicable." (*Ibid.*, Vol. XII, Part 3, page 844.)

About this time (April 11), Governor Brown of Georgia advised that he was shipping to Chattanooga 829 pikes and 321 side knives. (*Ibid.*, Vol. LII, Part 2, page 301.)

"All available arms have been issued. Arms for the regiment at Wilmington could be secured by issuing pikes to the men at the heavy batteries and giving these arms to the regiment as far as they could go. The centre companies to be armed with pikes." So stated Colonel Taylor, April 23. (*Ibid.*, Vol. IX.)

General Magruder in the Seven Days' Battles before Richmond recommended the "arming of cavalry with lances and shot-guns." (*Ibid.*, Vol. XI, Part 3, page 390.)

The *Confederate Veteran* (Vol. XXX, No. 2, February, 1922, page 54) records that DeGournay's Heavy Artillery was armed with pikes during the Seven Days' Battles. Undoubtedly there are other instances where these weapons were actually used in battle, but they have never been called to the writer's attention.

On January 13, 1863, General Wayne, C.S.A., in speaking of the various Home Guard units said: "What remains of the militia may be armed with pikes and knives or such shot-guns as they may pick up."

(*Official Records*, Vol. LIII, page 274.)

Although they were endorsed by practically everyone, the writer feels that General Beauregard on July 26, 1863, made the most reasonable suggestion as to what should be done with the pikes on hand. "There are about 3,000 lances or pikes in the Charleston (S.C.) Arsenal that could be of use as a *chevaux-de-frise*." (*Ibid.*, Vol. XXVIII, Part 2, page 232.)

Regardless of who thought what about pikes, and irrespective of their efficiency as a weapon, the fact still remains that they are without question as Confederate as General Robert E. Lee's sword. Although maybe not so desirable as Massa Bob's side arm, they nevertheless have a definite place in a Confederate collection of edged weapons and should be regarded accordingly.

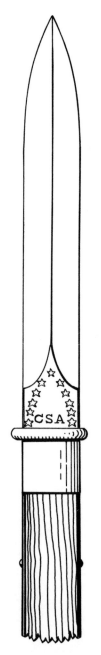

Fig. 104. Georgia Pike with "C.S.A." and eleven stars (B)

Confederate Pike—Maker Unknown

Figure 104

PIKES SUCH AS THE ONE illustrated were made by the thousands in practically every Southern State. The one illustrated has a 12-inch double-edged blade, diamond cross section. It is ornamented with the letters "C.S.A." beneath a semicircle of 11 stars. The blade is 1⅝ inches wide, under which is a brass collar from which run 2 wrought-iron straps 18 inches in length. These are riveted into the 7-foot ash pole by 3 rivets in each strap, spaced 6 inches apart.

Variations of this pike are numerous. Some are found with only one large star, others with the dotted outline of the Confederate flag. Some have white oak or hickory staffs rather than ash.

Another variation of this basic design is one which has an iron cross guard, from which run the same side straps of wrought iron as described above. The butt end is tipped with a 7-inch iron ferrule.

Although made all through the South, pikes answering this general description are usually referred to as "Georgia" or "Joe Brown Pikes," being named after the Governor of the State who had so many thousands made for home defense.

At the capture of the State Arsenal and Armory at Milledgeville, Ga., on November 22, 1864, a report of Colonel Hawley, 3rd Wisconsin Mounted Infantry, reflects that the following munitions were burned: "2,300 smooth-bore muskets, calibre .69, 5,000 lances and 1,500 cutlasses." (Moore's *Rebellion Record*, Vol. 9, page 147.) The "cutlasses" referred to by Colonel Hawley were probably "side knives" or "bowies," as they are better known today.

A number of pikes such as above described were purchased by Francis Bannerman & Co. on November 5, 1895, from the U.S. Ordnance Department at

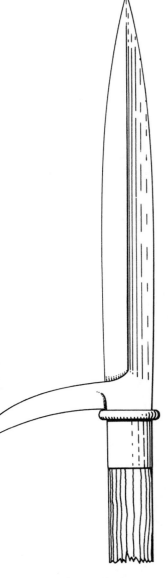

the Augusta, Ga., Arsenal, through the Arsenal's Commanding Officer, Major D. B. Taylor, U.S.A. It is my understanding that most of the pikes that have been offered by the Bannerman Co. for the past 60 years came from this source.

Confederate Bridle-Cutting Pike— Maker Unknown

Figure 105

IN GENERAL, the bridle-cutting pikes were only a variation of the pike previously described, except that the blade contained a sharp sickle attachment at its base which ran off roughly at right angles. This sickle blade was usually sharpened only on its underside, and was most frequently about half the length of the knife to which it was attached.

The specimen shown is the typical "Georgia" pike with the bridle-cutter attached. It has a 12-inch main blade, with a 5½-inch curved "bridle-cutter" at its base. The ash staff is 8 feet long, tipped on the butt end with a 7-inch iron ferrule. The blade end of the staff has a bronze collar from which extend two side straps of wrought iron, riveted to the staff. These, of course, are to give added strength to the weapon.

Most are unmarked and at this late date their makers have never been established.

Confederate Bridle-Cutting Pike— Maker Unknown

Figure 106

THE PIKE PREVIOUSLY DESCRIBED is the most common of the bridle-cutters but there are infinite variations. On some, the sickle blade is not attached to the main blade but to the collar fastened to the staff at the blade end. On these the main blade is usually pear-shaped, diamond cross section, although some have been

Fig. 105. Bridle-cutting pike (C)

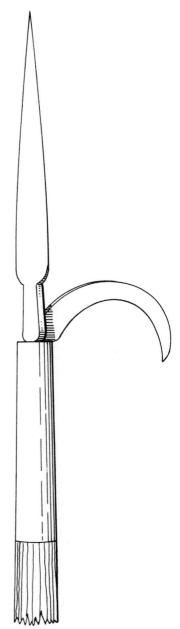

Fig. 106. Bridle-cutting pike (C)

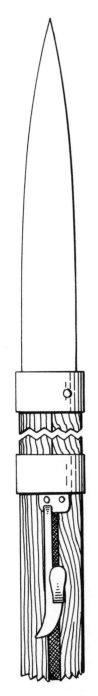

observed with a triangular "bayonet"-type main blade.

The pike pictured is this latter variation, the triangular blade being some 10 inches in length. This is inserted into a heavy iron collar or ferrule 7 inches long. The top portion of the ferrule contains a sickle-shaped 7-inch blade sharpened on both edges. The staff is 8 feet long and has no strengthening side straps.

Once again, the maker is unknown.

Confederate Retractable Pike—
Maker Unknown

Figure 107

GENERAL GORGAS commented upon a pike "in the shape of a stout wooden sheath containing a two-edged straight sword some two feet long. The sheath or truncheon could be leveled and the sword, liberated from the compression of a strong spring, by touching a trigger, leaped out with sufficient force to transfix an opponent." The weapon that Gorgas described was invented by a Rev. Graves (see Part III).

The nearest to a pike of this type the writer has ever seen is the one pictured. In general it follows the above except that it has a blade that is only retractable, and not one which jumps out at some unsuspecting enemy with "sufficient force to transfix" said opponent. In other words, it lacks the "strong spring."

This pike has a double-edged blade, 14 inches long, $1\frac{5}{8}$ inches wide. The wooden shaft is of pine, made from two half-rounded pieces recessed to contain the blade, which slips up or down at the owner's desire, held in either position by spring catches. The 6-foot staff is brass- and iron-mounted, the butt end capped with an iron ferrule.

Fig. 107. Retractable pike (C+)

Confederate Lance and Guidons—
Maker Unknown

Figure 108

Forest & *Stream*, March 17, 1881, page 130, contains the following inquiry:

Information Wanted. W.M.H., 712 Market St., Philadelphia, Pa., would be glad to get a letter from some one who can tell him accurately in what organization of the Confederate Army the lance was used. This weapon is about nine feet long, the Confederate States Flag (Stars and Bars) being attached to the staff near the steel spear-point. The pike for infantry of various shapes was usually heavy and longer as to its point, than the lance. Our correspondent was a soldier—then as now, a lover of historical things. He has two great boxes of these lances. The boxes (original) are addressed to Captain Getty, C.S.A., Lynchburg, Va. He would like to learn who this officer was and exactly where these curious weapons were abandoned or captured?

"W.M.H.'s" query is a good one. Many of us would like answers to the questions posed.

This we do know: Captain G. T. Getty, C.S.A., was the commanding officer of the C.S. Ordnance Depot at Lynchburg, Va., from 1862 until the end of the war.

As a young boy, the author remembers that steel-tipped (flat spear point) lances were reasonably

Fig. 108. Lance with swallow-tail pennant (B)

common in Richmond. All seen at that time were identical, having attached to the 8-foot ash staff, by means of three tacks, a small Stars and Bars Confederate flag which contained 11 four-pointed stars. The flag was of the swallow-tailed guidon variety and very poorly made, the stars being only on the left side of the flag, and secured to the flag only by stitches at their points. With very little use such pennants would surely have disintegrated. The fact that most were in fairly good shape indicated that they had seen very little service. Midway on the staff was a leather wrist strap indented into the wood. The butts had iron ferrules. The flat spear point was 10 inches long, 1¾ inches wide. Wrought-iron side straps riveted in four places ran from the iron collar at the top of the staff. The guidon measured 17 by 12 inches.

In the 1890s there operated in Richmond what might have been the first gun dealer. The shop was located at 1916 East Main Street in a small stone house which still lays claim to being the oldest building in the city. It was operated by W. S. Sclater and J. Jackson Chandler, former Confederate soldiers, and was called the "Washington's Headquarters Antiquarium." Here were sold all kinds of relics from the war. The prices would make today's collector water at the mouth: "Two-piece Confederate officer's buckle from Seven Pines, .50c," etc. The Messrs. Sclater and Chandler were considerably ahead of their time in that with each item sold they included an affidavit attesting to the genuineness of the article and its history when known. A lance purchased from this shop in 1896 bears the following notation: "Confederate Lance. Made in the South during the late Civil War. These weapons were among the munitions of war taken at the fall of Richmond in 1865. The pennons [sic], the wristloops, and the lanceboot were of poor materials, and in most cases, were lost or destroyed by the accidents of service."

Here, then, are two accounts which link these lances to Virginia, but who used them or made them remains unknown.

Figure 109

Another account, however, links this style lance and guidon to Missouri. *"Shelby and His Men,"* page 411, states:

The camp at Fulton, Mo., was delightful, amusing, instructive and retired. General Shelby never relaxed for a moment the vigor of his drill nor the manly exercises of his troopers. The short cavalry Enfields were here distributed to the troops, and the two brigades were splendidly armed, with the exception of Slayback's regiment, which had lances, tipped with steel and decorated with gay flags made by fair hands. This was one of General Magruder's ideas, and Shelby, to retain Slayback mounted, readily espoused it, and distributed the pikes among the men, fully determined however, to arm them as well as the others upon the occasion of another battle. It seemed very much like going back in the service of warfare two hundred years to see these fine, athletic Missouri marksmen handling the clumsy and unwieldy lances, more dangerous to horses and rear ranks of a column than they could ever be to the enemy, even in the opinions of their most sanguine advocates.

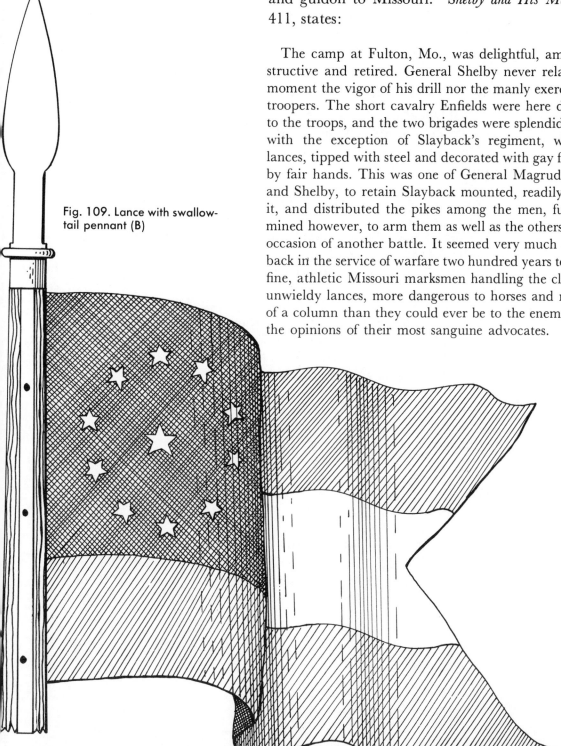

Fig. 109. Lance with swallow-tail pennant (B)

C. BAYONETS

TO DATE, writers have avoided the bayonet. The present work is no exception. Too little is yet known on the subject, and this is intended only as a starting point for some future historian. The variations and shades of variations are too numerous and diverse to include here.

Purposely we have omitted triangular bayonets, feeling that a basic book on American bayonets, period, is needed prior to their inclusion in any book which deals mainly with flat or sword-type blades. Here we have dealt only with the sabre bayonet, with no attempt to "match" them with their appropriate rifle, and once again we are concerned only with types and not their myriad variations.

We do include a few news items and accounts, obtained from various sources, apparently reliable. Possibly these will assist some future person in compiling the "basic book," but in the meantime are of interest to those who collect Confederate edged weapons.

You will please have all contracts for bayonets altered so as to require one-third of the amount contracted for made for the .69 calibre, model 1842, and two-thirds for the Enfield and Richmond Armory rifles. (Lt. Col. W. L. Brown, Comdg., Richmond Arsenal, April 20, 1862, to Capt. J. Dinwiddie, in Charge, Ordnance Department, *Captured Rebel Records*, Vol. 94, Chapter IV, page 54.)

Whenever there are no arms to repair, make bayonets and implements for arms. A Model bayonet of iron, tipped with steel will be sent you from here. (J. Gorgas, Chief of Confed. Ordn., to Macon Arsenal, March 6, 1863, *Captured Rebel Records*, Vol. 7, Chapter IV.)

J. D. Gray of Graysville, Ga., had contract to manufacture rifles with bayonets complete at $45.00 per. Weapons to be made by themselves and not imported or sub-contracted. (*Ibid.*, Vol. 4, Chapter IV, July 16, 1862.)

As of July 8, 1861, Jones & McElwain, Holly Springs, Miss., proposed to make lock making machinery for the construction of Belgium or Mississippi rifles with sword bayonet. (*Ibid.*, Vol. I, Chapter IV, page 425.)

May 7, 1862, received from Holly Springs, Miss., W. S. McElwain, 35 bayonets, 25 double-barrel shotguns, 20 percussion muskets, 20 Mississippi rifles, 15 muskets with bayonets. May 9, 1862, 40 double-barrel shotguns, 60 Mississippi rifles, 60 percussion muskets, 48 bayonets. May 13, 1862, 40 percussion muskets, 40 bayonets, 20 Tennessee rifles and 60 double-barrel shot-guns. These arms were received at Corinth, Miss., having been sent to Holly Springs for repair. These are not new manufacture, only repair. (*Ibid.*, Vol. 118, Chapter IV.)

Notice—proposals for the manufacture of 3,000 sabre bayonets of Harper's Ferry pattern will be opened at 12 M., the 4th Instant. The War Department. (Daily Richmond *Examiner*, July 2, 1861.)

General Orders No. 6, of January 14, 1864, substituted the triangular bayonet in all instances for the sabre bayonet. This, of course, was to conserve metal.

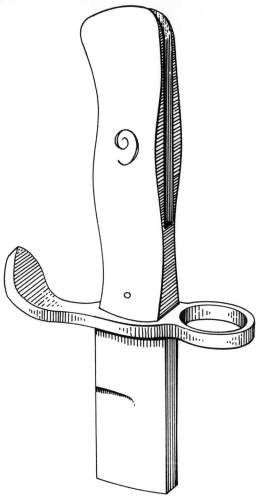

Fig. 110. Bayonet with smooth brass grip, iron guard (E+)

Confederate Bayonet—Maker Unknown

Figure 110

THE ONLY MARKING to be found on this well-made weapon is the number "6" neatly engraved in the smooth brass grip. Its significance is not known, but it is assumed to be a regimental marking. The guard is of iron. The single-edged yataghan blade is only 17¼ inches long, flat, without fullers.

A peculiarity of this bayonet is that the slot for the rifle lug extends two-thirds of the length of the grip, and no provision is made to "lock" the slot to the rifle lug.

Nothing is known of its background or maker, and the writer has never seen another like it.

Confederate Bayonet—Maker Unknown

Figure 111

PICTURED IS A BAYONET that could have been fitted to any type of gun, rifle or fowling piece by the simple addition of two right-angle lugs on the side of the gun barrel. It will be noted that the bayonet has no encircling ring on the guard for the gun barrel, but instead, has a projection containing a slot, this same feature being duplicated on the butt.

Grip and guard are of brass, and as shown, each has a squared slot which must have been for the engaging of an angle lug on the gun barrel. At the back of the grip and conforming in contour to it, is a spring, the male portion of which evidently fitted a female counterpart on the barrel lug, to lock the bayonet to the gun.

The pictured weapon has a single-edged yataghan-type blade, with an unstopped fuller on either side, but several have been seen with straight double-edged blades of diamond cross section. Blade length is usually about 20 inches. On the yataghan-style bayonets the blade is noted to have its cutting edge facing the rear of the grip.

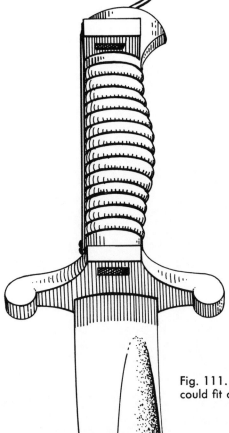

Fig. 111. Bayonet, type that could fit on any gun (D)

Although some have been stamped with a serial number on the grip near the guard, most appear to be unmarked.

The St. Louis, Mo., Museum includes in its collection a rifle on which a bayonet like this might fit, it having two right-angle lugs attached to the barrel. The rifle is a military piece constructed of sporting rifle parts. It is said to have come from North Carolina.

Confederate Bowie Bayonet—Maker Unknown

Figure 112

HERE IS A BAYONET that has puzzled top collectors for a number of years. Its origin or even its intended use are subject to much controversy. Few disagree that it is Confederate, but beyond that we seem to get nowhere. Obviously the weapon was originally intended as both a bowie and a bayonet, but as the latter it is completely unfinished.

The single-edged blade is beautifully made, 12 inches long. The grip appears to be of rosewood. The mounts to the grip (guard and pommel) are of cast brass, but unfinished. They could not possibly fit any known rifle or musket. The theory has been advanced that these rings were to encircle a pole or a pike but this is discounted by their size. They are too small to admit anything other than a very small rifle; certainly not large enough to admit a wooden staff of any description. The scabbard is leather, with belt loop sewed to its back and with brass mounts.

Despite the number that have survived the years no one has ever determined its maker. Back in the 1940s, Robert Abels, well-known gun dealer of New York, listed and pictured one of these bayonets in his catalogue. The price was then $5. We seriously doubt that Mr. Abels presently has very many left at this price.

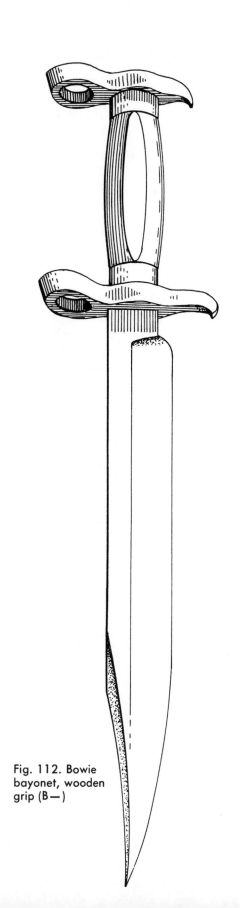

Fig. 112. Bowie bayonet, wooden grip (B—)

Confederate Bayonet—Maker Unknown
Figure 113

CONSIDERING THAT the Confederates were decidedly short of iron, the pictured bayonet is an odd one—it is all of iron, guard, grip and blade. It is entirely without markings, and its maker remains very much unknown. Note that the grip is serrated only at the front. Also note that the guard is considerably wider than the encircling ring at the rear.

The flat single-edged blade is of the yataghan variety, 20 inches long. The scabbard is of black leather with brass mounts.

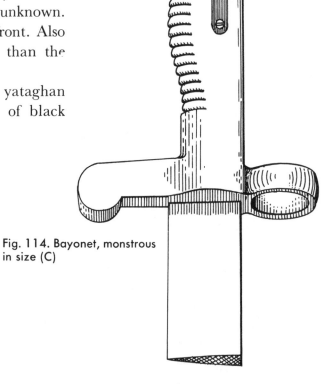

Fig. 114. Bayonet, monstrous in size (C)

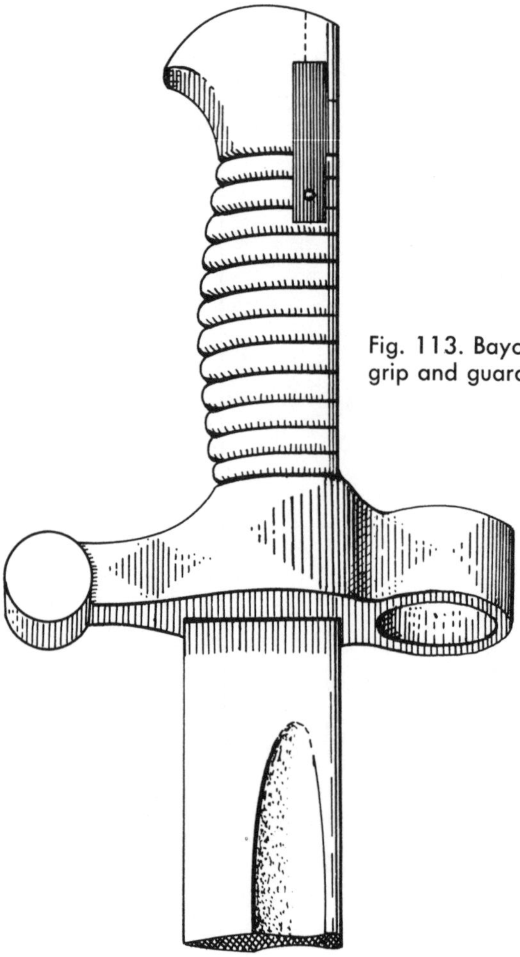

Fig. 113. Bayonet with iron grip and guard (C)

Confederate Bayonet—Maker Unknown
Figure 114

IN ORDER TO appreciate this "monster" it should be both seen and hefted. It is the most massive and awkward that has come to our attention. Brass grip and guard are one piece, poorly cast. The blade is very heavy and thick, 21 inches long with a shallow unstopped fuller on either side. Evidently intended to be straight, the blade has a decided "bend" at the point of juncture with its 6-inch false edge. In handling this weapon one has the feeling of holding a foot artillery sword.

Confederate Bayonet—Maker Unknown

Figure 115

IN MARKED CONTRAST to the bayonet just preceding is the one here shown. It is slim, light and graceful. The 20-inch yataghan blade has a deep unstopped fuller on either side. The guard and grip were cast in one piece. The casting is very poor. Although this bayonet is without marks, several of this same type have been observed with what appear to be serial numbers on the back of the grip, or on the encircling ring.

The scabbard is of brown leather, brass-mounted, the top mount having a stud for frog. One similar in the writer's collection has an all-leather scabbard, re-enforced leather throat with belt loop sewed on. Halfway down the scabbard is another leather tab having in it a brass ring. Evidently this bayonet was carried sword-fashion, with a sling.

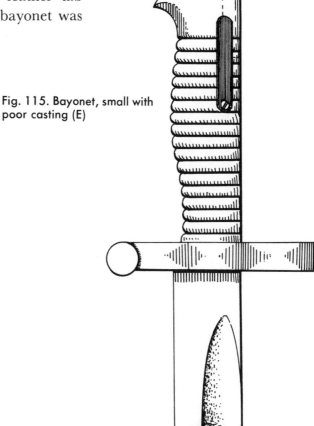

Fig. 115. Bayonet, small with poor casting (E)

D. KNIVES

IT IS A POPULAR misconception to believe that only Southern soldiers carried bowie (or side) knives. At the present time apparently all side knives of the Civil War period are termed "Confederate." Many of the Northern soldiers also carried side knives, particularly those from Wisconsin, Michigan and Illinois. Many of these were homemade and as of today it cannot actually be established whether a homemade knife was carried by a Northern or Southern soldier. However, it is not believed that the side knives were made in the North in the mass production, so to speak, that they were in the South. Those knives which appear to have been made on a production basis, therefore, are more likely to be Confederate than Union. Also, it is noted that because tin was easier to work than iron, the Confederate knives more frequently had tin mounts on their scabbards. Once again, while this is not a sure criterion, it is nevertheless indicative.

The Confederate Ordnance Department could not afford to waste anything. Many of the arms fashioned in the various C.S. armories were hand-finished by means of files. When these files wore out, the steel they contained was of too good quality to throw away, and they were subsequently used to make knives. While a production knife obviously made from a file is a good indication of Confederate background, a homemade knife made from a file is not at all a sure indication of the same background, for there were many thrifty Yankee blacksmiths who also employed worn-out files for this purpose.

One hundred years after the great American Civil War it is exceedingly difficult to determine the origin of any hand-made article. Any knife made in the North by unskilled, or semiskilled labor would, after all, closely resemble one made of the same materials in the South. However, by and large, the Southern-made knives were manufactured primarily for fighting. Utilitarian purposes were secondary. In the North it was the opposite. Knives were made primarily for purposes other than fighting. Thus, when we see a side knife with knuckle guard and branches, we assume it to be Confederate, for after all, a knuckle guard is not really needed to scale a fish or peel potatoes. Similarly, a production knife without hand guard is more apt to be Confederate than Yankee, for these were issued en masse to Confederate troops, but carried only individually by the Federal soldiers. Hand-made knives of no particular pattern will always be controversial.

In recent years a number of Filipino knives seem to have slipped into the ranks of "Confederate." Usually such knives have a water buffalo horn handle, copper guard and ferrule, and either a wavy blade or a blade narrow at the guard and point and wide in the center. A number of collectors, who should have known better, have been taken in by this slant-eyed merchandise. Because these knives were also made by hand there is no sure way of detecting them, but when buying a supposedly Civil War knife, the reader might well remember that instead of having been carried by Blue or Gray, it might have originally been thrust into the loincloth of one of our little brown brothers.

We will not attempt to establish the difference between a plain knife and a "bowie knife." Entire books have been devoted to this subject. Suffice it to say that most present-day collectors refer to any knife of the Civil War period as a "bowie." Oddly enough, so did the soldiers who fought in that war, regardless of style or type of manufacture. Officially, however, Confederate Ordnance referred to them as "side knives." Occasionally some witty newspaper correspondent called them "Arkansas toothpicks."

Below are excerpts which refer to this fascinating weapon.

The Tyler Rifles of New Orleans threw down their rifles and charged with their long knives. (Richmond *Examiner*, August 26, 1861.)

Received by T. M. Bradford, Military Storekeeper, Georgia State Arsenal and Armory, Milledgeville, Ga., from April 1 through August 5th, 1862, a total of 4,908 knives, of which 321 were sent to C.S. troops at Chattanooga, 60 to Colonel Phillips at Hardeeville, S.C., 900 to Colonel Brown at Macon, and 3,628 retained in Arsenal. (*Confederate Records of Georgia*, page 351.)

Where lies the necessity of soldiers parading our streets with revolvers and Bowie-knives, many of the latter as large as old fashioned scythe-blades? (Richmond *Examiner*, June 29, 1861.)

A Secession knife was shown in New York by a returned member of the 9th Infantry. It is made from a saw blade, 18 inches long with buckhorn grip. The back is ground sharp and the teeth arranged to act as barbs. (New York note in Richmond *Examiner*, August 7, 1861.)

Company C, First Georgia Infantry from Cass County, were known as the "Bowie-knife Boys." (Richmond *Examiner*, August 2, 1861.)

Act to prohibit the taxing of bowie-knives, sword canes and dirk-knives. (Chapter CXXV, *Regular Session Mississippi Legislature*, Jackson, November and December, 1861 and January, 1862.)

Recruits for the Wise Legion will bring a gun and a good Bowie-knife, or will be furnished a good flintlock musket. (Richmond *Examiner*, June 26, 1861.)

Richmond armorers are now making fine Bowie-knives in quantity and could as easily make swords. It is a mistake to pay fancy prices for Ames chilled iron. Patronize home industries. (Richmond *Examiner*, June 3, 1861.)

You must not wait for a magic weapon, but take the flintlock muskets, the double-barrel shotguns and buckshot. Make Bowie-knives from two-inch wagon springs with ash grips, or hickory, or oak, and have your blacksmith make pike heads from wagon tires. Do not wait for Minie or percussion muskets. (Richmond *Dispatch*, January 3, 1862.)

Confederate Bowie—Maker Unknown

Figure 116

DAVID M. REAM of Berkley, Va. (now West Virginia), at the outbreak of the American Civil War was a young man visiting relations in Mississippi. So afraid was he that he would miss the entire war if he waited to return home and join a Virginia unit that he volunteered in the 11th Mississippi Infantry Regiment.

The 11th Mississippi was attached to the Army of Northern Virginia and young Ream was wounded at Second Manassas. Upon recovering from his wounds he transferred to the 5th Virginia Cavalry, serving out the war as a lieutenant therein.

Pictured is the knife Ream carried throughout the war. The grip and guard are of brass, the former appearing to be an unmilled bayonet grip. Carefully scratched thereon is "D. M. Ream, 11th Miss. Regmt." The heavy single-edged blade has a clipped point and was originally 10½ inches long, 1¾ inches wide. The brown leather scabbard is hand-stitched.

This is a fine fighting knife. Its maker is unknown.

Confederate Side Knife— Maker Unknown

Figure 117

HERE WE HAVE a particularly fine side knife, a production job, and not made for killing buffalo, skinning rabbits or scraping mud off one's shoes. It was made for one purpose—killing one's fellow man. The blade is single-edged, spear-shaped, 12¾ inches long. Guard and grip are cast brass, made in one piece. The weapon is not unlike the brass-knuckled trench knife of World War I. The scabbard is of leather with no mounts. Over-all length is 17 inches. It is a very well-made piece.

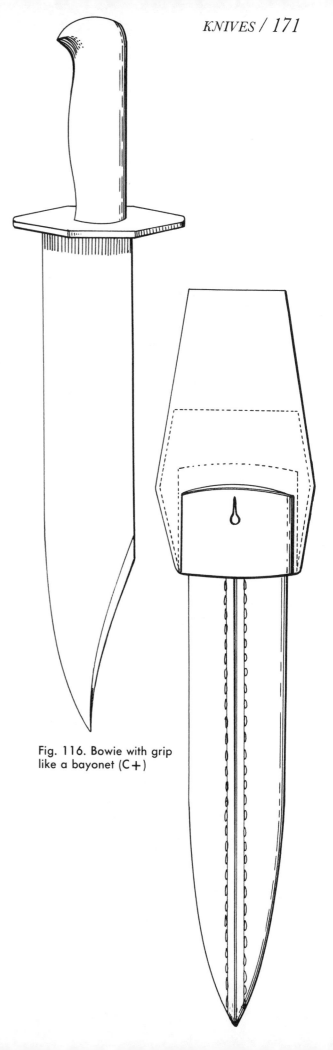

Fig. 116. Bowie with grip like a bayonet (C+)

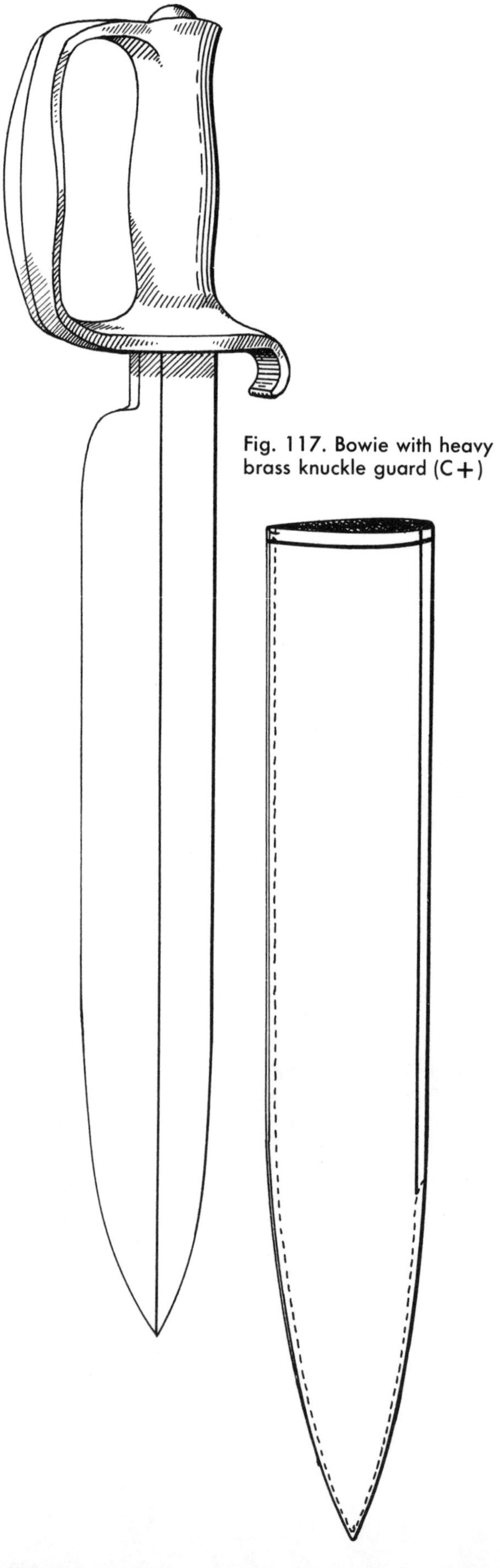

Fig. 117. Bowie with heavy
brass knuckle guard (C+)

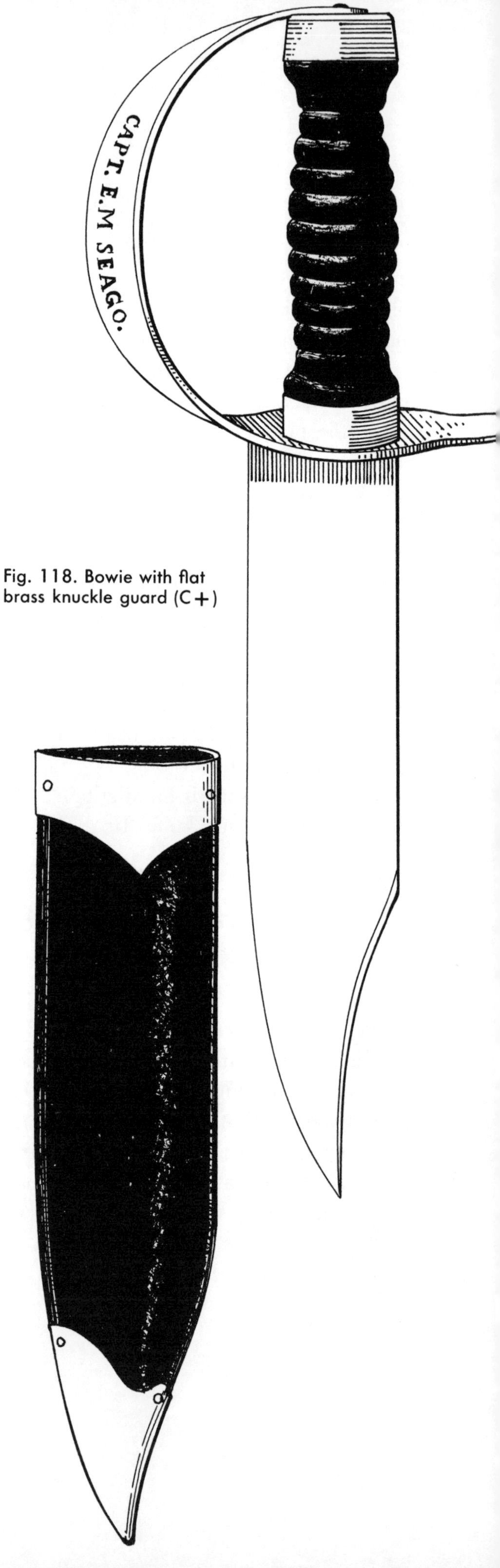

Fig. 118. Bowie with flat
brass knuckle guard (C+)

CAPT. E.M SEAGO.

Confederate Side Knife— Maker Unknown

Figure 118

THIS IS AN extremely well-made knife, which undoubtedly is a production job. The "D" guard, the encircling ring at the bottom of the grip and the pommel ring are all of brass, evidently secured from scrap as parts of these pieces contain a partial unrelated design from their unknown origin. The grip is of wood, painted black. The single-edged blade is 10 inches long with clipped point. Scabbard is of leather with brass mounts.

The weapon is stated to have been taken by a Maine soldier from a Confederate officer. Engraved on the knuckle guard is: "Capt. E. M. Seago." The identity of Captain Seago has not been established nor has the maker of the knife.

Confederate Side Knife— Maker Unknown

Figure 119

A VERY TYPICAL Confederate "Bowie" or side knife is here pictured. The blade is 16½ inches long, 2½ inches wide and ¼ inch thick! It has a clipped point but no false edge. The "D"-type guard is made of heavy wrought iron and the grip is of oak, riveted in two places to the tang of the blade. Although the blade is of poor metal and crudely fashioned, the weapon is a very heavy one and would have been deadly in close-up fighting.

The scabbard is of heavy brown leather, the outer seams being crudely stitched with heavy thread, and with a tin mount at throat and toe. On the underside of the scabbard is a belt loop, and in addition, a leather tab near the toe with an inserted brass ring. The weapon was evidently too heavy to carry from the belt strap and needed the additional support of a belt sling.

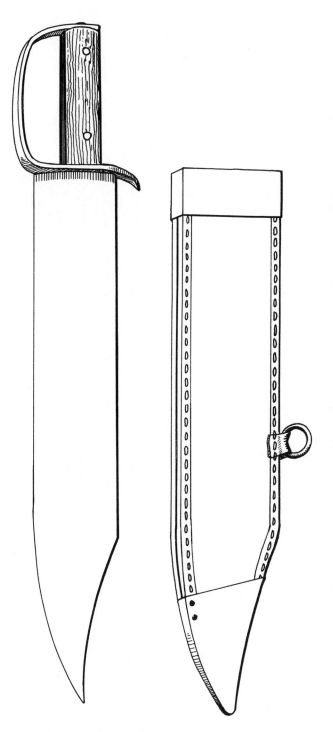

Fig. 119. Bowie with heavy iron "D" guard (D+)

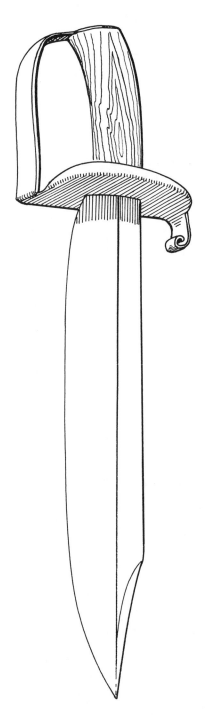

Fig. 120. Bowie with heavy iron guard (D+)

This "monster" came from the Shenandoah Valley of Virginia, scene of so many of "Stonewall" Jackson's activities. Its history is unknown, as is its maker.

Confederate bowies with "D" guards were made in infinite varieties, some with branches added to the basic "D" guard, some with the cutting edge of the blade facing the top of the guard, etc. A book itself could be written on such variations.

Confederate Side Arm— Maker Unknown

Figure 120

HERE IS WHAT APPEARS to be an armory side arm, and very definitely a production job. Its maker is unknown but its "feel" is certainly Confederate.

It has an over-all length of 22½ inches, the blade being 17½ inches long, with a clipped point and false edge. The guard is of wrought iron, the counterguard being a half-oval ending in a turned-down quillon. The knuckle guard is of strap iron which ends in an oval cap on the top of the oak grip.

Such a weapon would be deadly in hand-to-hand fighting as it could easily cut off a man's arm with a single chop.

Confederate Side Knife— Maker Unknown

Figure 121

THIS IS A well-made and handsome weapon, obviously made on a production basis and not the product of some crossroad smithy. It has a double-edged spear-shaped blade 13 inches long and 2 inches wide. The cross guard is of iron. The walnut grip is undecorated. The blade is held to the grip by a nut screwed to the tang. A small iron washer on the grip prevents the nut from sinking into the wood.

The scabbard is original, of leather with a tin mount

at the throat. The toe mount is missing. The knife has no markings. It came from the Valley of Virginia many years ago and surely belonged to some member of the Army of Northern Virginia.

Bowie Knife—Maker Unknown
Figure 122

A VERY BEAUTIFUL bowie knife is pictured here. Its single-edged clip-pointed blade is 10⅝ inches long, with an over-all of 15 inches. The guard and pommel are of brass, originally silver-plated. The grip is of old yellowed ivory. The knife is finely and beautifully made. It is included in this book only because of the name etched on the ricasso: "R. Alldeon, Memphis." Whether this be owner or maker is not known, although judging from the crudity of the etching compared with the fineness of the balance of the knife, Mr. Alldeon must have been the owner. The maker would have applied his name with more artistry to conform with the balance of the piece.

Southern Bowie Knife—
George Westenholm, Maker
Figure 123

A MOTTO NOT UNCOMMON in the 1850s was "Death to Abolition" or "Death to Abolitionists." Understandably, such a motto was particularly popular in the Southern States. Sitting, as I do, calmly on the middle of the fence, I cannot help but wonder how far we have advanced politically during the past hundred years. The wording of the motto may have changed but not its basic meaning. Possibly the next hundred years will change such a biased viewpoint to one considerably more liberal, such as: "Death to anyone who does not consider every man his brother," or "Death to everyone who will not share my liberal

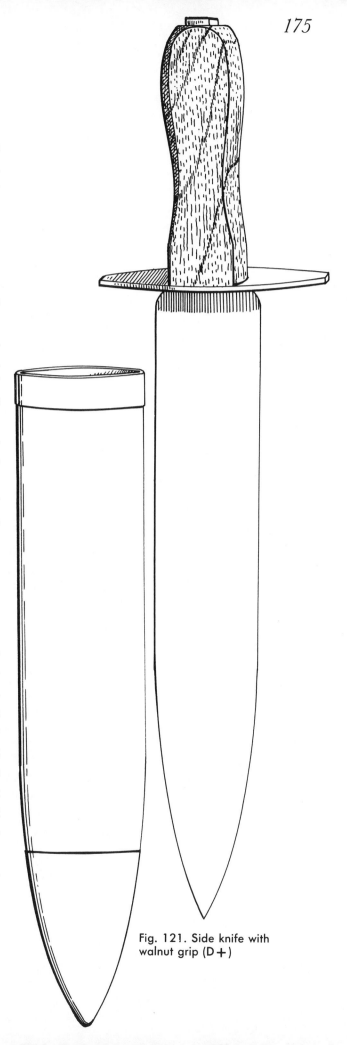

Fig. 121. Side knife with walnut grip (D+)

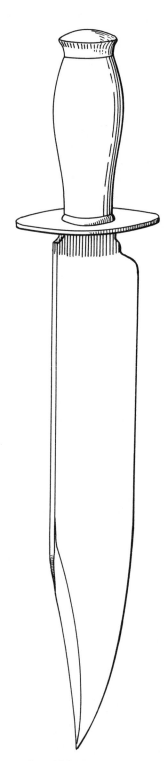

Fig. 122. Bowie with ivory grip (C+)

views." If anyone can stick around that long it will be interesting to note, and I would appreciate their comment at the end of this time.

At any rate here is a knife that made no bones as to its political feelings. It was made by George Westenholm & Sons, of Sheffield, England, makers of the famous "IXL" bowie knife.

This manufacturer lost no bets in supplying North and South in our struggle for States' rights, for at the same time he offered "Death to Abolition" knives to the South he was also giving the North a choice of bowies variously inscribed: "Death to Rebels," or "Kill all Traitors." Evidently it was of little difference to George Westenholm & Sons as to who killed whom, just so long as their bowie knives did the killing.

The pictured knife is quality merchandise. The single-edged bowie-type blade is 8¼ inches long, with the frosted design "Death to Abolition," and stamped on the ricasso: "Geo. Westenholm & Sons, Celebrated Cast Steel Bowie Knife, IXL." The blade is also stamped "Warranted of the best quality."

The ebony wood grip is checkered with a German silver guard, grip collar and shell pommel. The scabbard is of red leather with German silver mounts. Regardless of political affiliations, this is a beautiful knife.

Confederate Side Knife— Maker Unknown

Figure 124

IN HIS *History of the Ninth Regiment, Connecticut Volunteer Infantry* Thomas H. Murray describes the skirmish at Pass Christian on April 4, 1862. He states: "The regiment returned to the island in high spirits, bearing among their trophies sundry wrought-iron bowie-knives, one of which was marked 'Yankee Exterminator.'"

Although the pictured weapon is not marked "Yankee Exterminator," one senses that its inscription, "Death to Yankees," more or less conveys the same sort of meaning. Also inscribed on the blade is "Croskeys Maker." This last, however, does not begin to carry the impact of the first statement, which is understandable even to a child, or at least my children. It is supposed that "Croskey" is the maker of this very fine bowie knife, although this is strictly conjecture.

The knife is 16½ inches over-all, with a very heavy single-edged blade, the back of which is severely beveled, the final 4 inches containing a false edge. It is etched as stated. The grip is of cast brass, rounded and slim, ending in an octagonal shape. The guard is of heavy flat sheet brass.

Holding this knife in one's hand, one has the distinct feeling that judicious use of same by a number of dedicated persons might have extended the war considerably after April, 1865. What a shame its production was so limited.

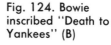

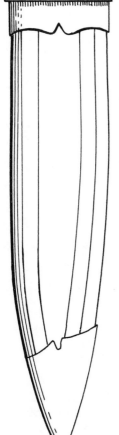

Fig. 123. Bowie inscribed "Death to Abolition" (B+)

Fig. 124. Bowie inscribed "Death to Yankees" (B)

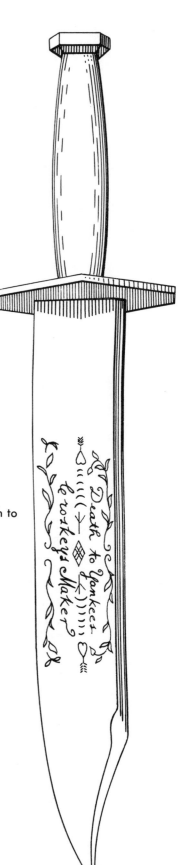

Confederate Side Knife— Maker Unknown

Figure 125

HERE WE HAVE another quality knife without the slightest indication of where it was made or by whom. An old label on the scabbard indicates that it was carried by W. T. Sherman of the "Greene Rough & Readys."

Originally known as Captain S. T. Dean's Company, Triplett's Battalion Heavy Artillery, the Greene "Rough & Readys" was composed of men from Greene County, Virginia. They were later absorbed into Captain L. B. McMullan's Artillery, Company D, 4th Regiment, Virginia Volunteers, Heavy Artillery.

The knife in question has an over-all length of 17 inches, with a double-edged spear-type blade 12 inches in length. The blade is finely made and severely hollow-ground. The guard is oval-shaped, of heavy flat iron. The grip is of cherry wood, on one side of which are carved the initials "W. T. S." At the top of the grip is a circular disk of flat iron which screws onto the tang of the blade, holding it secure. The scabbard is of tin, shaped to the hollow-ground spear-pointed blade.

This is a knife any Southerner would be proud to own, although as a general rule, anything belonging to a "W. T. Sherman" would be nothing to treasure by those with backgrounds "South of the Potomac."

Confederate Dirk—Maker Unknown

Figure 126

A WELL-FINISHED DIRK is the one pictured. It has an over-all length of 12 inches, with a 7½ double-edged blade, diamond in cross section at the guard, which slims down to flat at the point. The ricasso is stamped

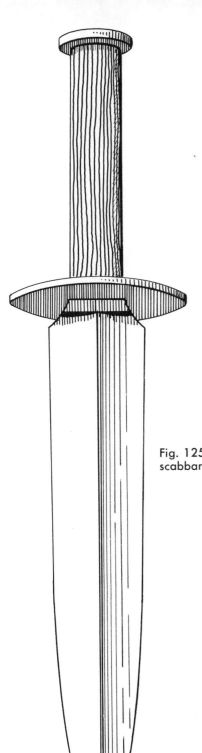

Fig. 125. Bowie with tin scabbard (C)

on either side "Winchester," but be this name or point of manufacture is not known.

The grip is of turned walnut with a flat iron disk at the top over which the tang of the blade is peened. The guard is of heavy flat brass, "S"-shaped, very similar to those cutlasses and knives supposedly made at Norfolk, Va. The scabbard is of leather with a belt loop attached to one side.

Records indicate that a Simon Dodge, of Winchester, Va., made bowie knives during the Civil War period. Possibly this is a specimen of his work.

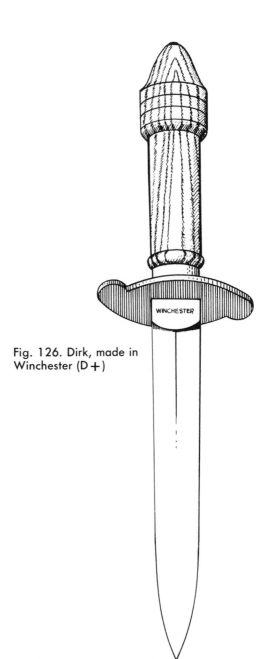

Fig. 126. Dirk, made in Winchester (D+)

PART III

DIRECTORY OF PERSONS AND PLACES

CONNECTED WITH THE

MANUFACTURE OF CONFEDERATE

EDGED WEAPONS

ALFRED, B. B.—Georgia

Delivered 18 pikes to the State Arsenal and Armory, Milledgeville, Ga., June 30, 1862. (*Confederate Records of Georgia*, page 352.)

BAKER, JOHN—Georgia

Made and delivered 296 bowie knives to the State Arsenal and Armory, Milledgeville, Ga., May 29, 1862. (*Confederate Records of Georgia*, page 351.)

BAYSER & STEBBINS & Co.—Columbia, S.C.

Had a large contract with the Confederate Government for bayonets. Delivered 215 on June 8, 1864. Kind or type not known. (*Captured Rebel Records*, Vol. 91, Chapter IV.

BELL & DAVIS—Atlanta, Ga.

The above, with the date "July 6, 1861," is inscribed on a "D"-guarded bowie knife.

BERRY, WILL—Georgia

Made pikes and bowie knives. Delivered 18 pikes to the State Arsenal and Armory, Milledgeville, Ga., May 27, 1862; 1 bowie knife on May 29 and 19 pikes September 28, 1862. (*Confederate Records of Georgia*, pages 351–352.)

BISSONNET, L.—Mobile, Ala.

Swordmaker. See under Part I.

BORUM, CHARLES—Norfolk, Va.

See under Part I. (Bayonets for double-barreled shotguns.)

BOYLE & GAMBLE, or BOYLE, GAMBLE & MACFEE—Richmond, Va.

See under Part I. (All types of edged weapons.)

BRADFORD, T. M.—Milledgeville, Ga.

Military Storekeeper (MSK) at the State Arsenal and Armory, Milledge-ville, Ga., who received a total of 4,908 knives made by the mechanics of Georgia from April 1 through August 5, 1862. (*Confederate Records of Georgia*, page 351.)

BURGER & BROS.—Richmond, Va.

The 1859 Richmond City Directory lists a firm of "Burger & Boyle, sawmakers, corner 8th and Arch Sts." The principals were Edwin Boyle (later associated with Boyle, Gamble & Mac-Fee) and P. and H. R. Burger, who during the war operated as "Burger & Bros." and were engaged in making all kinds of edged weapons. Specimens of their manufactory have never been identified as such.

The Richmond *Dispatch* of May 27, 1861, contained the following advertisement: "Wanted immediately, 2 cutlery grinders and a blacksmith to work on swords, bayonets, bowie knives. Call at our factory at the Petersburg R. R. Bridge, Burger & Bros."

CAMERON & WINN—Georgia

Bowie knife makers for the State of Georgia. Delivered 43 on April 8, 196 on May 24 and 219 on June 13, 1862, to the State Arsenal and Armory, Milledgeville, Ga. (*Confederate Records of Georgia*, page 351.)

CHRISTOPHER, C. J.—Atlanta, Ga.

The *Southern Confederacy*, Atlanta, Ga., of June 22, 1864, contained an advertisement of Mr. C. J. Christopher offering to "repair swords of every description with neatness and dispatch." He also declared himself to be a "fine finisher, spur-maker, gilder and burnisher." His address, according to the ad, was on Bridge Street "near the Bridge."

CLARKSON, ANDERSON & CO.—106 Main St., Richmond, Va.

Advertised in the Richmond *Dispatch* June 13, 1861: "Bowie-knives and pistols for sale." On December 31, 1861, the daily Richmond *Examiner* carried the following: "Clarkson & Co., 106 Main St.," offering "Virginia made bowie knives at reduced prices."

CLEVELAND, MARION—Georgia

Made and delivered 10 pikes to the State Arsenal and Armory, Milledgeville, Ga., April 16, 1862. (*Confederate Records of Georgia*, page 352.)

COLLEGE HILL ARSENAL—Nashville, Tenn.

See under Part I. (All types of swords.)

CONFEDERATE STATES ARMORY—Kenansville, N.C.

See under Part I. (All types of edged weapons.)

CONNING, JAMES—Dauphin & Water Sts., Mobile, Ala.

See under Part I. (All types of swords.)

COOK & BROTHER—New Orleans, La., and Athens, Ga.

See under Part I. (Bayonets and cutlasses.)

COOPER, MARK A.—Georgia

The above, as agent for an unknown party, delivered 5 pikes to the State Arsenal and Armory, Milledgeville, Ga., May 22, 1862. (*Confederate Records of Georgia*, page 352.)

COTTRELL, S. S. & CO.—Richmond, Va.

Furnished cartridge boxes, bayonet scabbards, belts and buckles to the Confederacy. (*Southern Historical Papers*, Vol. 29, page 145.)

COURTNEY & TENNANT—Charleston, S.C.

See under Part I. (Swords and cutlasses.)

CRUSH & WADE—Christiansburg, Va.

Chapter IV, Vol. 91, of *Captured Rebel Records* refers to the above in a letter dated June 2, 1864, from the Richmond Armory, as "Long time contractors with the Confederate Ordnance Department for sabres." The firm proposed to make bits at $10 per bit.

CUNNINGHAM, L. T.—Nashville, Tenn.

Operator of the College Hill Arsenal. See under Part I.

DABNEY, I. F., & BROTHER—Richmond, Va.

Had contract with the Richmond Armory for 2,500 scabbards and cap boxes. (*Captured Rebel Records*, Vol. 90, Chapter IV, page 159.)

DEVISME—Paris, France

Maker of the swords carried by Generals Robert E. Lee and John B. Hood. See under Part I.

DEWITT, A. H.—Columbus, Ga.

A letter in my files dated April, 1922, from George J. Burrus of Columbus, Ga., a Confederate veteran, advises DeWitt to have been a jeweler who with the war started a sword manufactory. According to this source DeWitt was in the sword business for only a short time before selling his factory to Greenwood & Gray, who used the premises for the manufacture of rifles. DeWitt evidently opened shop at another address for on May 22, 1862, Major M. H. Wright, commanding the Atlanta Arsenal, wrote him as follows: "I have received your sample sabre, and will give you a contract for sabre and belt at $20.00 per. I am having sabres manufactured here at a less price than I offer you, but would make a contract for more because they are needed." According to the *Confederate Veteran*, April, 1922, page 124, DeWitt had a contract with the State of Georgia to supply sabres. His arms have never been identified.

DODGE, SIMON—Winchester, Va.

Made bowie knives during the Civil War.

DORSETT, J. R.—Georgia

Manufactured pikes for the State of Georgia, delivering 45, 44 and 143 on March 27, April 8 and May 3, 1862, respectively, to the State Arsenal and Armory at Milledgeville, Ga. (*Confederate Records of Georgia*, page 352.)

DRISCOL, T. D.—Howardsville, Va.

According to DeBow's *Review* of March-April, 1862, the above firm was making swords with an output of 28 per week.

DUFILHO—New Orleans, La.

Swordmaker. See under Part I.

DUNLAP, T.—Georgia

Made 29 pikes for the State of Georgia, which he delivered to the State Arsenal and Armory, Milledgeville, Ga., May 1, 1862. (*Confederate Records of Georgia*, page 352.)

DURY, ROBERT—Nashville, Tenn.

Connected with L. T. Cunningham, operator of the College Hill Arsenal (see under Part I). Wrote the Secretary of War, June 29, 1861, that he and Cunningham could buy "muskets, pistols & sabres for gold, to be delivered in Nashville." (*Captured Rebel Records*, Vol. 20, Chapter VIII, Contract Book.)

EASTVAN (ESTVAN), B.—Wilmington, N.C.

A partner of Louis Froelich, owner of the Confederate States Armory. (See under Part I.)

ELDER, WILLIAM H., & D. H. WINN—Georgia

Made and delivered 50 pikes to the State Arsenal and Armory, Milledgeville, Ga., May 22, 1862. (*Confederate Records of Georgia*, page 352.)

ESPER, JOHN—Georgia

Made pikes for the State of Georgia. May 27, 1862, delivered 525 to the State Arsenal and Armory, Milledgeville, Ga., and another 290 the following June 10. (*Confederate Records of Georgia*, page 352.)

ETOWAH IRON WORKS—Etowah, Ga.

According to the daily Richmond *Examiner* July 2, 1861: "The Macon *Telegraph* says that the Hon. Mark A. Hooper has left for Virginia with a superb bowie for every member of the Atlanta Grays. These knives were made at the Etowah Iron Works under Maj. Hooper's personal supervision. They are handsomely mounted, of excellent workmanship and most beautiful finish."

In the writer's collection is a very crude foot officer's sword of standard design. The blade is crudely etched with floral designs, a shield with "C.S.A." upon it, a Stars and Bars flag and "Presented to Lieut. George W. Harris by his friends in the Atlanta Grays, 8th Ga. Regt. Infy." The other side of the blade has floral designs, a shield with a stand of arms and a large "C.S.A." The sword came from Winchester, Va. Nothing is known of its background or of Lieutenant George W. Harris.

EVE, J. C.—Georgia

Made pikes for the State of Georgia, delivering 126 to the State Arsenal and Armory at Milledgeville, Ga., on June 17, 1862. (*Confederate Records of Georgia*, page 352.)

EYLAND & HAYDEN—Charleston, S.C.

Firm of jewelers and military outfitters 1832 to 1835. Succeeded by Hayden & Whilden (see under Part I.)

FAYETTEVILLE ARMORY—Fayetteville, N.C.

See under Part I. (Bayonets.)

FIRMIN & SONS—London, England

See under Part I. (Swords.)

FITZPATRICK, Capt. REES—Natchez, Miss.

The Richmond *Examiner* of June 8, 1861, contained an article taken from the Natchez (Miss.) *Free Trader* as follows:

Capt. Rees Fitzpatrick, gunsmith of Natchez, Miss., is the manufacturer of the first Bowie knife ever made. He was then resident in Louisiana and made the knife from a pattern furnished by Colonel James Bowie, whose name this formidable weapon will ever bear. The millions of knives bearing this name and made in Sheffield and Birmingham, England, have no affinity to the real Bowie-knife as made by the original manufacturer, Fitzpatrick. He makes his knife of elastic tempered steel, and the knives have the spring and rebound of a Damascus blade, while the English knives are made so hard for the purpose of giving them the highest possible polish that they have no elasticity and in cutting will break out huge gaps in the edge as easily as pot metal. Last week Mr. Fitzpatrick made a powerful knife for Dr. L. P. Blackburn, precisely after the original pattern of Colonel Bowie. The blade weighed only one pound and was elastic enough to quiver at the touch and bore an unsurpassed edge, keen as lightning's flash. Dr. Blackburn intends to exhibit the knife to the armorers of Louisville as a pattern and will induce them to imitate its temper and perfection for State defence. Mr. Fitzpatrick is the first weapon artist who placed the Bowie-knife upon the rifle as a bayonet after the pattern of General Felix Houston, a kindred spirit to the brave brothers Bowie. He also made that gem of a sword presented to General Quitman, and is now making a duplicate of it on order of Gov. Pettus for presentation to General Earl Van Dorn.

FOLSOM, H. & CO.—St. Louis, Mo., and New Orleans, La.

Gunsmith and military outfitter, who in the late 1850s was located in St. Louis, Mo., and who for a time was there connected with H. E. Dimick, a gunsmith and dealer in imitation Colt navy revolvers bearing his name. For some unknown reason these revolvers are often referred to as "Confederate," although obviously revolvers made prior to the war by a man who was Northern in his sympathies, and who later had a contract to make muskets for the Union Army, should not be referred to as "Confederate."

As opposed to Dimick, Folsom was entirely Southern in feeling and about 1859 left St. Louis for New Orleans, La. There he opened up a shop at 55 Chartres Street. Imported revolvers are occasionally found bearing his name.

Also to be found with his name and the St. Louis address are various types of swords. It should be pointed out that these weapons were sold prior to the war and that it is impossible to tell whether they went into Northern or Southern hands. Thus, they can hardly be considered as Confederate.

FORD & DUMAS—Georgia

Made and delivered 90 pikes to the State Arsenal and Armory, Milledgeville, Ga., on April 14, 1862. (*Confederate Records of Georgia*, page 352.)

FORD, J. J.—Georgia

Made and delivered 136 bowie knives to the State Arsenal and Armory, Milledgeville, Ga., on June 5, 1862. (*Confederate Records of Georgia*, page 351.)

FREEMAN, B. P.—Macon, Ga.

Is stated to have done some of the etching on the sword blades of both E. J. Johnson and W. J. McElroy of Macon, Ga.

FROELICH, LOUIS—Wilmington and Kenansville, N.C.

Proprietor of the Confederate States Armory (see under Part I).

GEORGIA STATE ARSENAL & ARMORY—Milledgeville, Ga.

See under Part I. (Bayonets.)

GILLELAND, H.—Georgia

Made bowie knives for the State of Georgia. On May 9, 1862, he delivered 25 to the State Arsenal and Armory at Milledgeville, Ga., and another 15 on May 29. (*Confederate Records of Georgia*, page 351.)

GITTER & MOSS—Beal St., Memphis, Tenn.

The above firm advertised on December 12, 1861, as having fitted up an establishment for making army cutlery of all kinds. All who wanted a good sword or knife were invited to call at their address on Beal Street "next door to the Aldridge House."

GLAZE, WILLIAM—Columbia, S.C.

Proprietor of the Palmetto Armory (see under Part I). (Swords.)

GRAVES, Rev. Dr.—Georgia

A Methodist minister originally from Vermont, who at the time of the Civil War was residing in Georgia, and who, with true Christian ardor, invented a pike which sheathed an 18-inch blade. By means of a spring, this knife would fly forth with "sufficient force to transfix an enemy." The retractable pike pictured and described under Part II may be a variation of the one invented by this man of peace.

GRAY, JOHN D.—Graysville and Columbus, Ga.

From information available, Gray appears to have been a man far in advance of his time. Records concerning him are plentiful but most confusing. Apparently he was engaged in making: rifles, carbines, canteens, pikes, buckets, pole-slides, tents, bowie knives and sabres, along with various other sundries found necessary in the Confederate Army.

The *Confederate Records of Georgia* (pages 351–352) reflect that John D. Gray delivered 283 knives and 676 pikes to the State Arsenal and Armory at Milledgeville, Ga., on May 27, 1862, and an additional 317 knives and 769 pikes on August 5.

The *Official Records of the War of the Rebellion* show that as of October 15, 1862, "J. D. Gray of Graysville, Ga. made canteens for the Macon Arsenal," and obtained a contract for 15,000 to 20,000 Enfield type rifles. From October 1, 1863, to November 1, 1864, he supplied the State of Alabama with 176 Mississippi rifles, receiving $7,920 in payment. Under the name of Greenwood & Gray, he supplied the State of Alabama with 262 Mississippi rifles and 73 carbines and received $18,335 during the same period of time.

On May 30, 1862, Gray addressed a letter to Captain Richard Cuyler, commanding the Macon (Ga.) C.S. Arsenal:

I have a contract with the Ordnance Department at Knoxville, approved by the Department at Richmond for making 200 rifles and 1,000 carbines to be completed in 8 or 9 months. I am making 4,000 pikes and sabres under a contract with the State of Georgia (to be filled at Milledgeville). I am filling an order for 2,000 canteens for Captain Humphries at Chattanooga, and am likewise filling an order for 2,000 buckets for the Ordnance Department at Abington, Va. I am also making pole-slides and buttons for 1,000 tents to fill a contract undertaken by White & Co. of Dalton, Ga. for making canteens, buckets, poles, etc. I have no regular contract signed, sealed and delivered, but when the departments want these articles, they send the orders to me and I fill them as fast as I can. I have now more orders on hand than I can fill in six months.

Most of the hands employed in the wooden department of mfgr. at this place are negroes. I have only a few white men here (Graysville). These hands are employed at this place (Graysville) making pikes, sabres, gunstocks, canteens, buckets and poles. At Columbus, Ga. I have a number of men employed in the Armory. . . . I expect to increase the force in the Armory at Columbus to 300 men. (*Captured Rebel Records*, Vol. 36, Chapter IV.)

Obviously, Gray operated both at Graysville and Columbus, Ga., but his operations appear so vast that it is suspected he subcontracted a number of his contracts.

On October 15, 1864, Colonel Gorgas, Chief of Confederate Ordnance, mentioned Gray in a letter to Captain Cuyler saying: "J. D. Gray of Graysville, Ga. is manufacturing canteens for the Macon Arsenal and has also a contract to manufacture rifles with bayonets at $45.00 per. The contractors are prevented from importing from the provision in the contract that guns delivered are to be manufactured by themselves."

The *Confederate Veteran* of July, 1908, contains an article dealing with a visit by General Sherman to Georgia after the war. Upon reaching Graysville, Sherman, seeing a stone building by the Chicamauga River, commented, "In that house an Englishman made swords for the Confederacy."

Supposedly John P. Murray (see also in Part III) was the superintendent for John D. Gray and Greenwood & Gray. No weapons have ever been found bearing the name of either "Gray" or "Greenwood & Gray."

Official Records, Series 1, Vol. XXX, Part 1, page 520: "We found and destroyed at Graysville a large number of gun-stocks, bayonet scabbards, etc. partly fabricated. Gray's establishment is the one that has manufactured the celebrated Mexican lance of Governor Brown."

An advertisement in the Columbus, Ga., paper of March 19, 1863: "We are prepared to fill all orders for Superior Grind Stones of any size. Robinet & Co. at Greenwood & Gray's Sword Factory."

GREENWOOD & GRAY—Columbus, Ga.

Made swords, rifles and bayonets, etc. Principals were: Eldridge S. Greenwood, William C. Gray (both cotton warehousemen) and John D. Gray, formerly engaged in the furniture business at Graysville, Ga. See also under John D. Gray, Part III.

GRIER & MASTERSON—Georgia

Made pikes for the State of Georgia, delivering 80 on March 28, 1862, and an additional 33 on April 10 to the State Arsenal and Armory at Milledgeville, Ga. (*Confederate Records of Georgia*, page 352.)

The "Grier" of this firm may have been the brother-in-law of Samuel Griswold, whose revolvers for so long a time were referred to as Griswold & Griers.

GRISWOLD, SAMUEL—Griswoldville, Ga.

Pike and revolver maker. See under Part I.

GUNNISON, A. W.—Griswoldville, Ga.

Foreman of Samuel Griswold (see under Part I).

HABERSHAM, R. W.—South Carolina

Acts of the Confederate States Congress, May 9, 1861, make reference to "Certain papers from R. W. Habersham of S. Carolina, touching on a new artillery sabre, and asking it to be tested." Nothing further known.

HAIMAN, ELIAS—Columbus, Ga.

Brother to swordmaker Louis Haiman (see under Part I).

HAIMAN, LOUIS—Columbus, Ga.

Sword and revolver maker. See under Part I.

HALFMANN & TAYLOR—Montgomery, Ala.

Importers of military goods. See under Part I. (Swords.)

HALL, JAMES M.—Georgia

Maker of bowie knives and pikes for for the State of Georgia. Delivered 6 pikes and 15 bowie knives to the State Arsenal and Armory, Milledgeville, Ga., on April 16, 1862. (*Confederate Records of Georgia*, pages 351–352.)

HAMMOND, C.—unlocated.

Confederate swordmaker. See under Part I.

HATCH, NASON—Georgia (?)

Name found stamped on what appears to be a Georgia pike. Nothing further known.

HAYDEN, AUGUSTUS H.—Charleston, S.C.

Senior partner of Hayden & Whilden, military outfitters (see under Part I).

HAYDEN & WHILDEN—250 King St., Charleston, S.C.

Military outfitters of the Civil War period. See under Part I. (Swords.)

HAYNES, O. S.—Georgia

Made and delivered 49 bowie knives to the State Arsenal and Armory, Milledgeville, Ga., on April 12, 1862. (*Confederate Records of Georgia*, page 351.)

HECK, BRODIE & Co.—Raleigh, N.C.

Bayonet makers, who also operated under the name of Raleigh Bayonet Factory. Principal of the firm was Colonel J. M. Heck. Bayonets made by this firm have never been identified but they were of the triangular-musket variety as of September 6, 1864, for on that date in writing to the Richmond Ordnance Department, the firm stated they were sending samples of both blade and *socket* iron. On September 19 they shipped 2,000 bayonets stating that they had only to send an additional 3,800 to complete their original contract for 10,000. (*Captured Rebel Records*, Vol. 93, Chapter IV.) In April, 1864, the firm had written to the Richmond Ordnance Department requesting permission to finish their old contract for 10,000 bayonets before starting in on the "new type bayonet—with or without clasps." At the time of this writing, their establishment was at a standstill because, "the socket iron is too thin." (Vol. 94, Chapter IV.) What is meant by the "new type bayonet" is not known.

HECK, Colonel J. M.—Raleigh, N.C.

Principal of Heck, Brodie & Co., bayonet manufacturers.

HEINZ, C.—Columbia, S.C.

"C. Heinz, Columbia, S.C." is stamped on the ricasso of a knife apparently of Civil War vintage. It is double-edged, diamond cross section, spear-shaped, with heavy German silver cross guard. Grip is of polished ebony, oval in cross section, with German silver ferrule at juncture of guard. The leather scabbard has a brass stud for frog and also a loop for attaching to the belt. Nothing further known.

HERZOG, F.—Macon, Ga.

Stated to have etched some of the sword blades for E. J. Johnson and W. J. McElroy & Co. of Macon, Ga. (See these firms under Part I.)

HEYER, FREDERICK—Richmond, Va.

Information received from a grandson of the above indicates that he was a swordsmith in Richmond at the time of the Civil War and worked on the naval cutlasses of the type with heavy brass guard and grip with "C.S.N." on one side of the pommel and fouled anchor on the other. Several swords the ricassos of which are stamped "F.H." have been called to the author's attention, but are not believed to have any connection with Frederick Heyer.

HIGGINS, J. M.—Georgia

Made pikes for the State of Georgia. On May 16, 1862, delivered 104 to the State Arsenal and Armory, Milledgeville, Ga., and an additional 87 on May 23. (*Confederate Records of Georgia*, page 352.)

HIRSCHBERG, J. J.—Louisville, Ky.

A dragoon sabre of the Mexican War period bears the above name and address on the obverse of its ricasso. On the reverse appears the name of the maker, "W. Clauberg, Solingen" (of Germany). The blade is highly etched with flags, drums, trophies, stands of arms, etc. and "Lt. Col. I. W. M. Grayson, 4th Regt. East Tenn. Inf." The 4th Regiment, East Tennessee Regiment of Infantry, was Union, not Confederate.

HODGSON, E. R., & BRO.—Georgia

Made and delivered 28 pikes to the State Arsenal and Armory, Milledgeville, Ga. on September 30, 1862. (*Confederate Records of Georgia*, page 352.)

HOUSTON & LANEY—Monroe, N.C.

The above had a contract with the Richmond Armory for bridles, cartridge boxes, shoulder straps, waist belts, cap boxes and bayonet scabbards. (*Captured Rebel Records*, Vol. 90, Chapter IV, page 159.)

HUGHES, R. J.—Georgia

Bowie knife maker, who on April 16, 1862, delivered 1,294 knives and 1,103 belts to the State Arsenal and Armory, Milledgeville, Ga. On May 10, delivered an additional 175 knives. (*Confederate Records of Georgia*, page 351.)

HURT, JAMES—Georgia

Made and delivered 17 pikes to the State Arsenal and Armory, Milledgeville, Ga., April 15, 1862. (*Confederate Records of Georgia*, page 352.)

HYER, F. F.—Georgia

Made and delivered 80 pikes to the State Arsenal and Armory, Milledgeville, Ga., on April 21, 1862. (*Confederate Records of Georgia*, page 352.)

ISAAC & CO.—London, England

Identical with Isaac, Campbell & Co., military outfitters (see under Part I). (Swords.)

ISAAC, CAMPBELL & CO.—London, England

Military outfitters of the Civil War period, who sold only to the Confederate Government. See under Part I. (Swords.)

ISAAC, SAUL—New York and London

Principal in the firm of Isaac, Campbell & Co., military outfitters (see under Part I).

JOHNSTON, E. J., & CO.—Macon, Ga.

Large manufacturer of all types of edged weapons. See under Part I.

K. G. & K.—Columbia, S.C.

Initials of the firm of Kraft, Goldschmidt & Kraft, swordmakers (see under Part I).

KEAN'S SWORD SHOP—Columbus, Ga.

Made swords for the Confederacy, being located at the same address as the factory of Greenwood & Gray,

John P. Murray superintendent. It is possible that Kean made all swords under the Gray or Greenwood & Gray contract with the Confederacy. None of his weapons have been identified.

KIND, PETER—Columbia, S.C.

Proprietor of a brass foundry which cast the sword hilts and scabbard mounts for Kraft, Goldschmidt & Kraft (see under Part I).

KNIGHT'S BLACKSMITH SHOP—Amelia, Va.

Made bowie knives for Confederate soldiers. Is not believed to have had a contract with the Ordnance Department.

KRAFT, H. F.—Columbia, S.C.

One of the principals of Kraft, Goldschmidt & Kraft, swordmakers. See under firm name, Part I.

KRAFT, PETER W.—181 Richardson St., Columbia, S.C.

One of the principals of Kraft, Goldschmidt & Kraft, swordmakers. See under firm name, Part I.

KRAFT, GOLDSCHMIDT & KRAFT—181 Richardson St., Columbia, S.C.

Made many fine swords for the Confederacy. See under Part I.

LAN & SHERMAN—Cary St., above 9th, Richmond, Va.

The above, file manufacturers, advertised in the Richmond *Dispatch* of May 27, 1861: "Bowie knives in our manufactory of the finest English steel are now ready for sale. This is in answer to many inquiries and letters." A bowie knife apparently made by the above has an 8-inch clip-pointed blade, plain wood grip (hickory), and a crude "D"-type guard. The blade is stamped in large letters "Lan &

Sherman, Richmond, Va." (two lines).

LEECH & RIGDON—Memphis, Tenn., Columbus, Miss., and Greensboro, Ga.

Made swords and revolvers. See under Part I.

LEECH, THOMAS S.

Partner in the firm of Leech & Rigdon, sword and revolver makers. See under firm name, Part I.

LOWRY & WILDER—Georgia

Made and delivered 193 pikes to the State Arsenal and Armory, Milledgeville, Ga., on April 19, 1862. (*Confederate Records of Georgia*, page 352.)

MARSHALL BEACH & Co. Address undetermined.

The ledger of Colonel J. M. Payne, Collector of the Port of Wilmington, N.C., for the year 1864, is in the possession of the Confederate Museum, Richmond, Va. In this ledger the Colonel states that "250 interchangeable bayonets" were purchased from the above-named firm. The meaning of "interchangeable" is not known.

MARSHALL & RICE—Georgia

Made and delivered 52 pikes to the State Arsenal and Armory, Milledgeville, Ga., on April 1, 1862, and an additional 48 on April 7. (*Confederate Records of Georgia*, page 352.)

MARSHALL, H., & Co.—Atlanta, Ga.

The above, who made various edged weapons for the South, must have been a pretty sharp type of firm. Witness what the commanding officer of the Atlanta Arsenal, Major M. H. Wright, writes to Colonel Gorgas, Chief of Confederate Ordnance, on May 26, 1862:

I have the honor to acknowledge the receipt of a letter from H. Marshall & Co.,

with your endorsement directing me to contract for sabres with said parties. I am negotiating with them now and send this communication in order to place myself in proper light before you. Their letter written *under my certificate* would seem to intimate that I was cognizant of their proceeding to endorse their statement of personal losses, as a reason in part for giving them aid, etc. I desire simply to state that I knew nothing of the letter at all. I was requested to sign on the half sheet as he wished to get another certificate on the same.

It appears that the good Mr. Marshall had tricked the Major into signing a blank piece of paper, using this signature later on as an "endorsement" to a letter written afterward. (*Captured Rebel Records*, Vol. 12, Chapter IV.)

On August 11, 1862, Major Wright directs the following to "Messrs. H. Marshall & Co.":

I have broken up your scabbards this morning to a considerable extent and I must confess my astonishment at the inferiority of the work. Old burnt sheet iron or tin seem to be the material out of which they are made. Hereafter, I will not receive a lacquered scabbard until after it shall have been inspected by an officer of the Department. Burnt iron can not be used.

MARTIN, J. J.—Georgia

Made and delivered 12 pikes to the State Arsenal and Armory, Milledgeville, Ga., on April 19, 1862. (*Confederate Records of Georgia*, page 352.)

MASSEY, O. W.—Georgia

Made and delivered 63 pikes to the State Arsenal and Armory, Milledgeville, Ga., on April 14, 1862. (*Confederate Records of Georgia*, page 352.)

MATTHEWS, M. E.—Georgia

Made and delivered 10 pikes to the State Arsenal and Armory, Milledgeville, Ga., on May 21, 1862. (*Confederate Records of Georgia*, page 352.)

McELROY, WILLIAM J., & Co.—Macon, Ga.

Large manufacturer of all types of edged weapons. See under Part I.

McKENNIE & Co.—Charlottesville, Va.

According to DeBow's *Review* of March-April, 1862, this firm was established in July, 1861, and was located one mile from Charlottesville. They employed 4 hands and their capacity was 6 swords per week. No specimen has been identified.

McKINSTRY, ALEXANDER—Alabama

The Alabama State Legislature appropriated $6,000 in 1861 in order to purchase 1,000 bowie knife-shaped pikes and 1,000 bowie knives from the above to arm the 48th Regiment Alabama Militia for the defense of Mobile.

MITCHELL & TYLER—Richmond, Va.

A large firm of jewelers and military outfitters, who according to the 1859 Richmond City Directory were located at 108 Main Street.

On March 25, 1861, the firm advertised as follows in the Richmond *Dispatch*:

Military Notice. Arms for volunteers. Volunteer companies desiring arms (and Counties) are hereby informed that we have made arrangements for a supply of the best English and American guns, including the Minnie Musket, English Enfield rifle, rifled musket with either angular or sword bayonets. Fine navy pistols, also French cavalry sabres, a superior article at a low price. Samples may be seen at our store. Also on hand our usual variety of officer's swords, belts, sashes, epaulettes, passants, gloves, spurs, together with

buttons, laces, bidings, bindings and all necessary trimming for uniforms.

Many "Virginia" State seal buttons are found bearing this firm's name on the reverse. These buttons were made by Rowyer & Lavasseur of New Orleans. Mitchell & Tyler evidently had a contract with the sword firm of Boyle & Gamble as many of their swords contain the names of both firms.

Also see Boyle & Gamble under Part I.

MOLE, ROBERT, & SONS—Birmingham, England

Supplied the South with a number of brass-guarded "Enfield"-type swords and cutlasses. Most were imported through the firm of Courtney & Tennant, Charleston, S.C. See this firm under Part I.

MOORE, J. W. & L. L.—Georgia

Large manufacturer of bowie knives for the State of Georgia. Delivered 150 to the State Arsenal and Armory, Milledgeville, Ga., on April 2, 1862, 199 on May 9 and 504 on May 13. (*Confederate Records of Georgia*, page 351.)

MURRAY, JOHN P.—46 Broad St., Columbus, Ga.

Advertised as successor to Happolt & Murray in July, 1862: "Maker and dealer in shotguns, rifles, pistols, dram flasks, knives, powder flasks, shot pouches, shot belts, game bags, gunwads, powder, shot, caps, gun materials and everything in the sporting line. Restocking and repairing done with neatness and dispatch."

Murray also had some connection with the firm of Greenwood & Gray (see). It is the writer's opinion that Murray was subcontractor for this firm or for John Gray (see).

NASHVILLE PLOW WORKS—Nashville, Tenn.

Sword manufacturers. See under Part I.

NELSON, H. O. Address undetermined.

According to the magazine *Antique Firearms*, January, 1912, page 37, the above-named emigrated from Germany to this country in 1860 and became connected with the Confederate States Ordnance Department the following year. He "converted an old sawmill into an armory where flintlock guns were changed for percussion caps and where we made bowie-knives fashioned after an original in possession of our manager. A razor-like edge was put to every weapon that left our Armory, and with a cowhorn for a handle and copper guard from boiler tubes within the mill. A rawhide scabbard hid this vicious toothpick." The writer neglected to give the location of Mr. Nelson.

NISBET, T. C.—Georgia

Made and delivered 66 pikes to the State Arsenal and Armory, Milledgeville, Ga., on April 15, 1862. (*Confederate Records of Georgia*, page 351.)

PALMETTO ARMORY—Columbia, S.C.

See under Part I. Made all types of arms for the State of South Carolina in 1851–1852, including sabres.

PECK, JOHN C.—Atlanta, Ga.

Operated a planning mill and lumberyard at Decatur and Pratt Streets, Atlanta, Ga., and is believed to have furnished pikes to the State of Georgia. In September, 1861, operated as Peck & Bowman, and at a convention of gunsmiths held in Atlanta, it was stated that "Peck & Bowman had contemplated for sometime the establishment of an armory." In 1863 the establishment was purchased by the Confederate Ordnance Department and thereafter operated as the C. S. Atlanta Arsenal.

R. & C.

Initials supposedly standing for "Riggins and Cook." See Thomas Riggins, Part III.

RAINEY, W. L.—Georgia

Made and delivered 11 pikes to the State Arsenal and Armory, Milledgeville, Ga., on April 4, 1862. (*Confederate Records of Georgia*, page 352.)

RALEIGH BAYONET FACTORY—Raleigh, N.C.

Also known as Heck, Brodie & Co. Had a contract with the Confederacy for 10,000 bayonets. See Heck, Brodie & Co., Part III.

READ & DICKSON—Mississippi

"Act of Mississippi Legislature Called and Regular Sessions, Jackson and Columbus, Mississippi, December 1862–November 1863," Chapter XI, provided for the payment of $750 to Read & Dickson for 300 lances.

REID, HUMPHREY—Georgia

Made and delivered 76 pikes to the State Arsenal and Armory, Milledgeville, Ga., on April 24, 1862. (*Confederate Records of Georgia*, page 352.)

REUTER, Capt. FRANZ—Louisiana

According to the daily Richmond *Examiner* of January 3, 1862, the above-named invented a scythe-bladed pike with a sharp hook at the base of the blade. This in turn was mounted on a 10-foot pole.

RICHMOND ARMORY—Richmond, Va.

See under the name of Virginia Armory, Part I.

RIGDON, CHARLES H.

Partner in the firm of Leech & Rigdon, sword and revolver makers. See under firm name, Part I.

RIGGINS, THOMAS—McMinn County, Tenn.

An article in the *Confederate Veteran*, March 5, 1877, credits the above with substantial contribution to the war effort of Cook & Brother in their Armory at Athens, Ga. Riggins is stated to have used the "inspector's stamp" of "R. & C." (Riggins and Cook) on various arms, including swords. Little credence is placed in this account, which appears to fall into the same category as a book written by Private Brown entitled: "How me and General Lee almost won the Civil War."

Thomas Riggins was born in 1821, and was a gunsmith from McMinn County, Tenn., who as superintendent of the Knoxville Arsenal helped convert country rifles into military arms. Locally, he was known as "Armorer of the South," a title shared with several others, including Samuel Sutherland of Richmond, Va. After the fall of Knoxville, Riggins went into active service with the 3rd Tennessee Regiment.

If he made or marked swords, it is not known to the author.

ROBINSON, ADAMS & Co.—9th and Main streets, Richmond, Va.

Advertised in the daily Richmond *Examiner*, January 21, 1863, the "receipt by steamship *Modern Greece* of 13 new muskets with bayonets and 975 swords, comprising light and heavy cavalry and artillery swords."

S. & K.—Solingen, Germany

Initials for Schnitzler & Kirschbawer, swordmakers. See under firm name, Part III.

SCHLEY, W.—Georgia

Made and delivered 83 pikes to the State Arsenal and Armory, Milledgeville, Ga., on May 17, 1862. (*Confederate Records of Georgia*, page 352.)

SCHNITZLER & KIRSCHBAWER—Solingen, Germany

The initials of the above firm are to be found on much equipment used by both North and South during the war. Especially is it found upon various edged weapons.

On August 28, 1840, this firm wrote to the U. S. War Department offering to manufacture for the United States the following swords and sabres: 2,000 light cavalry sabres, price 3 thalers and 25 silver groschen each; 1,000 noncommissioned officer's swords, blades 32 inches long, price 4 thalers and 12 silver groschen; 100 infantry officer's swords, same as noncommissioned officer's but hilt to be chafed and mountings to be richly gilded, handle of silver and blade damasked, price 8 thalers and 25 groschen; 500 musician's swords like noncommissioned officer's but without coquilles and with blades 28 inches long and reduced proportionately to its shortened length, price 3 thalers and 22 groschen.

SHARP & HAMILTON—Nashville, Tenn.

Proprietors of the sword-making establishment better known as the Nashville Plow Works. See under firm name, Part I.

SHEPARD, MAXWELL & HOYT—Knoxville, Tenn.

Two thousand pikes were found in the Knoxville Arsenal and the machine shop of Shepard, Maxwell & Hoyt. (Report of January 1, 1864, *Official Records of the War of Rebellion*, Series 1, Vol. XXX, Part 2, page 571.)

SMITH, JOHN C.—Georgia

Bowie knife maker for the State of Georgia. On April 7, 1862, he delivered 50 to the State Arsenal and Armory, Milledgeville, Ga., and an additional 55 on May 21. (*Confederate Records of Georgia*, page 351.)

SPEAR, C. S.—Columbus, Ga.

Did the etching on many of the L. Haiman & Bro. swords. His name is occasionally to be found etched on the back of their blades.

SPELIERS, Professor A.—Exchange Hotel, Richmond, Va.

The above advertised in the Richmond *Dispatch* of May 27, 1861, as a graduate of the Sans Mur Military Institute, and offered to give lessons in fencing, broadsword practice and the Zouave bayonet exercise.

STATON, JOHN L.—Scottsville, Va.

The following advertisement appeared in the Richmond *Dispatch* of July 8, 1861: "Swords and bowie-knives. I am prepared to manufacture to order bowie-knives and swords of all kinds in the best manner at my shop in Scottsville, Albemarle county. John L. Staton."

STEVENS, H.—Richmond County, Ga.

Pike maker for the State of Georgia. See Part I.

T. G. & Co., N.O.

Initials found on some Confederate swords which stand for their maker, Thomas, Griswold & Co., New Orleans. See under this name, Part I.

THOMAS, GRISWOLD & Co.—Corner Canal & Royal streets, New Orleans, La.

Large manufacturers of edged weapons. See under Part I.

TODD, JOHN—New Orleans, La.

Another claimant for the title of having made a "bowie" for Colonel James Bowie in the 1830s.

TURNER & WEBB—Georgia

Made and delivered 11 pikes to the State Arsenal and Armory, Milledgeville, Ga., on April 19, 1862. (*Confederate Records of Georgia*, page 352.)

UNION CAR WORKS—Portsmouth, Va.

Manufactured: bowie knives, sabre bayonets, gun carriages, wagons, camp-stools, tent poles and tent pins for the Confederacy. Possibly made the knives and cutlasses with turned wooden handle and with the "S"-shaped iron or brass cross guard, pictured Plate #103.

UNION MANUFACTURING Co.—Richmond, Va.

A circular printed in Richmond, Va., and dated February 11, 1861, announces the formation of the Union Manufacturing Co., which "is prepared to manufacture fire-arms." The circular is signed by James S. Kent, president. The factory it occupied formerly made a product known as "Sloat's Great Southern Sewing Machine," and consequently the proposed gun manufactory became known as "Sloat's Rifle Factory" although no firearms were ever made here.

By July, 1861, some 200 hands were

employed and one of their first contracts with the Confederacy consisted of altering the old Virginia Manufactory rifles, pistols and muskets from flint to percussion. A number of machines for the C.S. Ordnance were also a product of this plant. The only edged weapons made by the Union Manufacturing Co. were bayonets, none of which have ever been identified. In March, 1865, they were charging the Ordnance Department $25 for these bayonets, making a net profit of $2.59 per. This, in accordance with estimates from other contractors, was not out of line. (*Captured Rebel Records*, Vol. 91½, Chapter IV, page 55.)

VIRGINIA ARMORY—Richmond, Va.

See under Part I. (Sabres.)

WALSONEID, W.—Solingen, Germany

Supplied the South with sabres and swords during the Civil War. See under Part I.

WATKINS, W. N.—Georgia

Made and delivered 12 pikes to the State Arsenal and Armory, Milledgeville, Ga., on May 23, 1862. (*Confederate Records of Georgia*, page 352.)

WEED, N.—Georgia

Made bowie knives and pikes for the State of Georgia. On April 1, 1862, delivered 84 knives and 15 pikes to the State Arsenal and Armory, Milledgeville, Ga., and 62 knives the following day. On April 16, he delivered 50 additional knives and 159 pikes. (*Confederate Records of Georgia*, pages 351–352.)

WELCH, JAMES—Richmond, Va.

The Richmond *Dispatch* of March 25, 1861, carried an advertisement by the above: "Life and property pre-

servers—I have received from the manufacturer a further supply of Colt's celebrated five-shooters in navy and pocket sizes. Also on hand a large assortment of duelling, self-cocking and rifle pistols. Bowie knives, dirks, sword-canes, travelers money belts, liquor flasks, drinking cups, shot belts, powder flasks, game bags, etc." The address was given as "7 doors above the St. Charles Hotel."

WELLS, URIAH—Petersburg, Va.

The Petersburg *Daily Express* of July 23, 1861, advises that the above manufactured a "most beautiful and serviceable sword to order by Major E. L. Brockett. The blade is made of highest tempered steel, is full thirty inches in length and brilliantly polished. Mr. Wells has been engaged for many weeks in the manufacture of very superior bowie knives, thousands of which he has disposed of, and we understand, has numerous orders for swords." Wells was the proprietor of the Petersburg Iron Works. According to local papers, he died, with "heavy loss to the community, September 3, 1864. Funeral at the Grace Episcopal Church."

WHILDEN, WILLIAM G.—Charleston, S.C.

Partner in the firm of Hayden & Whilden, military outfitters of the Civil War. See under firm name, Part I.

WHITE, JOHN G.—Macon, Ga.

Made and delivered 100 pikes to the State Arsenal and Armory, Milledgeville, Ga., on April 9, 1862, and an additional 105 on May 9 and still another 98 on September 28. (*Confederate*

Records of Georgia, page 352.) White also made shoe lasts, pegs, stocks and dies, spokes, rim hubs and gun carriages for the Confederate Army. His agent was a Mr. N. Weed.

WILLIAMS, E. P.—Georgia

Made a number of pikes for the State of Georgia, said to be of a "different pattern." Arms never identified. He delivered 107 to the State Arsenal and Armory on July 10, 1862, and 140 on September 16. *Confederate Records of Georgia*, page 350, notes that the above pikes were different in design from that afterward adopted by the Adjutant and Inspector General and Chief of Ordnance, State of Georgia.

WILSON, J. C.—Houston, Texas

Swordmaker. See Part I.

WINAN, Ross—Baltimore, Md.

Maker of the first Confederate pikes. See Part I.

WINN, D. H.—Georgia

Made pikes for the State of Georgia in connection with William H. Elder. See under Elder's name, Part III.

WOLFE, I. W.

Had a contract with the Richmond Armory for 10,000 cartridge boxes and bayonet scabbards. (*Captured Rebel Records*, Vol. 90, Chapter IV, page 160.)

WOODRUFF, D. B.—Georgia

Made pikes for the State of Georgia. Delivered 116 to the State Arsenal and Armory, Milledgeville, Ga., on March 18, 1862, and an additional 198 on April 15. (*Confederate Records of Georgia*, page 352.)

WYMAN, G. N., & Co.—Augusta, Ga.

Made pikes for the State of Georgia, delivering 7 to the State Arsenal and Armory at Milledgeville, Ga., on April 9, 1862. (*Confederate Records of Georgia*, page 352.) Wyman also made percussion cap boxes and cartridge boxes, which are stamped with his name and "Augusta, Ga."

ZIMMERMAN, J. C. & Co.—Georgia

Made pikes and bowie knives for the State of Georgia. On April 19, 1862, he delivered 14 knives and 29 pikes to the State Arsenal and Armory at Milledgeville, Ga., 91 knives and 45 pikes on April 18, 104 knives April 30, and 78 pikes on September 30. (*Confederate Records of Georgia*, pages 351–352.)